Adventure Awaits: The Ultimate F UK's Best Child-Friendly Sites

101 Perfect Locations with Playgrounds, Every Age

Table of Contents

Chapter 4: London & Thames Valley - Urban Adventures & Royal Retreats

- 8 featured campsites within easy reach of London
- Cultural experiences and royal connections
- Museum visits and river trips
- Windsor Castle, Legoland, and Kew Gardens
- Palace tours and urban adventures

Chapter 5: Heart of England - Peaks, Valleys & Literary Landscapes

- 12 featured campsites across Cotswolds, Peak District, Midlands
- Walking trails and literary connections
- Traditional villages and hill walking
- Storytelling and craft workshops
- Alton Towers, Warwick Castle, and Shakespeare Country

Chapter 6: Eastern England - Wide Skies, Gentle Rivers & Seaside Fun

- 10 featured campsites across Norfolk, Suffolk, Cambridgeshire, Essex
- The Broads and seaside resorts
- Wildlife reserves and boat trips
- Seal watching and beach games
- Great Yarmouth, Norfolk Broads, and Colchester Zoo

Chapter 7: Northern England - Lakes, Dales & Industrial Heritage

- 15 featured campsites across Lake District, Yorkshire Dales, Northumberland
- Outdoor adventures and heritage sites
- Lake cruises and fell walking
- Castle exploring and mountain adventures
- Hadrian's Wall, Blackpool, and Lake Windermere

Chapter 8: Wales - Dragons, Castles & Coastal Wonders

- 13 featured campsites across North, Mid, and South Wales
- Mountain adventures and Welsh culture
- Coastal paths and castle quests
- Seaside adventures and mountain railways
- Snowdonia, Pembrokeshire Coast, and Cardiff Castle

Chapter 9: Scotland - Highland Adventures & Island Magic

- 12 featured campsites from Lowlands to Highlands and Islands
- Dramatic landscapes and Scottish heritage
- Wildlife watching and loch monster hunting
- Highland games and island hopping
- Edinburgh Castle, Loch Ness, and Isle of Skye

Chapter 10: Seasonal Camping & Year-Round Adventures

- Spring camping: Bluebells and baby animals
- Summer camping: Festivals and beach fun
- Autumn camping: Harvest time and changing colours
- Winter camping: Cozy retreats and Christmas markets
- Weather-appropriate gear and seasonal activities
- Seasonal safety considerations

Conclusion: Creating Lasting Family Memories

- Reflecting on camping adventures
- Building camping traditions
- Growing with your children's needs
- The environmental benefits of camping

Appendices

Appendix A: Essential Packing Checklists by Age Group

Appendix B: Campfire Cooking Recipes for Families

Appendix C: Rainy Day Activities and Games

Appendix D: Emergency Contacts and Safety Information

Appendix E: UK Camping Associations and Resources

Appendix F: Seasonal Activity Calendar

Appendix G: Budget Planning Worksheets

Introduction

Picture this: your eight-year-old has just discovered her first slow worm under a log, your teenager has actually put down his phone to help build the campfire, and your toddler is giggling as he chases bubbles across a sun-dappled meadow. The tent might be slightly wonky, there's sand in absolutely everything, and someone definitely needs a wash, but right now, in this moment, your family is creating the kind of memories that will be talked about for years to come.

This is the magic of family camping in the UK – and it's exactly why you're holding this book.

Why Family Camping is Booming in the UK

Family camping has experienced an extraordinary renaissance in recent years, and it's not hard to understand why. After years of complicated overseas holidays, passport queues, and the unpredictability of international travel, British families are rediscovering the simple joy of pitching up somewhere beautiful within our own borders.

The statistics tell an incredible story. According to recent industry reports, family camping bookings have increased by over 60% since 2020, with nearly three-quarters of UK families now considering camping as their preferred holiday option. But this isn't just about convenience or cost – though both are significant factors. There's something deeper happening here.

In our increasingly digital world, camping offers families something precious: genuine connection. Away from the constant ping of notifications and the endless scroll of social media, families are finding space to actually talk, play, and discover together. Children who might normally beg for screen time are suddenly fascinated by beetle hunting, star gazing, or learning to light a fire safely.

The UK camping scene has transformed dramatically too. Gone are the days when camping meant basic facilities and crossed fingers about the weather. Today's family campsites are sophisticated operations offering everything from heated toilet blocks and adventure playgrounds to on-site cafés and activity programmes designed specifically for different age groups. Many sites now provide luxury alternatives like safari tents and shepherd's huts for families wanting the camping experience without the tent-pitching stress.

Perhaps most importantly, camping has become accessible to families who might never have considered it before. Single parents are finding welcoming communities on family-friendly sites. Grandparents are discovering they can enjoy comfortable camping experiences with their grandchildren. Families with children who have additional needs are finding sites that truly cater to everyone.

How to Use This Guide Effectively

This isn't just another list of campsites with basic descriptions. Every single location in this guide has been chosen specifically because it excels at making families feel welcome, engaged, and excited about their camping adventure.

Each campsite review is structured to give you exactly the information you need as a parent. You'll find honest assessments of facilities (yes, we'll tell you if the shower blocks need updating), detailed breakdowns of what each site offers for different age groups, and insider tips that only come from extensive research and real family experiences.

The regional chapters aren't just geographical divisions – they're themed around the unique experiences each area offers. Southwest England focuses on coastal magic and beach adventures. The Heart of England emphasizes literary landscapes and traditional village experiences. Scotland delivers highland adventures and island magic. This thematic approach helps you choose not just where to go, but what kind of experience you want your family to have.

Look out for special features throughout each review:

Family Facilities Rating: A realistic assessment of playgrounds, toilet blocks, shops, and swimming facilities, with specific notes about what works well for different ages.

Age-Specific Activities: Detailed suggestions broken down by age group, from toddler-safe play areas to teen-friendly independence opportunities.

Local Attractions Within 30 Minutes: Carefully selected recommendations including free options, educational opportunities, and weather-backup plans.

Parent Tips & Insider Knowledge: The kind of advice you'd get from experienced camping friends – which pitches to request, when to avoid peak times, and how to save money.

Weather Contingency Plans: Because let's be honest, this is Britain, and rain happens. Every region includes specific recommendations for keeping children happy whatever the weather brings.

Understanding the Rating System

Rather than using generic star ratings that don't really tell you what you need to know as a parent, this guide uses a practical assessment system based on what actually matters to families:

Playground & Play Areas: Evaluated on safety, age-appropriateness, and maintenance standards. We'll tell you if it's suitable for toddlers, exciting enough for older children, or if teens will find it babyish.

Toilet & Shower Facilities: Assessed for cleanliness, family-friendly features (baby changing, family shower rooms), and accessibility. We'll be honest about facilities that are showing their age.

On-Site Amenities: Realistic reviews of shops, cafés, swimming pools, and other facilities, with notes about pricing and quality.

Local Attractions Access: Measured by actual travel times, public transport links, and suitability for families with different mobility needs.

Value for Money: Not just about being cheap, but about getting good value for what you pay, with consideration of what's included and local pricing.

Essential Pre-Trip Planning

The difference between a camping disaster and a camping triumph often comes down to preparation – but not the kind that requires military precision and endless lists. Smart preparation is about knowing what's essential, what's nice to have, and what you can definitely buy when you get there.

Age Considerations Are Everything: A campsite that's perfect for a family with teenagers might be utterly wrong for parents with toddlers. Throughout this guide, you'll find specific advice about age-appropriate expectations and how to set everyone up for success.

Seasonal Planning Matters: A Lake District campsite that's magical in summer might be challenging in April. Each regional chapter includes specific guidance about the best times to visit, what weather to expect, and how to make the most of each season.

Booking Strategy: Family camping has become popular enough that the best sites book up quickly, especially during school holidays. We'll share insider knowledge about when to book, how to find last-minute availability, and which sites offer the best value at different times of year.

Gear Philosophy: You don't need to own a camping shop to enjoy family camping, but having the right basics makes everything easier. Chapter 1 covers essential gear recommendations, but more importantly, it explains the thinking behind smart gear choices for families.

Expectation Management: Perhaps the most important preparation is mental. Family camping isn't about perfection – it's about adventure, flexibility, and creating positive experiences together. The best camping families are those who can laugh when things don't go exactly to plan.

What Makes This Guide Different

This guide was born from a simple frustration: existing camping guides either treated families like smaller adults or focused so heavily on facilities that they forgot about fun. We wanted to create something different – a guide written by parents, for parents, with honest advice about what really works when you're camping with children.

Every campsite has been visited by families with children of different ages. Every recommendation comes from real experience, not just website descriptions. Every tip has been tested by parents who understand that camping with a baby is completely different from camping with teenagers, and both are different again from camping with the whole extended family.

Most importantly, this guide recognizes that families come in all shapes and sizes. Single parents, grandparents, families with children who have additional needs, families on tight budgets, and families looking for luxury experiences – everyone deserves to find their perfect camping adventure.

The 101 campsites in this guide represent the very best of what UK family camping has to offer. From wild coastal spots in Cornwall to cozy farm sites in the Cotswolds, from adventure-packed locations near theme parks to peaceful retreats perfect for digital detox, there's something here for every family at every stage.

But beyond the practical information, this guide is about inspiration. It's about recognizing that some of childhood's most treasured memories happen around campfires, in makeshift dens, and during those golden hour moments when the tent is finally up and everyone's actually happy.

Your family's perfect camping adventure is waiting somewhere in these pages. Let's go find it together.

_____

Ready to start planning? Chapter 1 will equip you with everything you need to know about making family camping work, whatever ages and stages you're dealing with. But if you're eager to start browsing destinations, feel free to jump straight to any regional chapter that catches your imagination. This is your guide – use it however works best for your family.

Chapter 1: Getting Started - Your Family Camping Foundation

Picture this: your six-year-old daughter is roasting her first marshmallow over a campfire, her face glowing with wonder as the flames dance in her eyes. Your teenager, who's been glued to his phone for months, is actually engaged in building the perfect den with his younger brother. Meanwhile, you're sitting back with a cup of tea, watching the sunset paint the sky in impossible colors, feeling more relaxed than you have all year.

This isn't a fantasy—it's what happens when family camping goes right. But here's the thing: successful family camping doesn't happen by accident. It requires understanding what works for different ages, having the right gear, knowing how to choose suitable sites, and most importantly, setting realistic expectations.

After camping with families across the UK for over fifteen years, I've learned that the difference between a magical adventure and a stressful ordeal often comes down to preparation and mindset. This chapter will give you the foundation you need to create those golden moments while avoiding the common pitfalls that can turn a weekend away into a family legend for all the wrong reasons.

Age-Appropriate Expectations: Setting Your Family Up for Success

The Toddler Years (0-3): Little Steps, Big Adventures

Camping with toddlers requires a complete shift in perspective. Forget about conquering mountain peaks or covering miles of countryside—with this age group, success is measured in small victories and precious moments.

What to expect: Your toddler won't remember the stunning views from Dartmoor or the historical significance of Hadrian's Wall, but they will remember the excitement of sleeping in a tent, the thrill of eating beans straight from the tin, and the magic of watching daddy light a campfire. At this age, the camping experience itself is the adventure.

Realistic daily schedule: Plan for a maximum of two activities per day, and build in plenty of flexibility. A typical day might involve a short walk to find interesting sticks and stones in the morning, followed by lunch back at the tent, an afternoon nap (essential for everyone's sanity), and an early evening around the campfire. That's plenty.

Sleep considerations: Be prepared for disrupted sleep patterns. The excitement, different surroundings, and outdoor sounds can make settling difficult. Bring familiar comfort items, maintain usual bedtime routines as much as possible, and consider your tent placement carefully—away from main pathways and near facilities for those inevitable middle-of-the-night bathroom runs.

Safety priorities: Constant supervision is non-negotiable. Toddlers are naturally curious and have no concept of danger. Choose sites with secure boundaries, avoid camping near water features, and always have a plan for containing wandering little ones. A travel cot or pop-up tent can create a safe space when you need to focus on other tasks.

The Inquisitive Phase (4-8): Natural Born Explorers

This is arguably the golden age for family camping. Children at this stage are old enough to actively participate in camping activities but young enough to find genuine wonder in simple outdoor experiences.

What to expect: Endless questions, boundless energy, and an insatiable curiosity about everything from why worms come out when it rains to whether badgers really live in those holes. These children will want to help with everything—pitching the tent, collecting firewood, cooking dinner—which means everything takes twice as long but is infinitely more rewarding.

Activity planning: This age group thrives on variety and discovery. Plan for 3-4 activities per day, mixing physical challenges with quiet exploration. A morning nature scavenger hunt, afternoon stream paddling, evening storytelling session, and nighttime star gazing create a perfect rhythm without overwhelming anyone.

Learning opportunities: Four to eight-year-olds are natural scientists. They'll collect rocks, study insects, and create elaborate theories about how clouds form. Encourage this curiosity with simple nature identification books, magnifying glasses, and collection containers. The outdoors becomes their laboratory.

Independence building: This is when children can start taking genuine responsibility—carrying their own small backpack, helping to tidy the tent, or being responsible for remembering their water bottle. These small tasks build confidence and investment in the camping experience.

The Adventure Seekers (9-12): Ready for Real Challenges

Pre-teens bring a different energy to family camping. They're physically capable of more demanding activities but emotionally still need security and family connection. This age group can handle genuine adventures while still enjoying the cozy aspects of family camping.

What to expect: Increased stamina for hiking, genuine interest in skill-building activities like fire lighting or map reading, and the beginning of independence desires. They might want to explore slightly ahead of the family group or stay up later around the campfire. They're also more aware of weather discomfort and might need extra encouragement during challenging conditions.

Activity escalation: This is when you can introduce more adventurous elements—longer hikes, basic orienteering, bike rides, or water sports. They can handle 4-5 activities per day and enjoy challenges that require problem-solving and skill development.

Responsibility expansion: Nine to twelve-year-olds can take on significant camping responsibilities. They can help with meal planning, be responsible for their own packing lists, assist with tent setup, and even lead younger siblings in activities. This responsibility builds ownership of the camping experience.

Social considerations: Friendship groups become increasingly important. If possible, consider camping with other families or choosing sites with good facilities where they might meet other children. The social element often determines their overall enjoyment of the trip.

The Teen Years (13+): Balancing Independence and Family Time

Camping with teenagers requires delicate navigation between respecting their growing independence and maintaining family connection. Get it right, and you'll find they become your best camping companions.

What to expect: Initial resistance ("Do we have to?"), followed by grudging participation, and often ending with genuine enjoyment. Teenagers appreciate the freedom that camping provides from daily routines, the opportunity to develop real outdoor skills, and surprisingly, the chance to spend quality time with family away from normal distractions.

Technology balance: Rather than fighting the technology battle, create reasonable boundaries. Many sites have limited phone signal anyway, which often comes as a relief to everyone. Consider designated phone-free times (during meals and activities) and phone-allowed times (evening relaxation).

Independence opportunities: Give teenagers genuine responsibility and decision-making power. Let them plan a day's activities, be responsible for cooking a meal, or navigate a walking route. This investment in the trip's success changes their perspective from passive participant to active contributor.

Skill development: Teenagers can handle advanced camping skills—fire management, outdoor cooking, basic navigation, weather prediction, and emergency procedures. These practical life skills often appeal to their desire to feel capable and adult.

Essential Gear for Families: What You Really Need

The camping gear market can be overwhelming, especially for families. You'll see everything from titanium tent pegs to solar-powered camping showers, but the truth is, successful family camping relies more on the right basics than expensive gadgets.

The Non-Negotiable Essentials

Family-sized tent: This is where you'll spend roughly half your camping time, so it's worth investing properly. For a family of four, consider a six-person tent—the extra space makes an enormous difference for comfort and sanity. Look for tents with separate sleeping areas, adequate headroom for adults, and multiple entrances to reduce disruption during nighttime bathroom runs.

Key features to prioritize:

- Sewn-in groundsheet (keeps out moisture and drafts)
- Dual-layer construction (better temperature control)

- Large porch area (essential for wet weather and gear storage)
- Color-coded pole system (makes setup with "helpers" less stressful)
- Windows with mesh screens (ventilation without bugs)

Sleeping system: Comfortable sleep makes or breaks a camping trip, especially for children. Invest in quality sleeping bags appropriate for UK conditions—look for bags rated to at least 5°C, even for summer camping. Self-inflating mats provide crucial insulation and comfort; don't underestimate how much difference they make to sleep quality.

For families, consider:

- Child-specific sleeping bags (properly sized, often warmer)
- Pillows or inflatable pillows (comfort items are worth the space)
- Extra blankets for added warmth and security
- Foam mats as backup insulation

Cooking equipment: Family camping means feeding multiple people with varying tastes and dietary requirements. A two-burner camping stove provides flexibility and speed—essential when hungry children are waiting. Bring more fuel than you think you'll need; it's frustrating to run out halfway through cooking dinner.

Essential cooking kit:

- Lightweight pots and pans (non-stick makes cleaning easier)
- Sharp knife and cutting board
- Plates, bowls, and cups for everyone (lightweight melamine works well)
- Plenty of utensils (items get dropped and lost)
- Can opener and bottle opener
- Washing up bowl and eco-friendly soap

Clothing and Weather Protection

UK weather is famously unpredictable, and being prepared for all conditions is essential for family comfort and safety. The key principle is layering—multiple thin layers that can be added or removed as conditions change.

Base layer system: Everyone needs moisture-wicking base layers. Merino wool is excellent but expensive; synthetic alternatives work well for growing children. Avoid cotton base layers—once wet, they stay wet and become uncomfortably cold.

Insulation layers: Fleece or synthetic insulation jackets for everyone. Down is warmer and lighter but loses effectiveness when wet—not ideal for UK conditions. Look for layers that work together; a lightweight fleece under a waterproof jacket provides excellent versatility.

Waterproof protection: Invest in quality waterproof jackets and trousers for everyone. Look for "breathable" waterproofs—they prevent the clammy feeling that comes with cheaper alternatives. Waterproof over-trousers are often overlooked but essential for keeping children comfortable during outdoor activities in wet conditions.

Footwear strategy: Everyone needs at least two pairs of shoes—walking boots for activities and casual shoes for around the campsite. Wellies are invaluable for wet conditions and muddy sites. Pack extra socks—wet feet make everyone miserable.

Family-Specific Gear

First aid and medications: Create a comprehensive first aid kit that covers common childhood injuries and ailments. Include plasters in various sizes, antiseptic wipes, children's paracetamol, any prescription medications, thermometer, and emergency contact information.

Entertainment and comfort: While outdoor activities fill most of the time, you'll need backup entertainment for rest periods and bad weather. Pack books, card games, travel board games, and comfort items for younger children. A deck of cards takes virtually no space but provides hours of entertainment.

Practical additions: Headtorches for everyone (hands-free lighting is crucial), portable phone charger, washing line and pegs, rubbish bags, wet wipes, and a small camping table if your tent doesn't have adequate surfaces.

Safety Fundamentals: Keeping Your Family Secure

Safety in family camping isn't about wrapping everyone in bubble wrap—it's about understanding risks, preparing for common scenarios, and creating systems that allow everyone to enjoy adventures safely.

Risk Assessment and Prevention

Campsite hazards: Upon arrival, walk the campsite with your children, identifying potential hazards together. Look for uneven ground, low branches, water features, boundaries, and vehicle areas. This family safety tour helps children understand the environment and demonstrates your commitment to their wellbeing.

Fire safety: If campfires are permitted, establish clear fire safety rules from the start. Children must ask permission before approaching the fire, never leave a fire unattended, and always have water available for extinguishing. Teach children to recognize hot surfaces and maintain safe distances.

Water safety: Any water feature—streams, lakes, or coastal areas—requires specific safety protocols. Establish boundaries, ensure adequate supervision, and consider life jackets for non-confident swimmers even in shallow water. UK water temperatures remain cold year-round; hypothermia is a real risk.

Weather awareness: Teach your family to recognize changing weather conditions and understand appropriate responses. Lightning, sudden temperature drops, and high winds require specific actions. Have shelter plans and ensure everyone knows severe weather procedures.

Emergency Preparedness

Communication plans: Mobile phone coverage can be patchy in rural camping areas. Identify the nearest reliable phone signal, know the location of the nearest hospital, and ensure someone knows your camping plans and expected return date.

First aid skills: Basic first aid knowledge is invaluable when camping with children. Consider taking a family first aid course before your first major camping trip. Know how to treat common camping injuries: cuts, burns, insect stings, and sprains.

Emergency contacts: Keep a written list of emergency contacts, including local emergency services, NHS Direct, your GP, and family contacts. Include details of any medical conditions or allergies within your family.

Teaching Safety to Children

Age-appropriate responsibility: Gradually increase safety responsibilities as children mature. Young children learn simple rules ("Stay where you can see Mummy"), while older children can learn navigation skills and emergency procedures.

Buddy system: Implement a buddy system where children are responsible for keeping track of each other. This builds mutual responsibility and ensures no one wanders off unnoticed.

Safety equipment familiarity: Teach children to use safety equipment—whistles for emergencies, how to operate torches, and basic first aid techniques appropriate to their age.

Choosing the Right Campsite Type: Matching Sites to Family Needs

Not all campsites are created equal, and choosing the right type for your family's specific needs can make the difference between a successful adventure and a stressful experience.

Traditional Camping Sites

Family-focused sites: These purpose-built sites cater specifically to families, offering playgrounds, family bathrooms, on-site shops, and organized activities. They're ideal for first-time camping families or those with younger children who need reliable facilities and entertainment options.

Advantages: Consistent facility quality, child-friendly environments, other families for social opportunities, usually well-maintained and secure.

Considerations: Can be crowded during peak times, less natural settings, higher costs, potentially noisy with many children.

Farm camping: Camping on working farms provides authentic rural experiences with opportunities to see animals and understand countryside life. Many offer basic facilities while maintaining a more natural environment.

Advantages: Educational opportunities, often more spacious pitches, authentic rural experience, usually family-friendly atmosphere.

Considerations: Facilities may be more basic, animal-related safety considerations, seasonal availability, potential for early morning farm noises.

Wild and Natural Camping

National park campsites: Camping within national parks offers stunning natural settings with good access to hiking trails and outdoor activities. These sites often balance natural beauty with adequate facilities for families.

Advantages: Spectacular locations, excellent walking access, educational opportunities, often well-managed and maintained.

Considerations: Can be busy during peak season, strict rules and regulations, weather exposure, advance booking usually essential.

Coastal camping: Sites near beaches or coastal paths provide unique opportunities for seaside activities and maritime exploration. Consider wind exposure and salt air effects on equipment.

Advantages: Beach access, water activities, often stunning views, different environment from inland camping.

Considerations: Weather exposure, salt air equipment effects, seasonal availability, potential for crowding during good weather.

Glamping and Upgraded Camping

Glamping sites: Pre-pitched tents, cabins, or pods provide a middle ground between camping and hotels. These can be excellent for families transitioning to camping or those wanting comfort without sacrifice of outdoor experience.

Advantages: Eliminates gear requirements, often includes bedding and basic cooking equipment, combines outdoor experience with comfort, good for first-time campers.

Considerations: Higher costs, less authentic camping experience, limited availability, less flexibility in location choice.

Weather Considerations: Embracing Britain's Variable Climate

UK weather is famously unpredictable, but this variability shouldn't deter family camping—it just requires preparation and the right mindset. Some of our best camping memories come from weathering storms together or discovering the magical beauty of misty mornings.

Seasonal Planning

Spring camping (March-May): Spring offers the excitement of nature awakening—bluebells carpeting woodland floors, lambs in fields, and longer daylight hours. However, weather remains unpredictable with potential for cold snaps and wet conditions.

Preparation: Pack for winter conditions but hope for spring weather. Waterproofs are essential, as are warm layers. Choose sites with good drainage and shelter options.

Summer camping (June-August): Peak camping season brings warmest weather, longest days, and highest site availability. However, popularity means crowded sites and advance booking requirements.

Preparation: Don't assume hot weather—pack layers and waterproofs. Consider sun protection, insect repellent, and extra water supplies. Book sites well in advance.

Autumn camping (September-November): Often overlooked, autumn provides some of the year's best camping conditions. Fewer crowds, stunning colors, mild temperatures, and harvest season create magical experiences.

Preparation: Shorter days require more lighting equipment. Weather becomes more variable, so pack for all conditions. Heating systems become more important.

Winter camping (December-February): Challenging but rewarding for experienced families. Fewer crowds, different landscapes, and cozy evening experiences create unique memories.

Preparation: Requires significant additional equipment and experience. Not recommended for first-time family campers.

Weather Response Strategies

Rainy day planning: Every camping trip should include rainy day alternatives. Research local museums, indoor attractions, and covered activities near your chosen campsite. Pack additional entertainment and indoor games.

Wind management: Strong winds affect tent stability, cooking safety, and general comfort. Learn proper tent guy-rope management, secure all loose items, and understand when conditions become dangerous.

Temperature fluctuations: UK temperatures can vary dramatically within single days. Layering systems allow families to adapt quickly to changing conditions without returning to the tent constantly.

Making Weather Part of the Adventure

Rather than viewing variable weather as an obstacle, frame it as part of the authentic British camping experience. Children often remember dramatic weather events more vividly than perfect sunny days.

Teach your family to find beauty in mist-shrouded valleys, excitement in approaching storm clouds, and magic in frost-covered morning landscapes.

Weather watching skills: Develop family weather prediction abilities. Learn to read cloud formations, understand wind direction changes, and recognize pressure system movements. This knowledge builds confidence and creates educational opportunities.

Adaptation strategies: Develop flexible activity plans that work in various weather conditions. Indoor alternatives, covered activity areas, and weather-appropriate gear ensure that no weather condition ruins your camping adventure.

Building Confidence: Your First Steps to Camping Success

Starting your family camping journey can feel overwhelming, but every expert camper began with their first nervous night under canvas. The key is building confidence gradually through preparation, realistic expectations, and celebrating small successes.

Start small: Your first family camping trip doesn't need to be a week-long expedition to the Scottish Highlands. Consider a single night at a local site with good facilities and easy escape options if things don't go according to plan.

Practice at home: Set up your tent in the garden and let the children sleep outside for a night. This familiarizes everyone with camping equipment, sleeping arrangements, and outdoor sounds in a safe, familiar environment.

Involve everyone: Include all family members in planning and preparation. Children who help choose the destination, plan activities, and pack equipment feel more invested in the experience's success.

Prepare for challenges: Things will go wrong—that's part of camping's character-building charm. Approach challenges as adventures and learning opportunities rather than disasters. Your attitude significantly influences how your children perceive and remember difficulties.

Document the journey: Keep a family camping journal, take photos, and encourage children to record their experiences. This documentation helps build camping identity and creates anticipation for future adventures.

The foundation you build through careful planning, appropriate expectations, and gradual confidence building will support years of family camping adventures. Remember, the goal isn't perfection—it's connection, adventure, and the creation of lasting family memories.

In the following chapters, we'll explore specific regions across the UK, each offering unique opportunities for family camping adventures. From Cornwall's dramatic coastlines to Scotland's mystical highlands, you'll discover 101 carefully selected sites that provide perfect bases for family exploration and memory-making.

Your adventure awaits—let's begin exploring the incredible diversity of family camping opportunities that the UK offers.

Chapter 2: Southwest England - Coastal Magic & Moorland Adventures

Southwest England is where family camping dreams come alive. From the dramatic granite tors of Dartmoor to the golden beaches of Cornwall, this region offers an intoxicating blend of wild landscapes, gentle countryside, and some of Britain's most spectacular coastline. For families, it represents the perfect storm of adventure, safety, and sheer natural beauty that creates those "pinch me" moments you'll treasure forever.

The Southwest has always held a special place in British hearts, but for camping families, it's nothing short of magical. Where else can you wake up to the sound of waves crashing against ancient cliffs, spend your morning exploring rock pools with excited toddlers, enjoy a pasty lunch while watching seals bask on distant rocks, and end your day toasting marshmallows around a campfire as the sun sets over the Atlantic?

This chapter will guide you through twelve carefully selected campsites across Cornwall, Devon, Dorset, and Somerset – each chosen not just for their stunning locations, but for their genuine understanding of what families need. We're talking about sites where the playground equipment is regularly maintained and age-appropriate, where the shower blocks are spotlessly clean with baby-changing facilities, and where the site owners genuinely care about creating magical experiences for children.

What makes Southwest camping special isn't just the scenery – though watching your children's faces light up as they spot dolphins from a clifftop campsite never gets old. It's the way this region seems designed for family adventures. The South West Coast Path provides endless walking opportunities suitable for every age, from pushchair-friendly sections to challenging cliff walks for teenagers. Beach access is often direct from campsites, meaning you can be building sandcastles within minutes of leaving your tent.

The cultural richness adds another layer to your family camping experience. This is the land of King Arthur and Cornish pasties, of smugglers' caves and ancient stone circles. Your children won't just be camping – they'll be living in the middle of stories that have captured imaginations for centuries. And unlike some heritage-heavy destinations, Southwest England wears its history lightly, making it accessible and exciting for young minds.

Understanding the Southwest Advantage

Before we dive into specific sites, it's worth understanding what makes this region so family-friendly. The Gulf Stream's warming influence means milder weather than you might expect, extending the camping season and making coastal camping comfortable even in shoulder seasons. The region's tourism infrastructure is incredibly family-oriented – developed over generations of welcoming families on holiday.

From a practical standpoint, the Southwest offers excellent value for families. Many campsites here have been family-run for generations, meaning they understand the real needs of camping families rather than just providing generic facilities. You'll find site owners who remember your children's names, who can recommend the best spots for crabbing, and who keep a weather eye on conditions to suggest the perfect activities for each day.

The region's compact nature means you can base yourself at one excellent campsite and explore multiple areas. A well-chosen site in Devon, for instance, can give you access to both dramatic moorland and stunning coastline within a twenty-minute drive.

---

1. Wowo Camping - Devon's Hidden Coastal Gem

Location: Near Dartmouth, South Devon
Best For: Families seeking luxury camping with spectacular views
Age Sweet Spot: All ages, particularly 4-12 years

Site Overview

Perched on the cliffs above Start Bay, Wowo Camping redefines what glamping can be for families. This isn't your typical campsite – it's a carefully curated experience where luxury meets adventure in the most natural way possible. The site occupies a stunning position with panoramic views across the English Channel, where you can watch fishing boats heading out at dawn and pleasure craft returning at sunset.

The accommodation here consists of beautifully designed safari tents, each positioned to maximize privacy and views. What sets Wowo apart is how they've thought about families at every level. The tents are spacious enough for family life but cozy enough to feel like a real adventure. Most importantly, they've managed to create luxury without losing that essential camping connection to the outdoors.

The site maintains an exclusive feel with just twelve pitches, meaning your children can roam safely while you maintain that crucial parental awareness. The atmosphere is sophisticated but never stuffy – think middle-class families who appreciate good design and stunning locations but still want their kids to get properly muddy.

Family Facilities Rating

Playground & Activities: ★★★★☆
Rather than a traditional playground, Wowo offers something better – a vast natural playground. The cliff-top location provides endless exploration opportunities, with safe paths leading to hidden coves and rock formations that seem designed for imaginative play. The site provides outdoor games equipment and has created natural play areas using logs and rope swings.

Facilities: ★★★★★
The shower blocks are exceptional – spotlessly clean, heated, and designed with families in mind. Spacious family bathrooms include baby-changing facilities, and the design aesthetic is more boutique

hotel than typical campsite. The shop is small but perfectly curated, focusing on local products and essentials.

Swimming & Water: ★★★★☆

No on-site swimming pool, but direct access to secluded beaches more than compensates. The private beach access is a huge draw – imagine having a virtually private cove where your children can play safely while you relax with a coffee and that million-pound view.

Age-Specific Activities

Ages 0-3: This age group will love the gentle adventures Wowo offers. The site's elevated position means stunning views but also safety – toddlers can't wander toward dangerous cliff edges due to careful fencing. The beach access involves a short walk (manageable with a good all-terrain buggy), and the protected coves provide perfect paddling opportunities. Site owners Sarah and Tom are parents themselves and have created quiet zones where naptime can happen peacefully even when older children are playing nearby.

Ages 4-8: This is where Wowo really shines for families. Children this age are perfectly placed to enjoy the site's adventure opportunities while being safe enough for parents to relax. Rock pooling becomes a daily obsession – the protected coves below the site teem with crabs, anemones, and small fish. The site provides identification charts and buckets, turning each expedition into a learning experience. Natural play areas include rope swings and climbing logs, while the cliff-top location provides endless space for ball games and kite flying.

Ages 9-12: Pre-teens often struggle with the balance between adventure and safety, but Wowo gets this right. Older children can explore further along the coastal path (with parental permission), participate in organized beach activities like surf awareness sessions, and enjoy the responsibility of helping younger siblings with rock pooling. The site's location near Dartmouth means day trips can include sailing experiences and maritime museums that capture this age group's growing interest in real-world skills.

Ages 13+: Teenagers appreciate Wowo's sophisticated atmosphere – this isn't a place where they'll feel embarrassed to be seen camping with family. The site provides WiFi (though encourages digital detoxing), and the nearby town of Dartmouth offers independent exploration opportunities. Photography becomes a natural activity with such stunning scenery, and many families report teenagers becoming genuinely enthusiastic about coastal walks and wildlife spotting.

Local Attractions Within 30 Minutes

Free & Low-Cost Options: The South West Coast Path provides unlimited walking opportunities, with sections suitable for every fitness level. Start Point Lighthouse offers guided tours (small fee) and spectacular views. Blackpool Sands is a beautiful family beach just ten minutes away, with excellent facilities and safe swimming. The medieval town of Dartmouth itself is perfect for wandering, with narrow streets, a working harbor, and plenty of opportunities for ice cream stops.

Educational Opportunities: Dartmouth's maritime heritage provides numerous learning opportunities. The Royal Naval College offers occasional tours, while the town museum focuses on local maritime history in an accessible way. Coleton Fishacre (National Trust) combines beautiful gardens with 1930s house tours that capture children's imaginations with stories of Art Deco glamour.

Weather Alternatives: When coastal weather turns, the nearby market town of Totnes provides covered shopping, cafes, and the fascinating Totnes Castle. The Dartmouth Steam Railway runs in most weather conditions and provides a magical journey through the Devon countryside. For families with older children, the indoor climbing center in Newton Abbot offers rainy day adventures.

Parent Tips & Insider Knowledge

Book well in advance – Wowo's reputation means peak season dates disappear quickly. The best pitches offer the most spectacular views but can be windier in adverse weather; families with very young children might prefer slightly more sheltered options. Local knowledge from site owners is invaluable – they'll recommend the best tides for rock pooling and warn you about weather changes before they become obvious.

The nearby village of Stoke Fleming has an excellent pub (The Green Dragon) that welcomes families and serves locally-sourced food. However, most families find themselves cooking more often than usual at Wowo – something about the location and the luxury tents makes outdoor dining feel special rather than necessary.

For groceries, the Dartmouth Farmers Market (Saturdays) offers local produce and becomes a morning adventure for the whole family. The larger Tesco in Dartmouth covers all essentials, but many families report enjoying the slower pace of shopping locally and involving children in choosing ingredients for campfire cooking.

Practical Information

Contact: Book through their website (woow.co.uk) or phone 01803 770111
Booking Strategy: Opens for bookings in January; peak summer weeks often book within hours
Price Range: Premium (£200-£400 per night for family safari tent)
Accessibility: Limited mobility access due to natural terrain; contact directly to discuss specific needs

---

2. River Dart Country Park & Campsite - Adventure Central for Active Families

Location: Buckfastleigh, Devon
Best For: Families with energetic children who love outdoor adventures
Age Sweet Spot: 4-14 years (though facilities for all ages)

Site Overview

If your family measures a successful holiday by how muddy the children get and how soundly they sleep,

River Dart Country Park is your perfect base. This isn't just a campsite – it's a 90-acre adventure playground where your tent happens to be pitched. The River Dart flows through the site, creating a natural boundary and providing the soundtrack of running water that makes this one of the most peaceful places to fall asleep under canvas.

The site operates on a simple principle: children need space, adventure, and safety in equal measure. The campsite itself is spacious and well-organized, but it's the immediate access to adventure activities that sets it apart. Your children can literally roll out of their sleeping bags and into treetop adventures, river activities, and woodland exploration.

What parent visitors consistently praise is the site's understanding of family rhythms. They know that 6 am is a perfectly reasonable time for excited children to start their day, that muddy clothes are a sign of success, and that sometimes parents need a coffee and five minutes' peace while children exhaust themselves safely nearby.

Family Facilities Rating

Adventure Activities: ★★★★★

This is where River Dart excels beyond almost anywhere else in the Southwest. The High Ropes course is suitable for children from 4 years up (with different difficulty levels), while the Zip Wire provides thrills for older children. The Adventure Playground is vast and varied, with natural wooden structures that blend seamlessly into the woodland setting. Most activities are included in your camping fee, making this exceptional value for families.

Basic Facilities: ★★★☆☆

The shower blocks are clean and functional rather than luxurious. Family bathrooms are available, and hot water is reliable. The laundry facilities are particularly useful for families staying longer or after particularly muddy days. The on-site cafe serves hearty, child-friendly food, though options are limited.

Natural Features: ★★★★★

The river access is carefully managed for safety while maintaining the adventure element. Shallow areas are perfect for paddling and dam-building, while deeper sections are clearly marked and supervised during organized activities. The woodland setting provides natural shade and endless exploration opportunities.

Age-Specific Activities

Ages 0-3: While this site is really designed for older children, toddlers aren't forgotten. The adventure playground includes a dedicated area for smaller children with low-level climbing frames and safe surfaces. The riverside areas have shallow, slow-moving sections perfect for paddling under careful supervision. The natural setting provides endless fascination – collecting sticks, watching wildlife, and simply experiencing the sights and sounds of woodland and water.

Ages 4-8: This age group finds paradise at River Dart. The High Ropes course includes courses specifically designed for smaller children, building confidence and physical skills. River activities like raft building (supervised) combine creativity with outdoor skills. The woodland provides perfect den-building territory, while organized activities include nature trails and treasure hunts. Many parents report children as young as four becoming genuinely competent at outdoor skills they've never attempted before.

Ages 9-12: Pre-teens can access more challenging ropes courses and zip wire experiences while developing genuine outdoor skills. Bushcraft activities teach practical abilities like fire-lighting and shelter-building. The site's education program includes wildlife identification and countryside skills. This age group often becomes protective of younger siblings, taking pride in helping them navigate easier courses and sharing their newly-acquired knowledge.

Ages 13+: Teenagers who might normally grumble about family camping often surprise parents with their enthusiasm at River Dart. The more challenging adventure activities provide genuine thrills and opportunities to push personal boundaries. The site offers Young Leader programs where teenagers can help with younger children's activities, providing responsibility and social interaction. Many families report teenagers requesting to return, which is the ultimate endorsement.

Local Attractions Within 30 Minutes

Buckfast Abbey: This working monastery offers peaceful walks, a gift shop full of interesting items (the famous Buckfast Bee products), and occasional guided tours that provide insights into monastic life. Children are often fascinated by the working aspects of the abbey, particularly the beehives and gardens.

Dartmoor National Park: The site provides an excellent base for exploring Dartmoor's gentler areas. Widecombe-in-the-Moor offers classic Dartmoor scenery with safe walking and the famous fair (if you're visiting in September). The nearby Buckfast to Lavington railway walk provides level ground for family cycling.

South Devon Railway: The steam railway between Buckfastleigh and Totnes provides a magical journey through the Dart Valley. Children love the authentic steam experience, while parents appreciate the gentle pace and stunning scenery. The Buckfastleigh station includes a small museum and model railway that can easily occupy an hour.

Totnes: This historic market town provides culture and shopping opportunities. The castle ruins are perfect for imaginative play, while the town's alternative culture (it was Britain's first Transition Town) provides interesting shops and cafes that welcome families.

Parent Tips & Insider Knowledge

River Dart works best for families staying three nights or more – there's so much to do on-site that shorter stays feel rushed. Book pitch 15-25 for the best river access while maintaining safety for smaller children. The site gets busy during school holidays, but the space is so vast that it rarely feels crowded.

Pack old clothes and plenty of them – children will get muddy, wet, and thoroughly adventurous. The site has good drying facilities, but having backup clothes allows for multiple adventures per day. Waterproof shoes are essential; wellies are better than walking boots for the shallow river sections.

The on-site cafe is reasonably priced and child-friendly, but many families enjoy the extra adventure of cooking over campfires (permitted in designated areas). Local shopping is limited – stock up in Totnes or Newton Abbot before arriving.

Consider combining your stay with local accommodation if you have family members who prefer comfort – nearby pubs and B&Bs mean grandparents can join the adventure without roughing it under canvas.

Practical Information

Contact: 01364 652511 or book online at riverdart.co.uk
Booking Tips: Peak season books early; mid-week breaks offer better value and smaller crowds
Price Range: Mid-range (£15-25 per tent per night plus activity fees)
Accessibility: Some adventure activities accessible for limited mobility; contact for specific requirements

---

3. Halse Farm Camping - Cornwall's Authentic Farm Experience

Location: Near St. Ives, Cornwall
Best For: Families wanting authentic farm life combined with beach access
Age Sweet Spot: All ages, particularly magical for 3-10 years

Site Overview

Halse Farm represents everything wonderful about traditional Cornish farming culture, wrapped up in a genuinely family-friendly camping experience. This working farm has been in the same family for four generations, and their understanding of both agriculture and family camping creates something genuinely special. The farm sits in a protected valley just two miles from St. Ives, offering the perfect combination of rural tranquility and coastal adventure.

What makes Halse Farm unique is its authenticity. This isn't farming themed for tourists – it's a real working farm that happens to welcome camping families with enormous warmth and expertise. Children don't just see farm animals; they participate in daily routines, learn about agricultural cycles, and develop genuine understanding of where food comes from.

The camping areas are generous and well-drained, with different fields offering varying levels of facilities and proximity to farm activities. The farm buildings provide natural windbreaks and create cozy, sheltered camping spots that feel secure rather than exposed.

Family Facilities Rating

Farm Experience: ★★★★★
This is what sets Halse Farm apart from virtually every other campsite in the Southwest. Daily farm

activities include egg collecting, feeding animals, and learning about seasonal farming tasks. Children can help with (safe, supervised) farm chores and develop genuine agricultural knowledge. The farm includes traditional Cornish breeds, providing educational opportunities about conservation and local heritage.

Basic Facilities: ★★★★☆

Clean, functional shower blocks with reliable hot water and family bathrooms. The farm shop sells fresh produce from the farm alongside camping essentials. Laundry facilities are available, particularly useful after muddy farm adventures. The site maintains high standards while preserving its working farm character.

Beach Access: ★★★★☆

A gentle twenty-minute walk through farmland leads to Carbis Bay, one of Cornwall's most beautiful beaches. The route is pushchair-friendly and becomes part of the daily adventure. Alternative access to St. Ives is via the scenic coastal footpath (more challenging but spectacularly beautiful).

Age-Specific Activities

Ages 0-3: Toddlers find endless fascination in farm life. Daily routines like feeding chickens and collecting eggs become major adventures. The farm's gentle animals (including particularly docile sheep and friendly farm cats) provide safe animal interaction opportunities. Pushchair access throughout most of the farm means nap times don't interrupt exploration. The protected valley location provides natural safety boundaries while offering space for energetic toddlers to run freely.

Ages 4-8: This age group often describes Halse Farm as their favorite holiday ever. Participating in real farm work – from feeding animals to helping with harvest activities (seasonally) – provides genuine responsibility and pride. The farm includes a play area with traditional wooden equipment, but most children prefer the endless natural play opportunities. Learning where food comes from becomes hands-on education, often changing eating habits long after the holiday ends.

Ages 9-12: Pre-teens can take on more responsible farm tasks and genuinely help with animal care. Many develop particular relationships with specific animals and take pride in their farming knowledge. The nearby coastal path provides appropriate walking challenges, while St. Ives offers cultural experiences and independent exploration opportunities. This age group often becomes passionate about sustainable living and agricultural conservation.

Ages 13+: Teenagers initially skeptical about farm camping often become the most enthusiastic converts. The authenticity appeals to their developing social consciousness, while the combination of responsibility (through farm work) and freedom (exploring the coastal area) provides ideal balance. Many teenagers report that Halse Farm changes their perspective on food, agriculture, and environmental issues.

Local Attractions Within 30 Minutes

St. Ives: One of Britain's most beautiful seaside towns, combining stunning beaches with world-class art galleries. The Tate St. Ives provides excellent family programs, while the town's narrow streets and harbor offer endless exploration opportunities. The St. Ives Museum includes fascinating displays about local history and culture.

Carbis Bay Beach: Accessible on foot from the farm, this award-winning beach offers safe swimming, excellent facilities, and the kind of golden sand that makes Cornwall famous. The beach cafe serves good family food, while the nearby coastal path provides spectacular walks suitable for all fitness levels.

Barbara Hepworth Museum & Sculpture Garden: This unique attraction combines art appreciation with garden exploration. Children often respond surprisingly well to Hepworth's sculptures, particularly when they can explore the artist's actual workspace and garden.

Seal Island Boat Trips: Weather permitting, boat trips from St. Ives harbor provide wildlife watching opportunities and spectacular coastal views. Children love spotting seals, while parents appreciate the professional, safety-conscious operators.

Parent Tips & Insider Knowledge

The farm experience varies significantly by season – spring brings lambing, summer provides full agricultural activity, autumn includes harvest participation, and winter offers cozy, intimate experiences with reduced crowds. Book according to what experiences most appeal to your family.

Wellingtons are absolutely essential – the farm provides authentic muddy experiences that require proper footwear. Pack clothes that can get genuinely dirty and consider bringing extra layers for changeable coastal weather.

The farm shop sells excellent local produce at reasonable prices – many families report eating better than usual by incorporating fresh farm eggs, milk, and vegetables into their camping meals. The owner, Helen, provides excellent local knowledge and can recommend activities based on your children's interests and weather conditions.

St. Ives parking can be challenging during peak season – the walk from the farm is actually preferable to driving and searching for spaces. The coastal footpath provides spectacular scenery and good exercise, though it's more challenging with younger children or pushchairs.

Practical Information

Contact: 01736 795583 or email bookings@halsefarm.com
Booking Strategy: Accepts bookings from February; Easter and summer holidays book quickly
Price Range: Budget-friendly (£12-18 per tent per night)
Accessibility: Limited access for wheelchairs due to working farm terrain; discuss requirements directly

---

4. Wooda Farm Holiday Park - North Devon's Family Paradise

Location: Near Bude, North Devon/Cornwall border

Best For: Families wanting comprehensive facilities with countryside and coast access
Age Sweet Spot: All ages, exceptional for 5-12 years

Site Overview

Wooda Farm proves that family holiday parks can maintain heart and character while providing comprehensive modern facilities. This 120-acre site occupies rolling countryside just three miles from Bude's spectacular beaches, creating the perfect balance between rural tranquility and coastal adventure. What sets Wooda apart from generic holiday parks is its genuine family ownership and operation – this is a family business that truly understands family needs.

The site layout is thoughtfully designed with different areas catering to various family preferences. Quiet zones suit families with younger children or those seeking more peaceful camping experiences, while livelier areas accommodate families wanting full holiday park atmosphere. The facilities are comprehensive without being overwhelming, and the natural Devon countryside setting prevents any feeling of artificial resort atmosphere.

The park's size allows for extensive facilities while maintaining personal service. Site owners and staff know returning families by name and remember children's preferences from previous visits. This combination of professionalism and personal touch creates the secure, welcoming environment that allows both parents and children to relax completely.

Family Facilities Rating

Swimming Complex: ★★★★★
The indoor swimming pool complex includes dedicated children's areas, teaching pool, and accessible facilities. The outdoor splash pad provides summer fun for all ages, while the pool heating ensures year-round use. Qualified lifeguards maintain safety while encouraging fun, and the changing facilities are spacious and family-friendly.

Adventure Activities: ★★★★☆
The adventure playground is vast and varied, with equipment suitable for toddlers through teenagers. The 9-hole golf course provides family putting opportunities, while the sports field accommodates everything from football to kite flying. Organized activities during peak season include treasure hunts, craft sessions, and evening entertainment suitable for families.

Essential Facilities: ★★★★★
Shower blocks are maintained to exceptionally high standards with family bathrooms, baby-changing facilities, and accessible options. The site shop stocks everything from fresh bread and milk to camping equipment and beach toys. Laundry facilities include large-capacity machines and reliable dryers.

Age-Specific Activities

Ages 0-3: Toddlers thrive at Wooda with dedicated play areas featuring age-appropriate equipment and safe surfaces. The teaching pool provides perfect first swimming experiences, while the splash pad offers water play without swimming concerns. Pushchair-friendly paths throughout the site mean easy access to all facilities. Quiet camping areas ensure afternoon naps aren't disrupted by livelier family activities.

Ages 4-8: This age group finds endless entertainment at Wooda. The main swimming pool provides safe, supervised fun, while the adventure playground offers challenges appropriate for developing physical skills. Organized activities during school holidays include craft sessions, treasure hunts, and nature walks. The site's size means children can safely explore while parents maintain visual contact.

Ages 9-12: Pre-teens appreciate Wooda's balance of independence and safety. The 9-hole golf course provides skill development opportunities, while the sports facilities accommodate team games and individual challenges. Swimming becomes more adventurous with diving boards and deeper areas. This age group often takes responsibility for younger siblings while gaining confidence in a secure environment.

Ages 13+: Teenagers find surprising enjoyment at Wooda, particularly with the swimming facilities and sports options. The site's WiFi allows digital connectivity while the extensive grounds provide space for independence. Many teenagers become enthusiastic about the golf course and take pride in improving their skills across the holiday.

Local Attractions Within 30 Minutes

Bude Beaches: Multiple spectacular beaches within easy reach, each offering different experiences. Summerleaze Beach provides safe family swimming and excellent facilities, while Widemouth Bay offers surfing opportunities and dramatic coastal scenery. The coastal path connecting the beaches provides excellent walking with spectacular views.

Bude Castle & Heritage Centre: This unique hexagonal castle houses local history exhibitions that bring North Devon's heritage to life for families. The surrounding parkland includes play areas and provides perfect picnic settings.

The Big Sheep: Devon's woolly theme park combines education with entertainment. Children learn about farming and wool production while enjoying rides, shows, and animal encounters. The indoor facilities provide excellent wet-weather alternatives.

Tamar Lakes: These two reservoirs provide excellent family walking opportunities with level paths suitable for all ages. Wildlife watching includes various bird species, while the visitor center provides educational information and refreshments.

Parent Tips & Insider Knowledge

Wooda works well for extended stays – the comprehensive facilities mean you can easily occupy a week without feeling limited. Book pitches in the quieter areas (Fields 1-3) for more peaceful experiences, or choose Fields 4-6 for proximity to facilities and livelier atmosphere.

The site shop is well-stocked but expensive for major shopping. Bude's supermarkets (Morrisons and smaller options) provide better value for weekly shops. However, the convenience of on-site shopping for daily essentials and forgotten items is invaluable.

Swimming pool sessions can get busy during peak times – early morning or early evening provides more relaxed experiences. The pool complex includes spectator areas where parents can supervise while enjoying coffee and WiFi.

Peak season entertainment is comprehensive but optional – families preferring quieter experiences can easily avoid organized activities while still accessing all facilities.

Practical Information

Contact: 01288 352069 or book online at woodafarm.co.uk
Booking Timeline: Opens January for peak season; popular weeks book within weeks
Price Range: Mid-range (£18-35 per night depending on pitch type and season)
Accessibility: Excellent accessibility throughout with designated pitches and adapted facilities

---

5. Golden Cap Holiday Park - Dorset's Coastal Crown Jewel

Location: Near Bridport, Dorset
Best For: Families seeking dramatic coastal scenery with comprehensive facilities
Age Sweet Spot: All ages, particularly stunning for 8+ years

Site Overview

Golden Cap Holiday Park occupies one of the most spectacular positions in the Southwest, sitting directly on the Jurassic Coast within an Area of Outstanding Natural Beauty. The park takes its name from Golden Cap itself – the highest point on the south coast of England – which provides a dramatic backdrop and endless walking opportunities for adventurous families.

What makes this site exceptional isn't just its UNESCO World Heritage coastline location, but how thoughtfully it's been developed to enhance rather than dominate the natural environment. The pitches are generously spaced across natural terraces, meaning every family enjoys spectacular sea views while maintaining privacy and space.

The park successfully balances comprehensive modern facilities with respect for its stunning natural setting. This isn't a site where facilities dominate the landscape – instead, everything is designed to help families make the most of one of England's most beautiful coastlines while ensuring comfort and safety.

Family Facilities Rating

Location & Views: ★★★★★
Simply unbeatable. Every pitch offers sea views, while the elevated position provides panoramic vistas

across Lyme Bay. Spectacular sunsets are visible from your tent, while the immediate access to the South West Coast Path opens up unlimited exploration opportunities.

Swimming & Recreation: ★★★★☆

The heated indoor swimming pool complex includes children's areas and accessible facilities. While not as extensive as some holiday parks, the pool provides perfect respite after coastal walking or beach adventures. The recreation room offers wet-weather alternatives with games and seating areas.

Essential Facilities: ★★★★★

Exceptionally clean and well-maintained facilities throughout. Shower blocks include family bathrooms and baby-changing facilities. The site shop covers essentials and local products, while the restaurant provides family-friendly dining with spectacular views.

Age-Specific Activities

Ages 0-3: Toddlers can safely enjoy the site's elevated position with careful supervision. The indoor pool provides perfect early swimming experiences, while the site's layout allows safe exploration. Pushchair access is good throughout the main areas, though coastal path walking requires more robust buggies and careful route planning.

Ages 4-8: This age group begins to appreciate the site's spectacular setting while safely enjoying coastal adventures. Supervised beach trips to nearby Seatown provide rock pooling and safe swimming opportunities. The coastal path includes easier sections suitable for developing walking skills, while the site's facilities provide secure base for adventures.

Ages 9-12: Pre-teens can begin to access more challenging coastal walking while developing genuine appreciation for the natural environment. This age group often becomes fascinated with the Jurassic Coast's geological significance and fossil hunting opportunities. Swimming becomes more adventurous, while the site's position allows for independence within safe boundaries.

Ages 13+: Teenagers often find Golden Cap their favorite family camping experience. The dramatic coastal scenery provides perfect photography opportunities and social media content they're proud to share. More challenging walking routes and the area's World Heritage status appeal to developing intellectual curiosity.

Local Attractions Within 30 Minutes

Charmouth Beach: Famous for fossil hunting, this beach provides endless fascination for all ages. The Charmouth Heritage Coast Centre offers expert guidance on fossil identification and provides tools for safe collecting. The beach itself is excellent for family use with good facilities and safe swimming areas.

Lyme Regis: This historic seaside town combines beautiful beaches with cultural attractions. The Lyme Regis Museum brings local geological history to life, while the town's narrow streets and harbor provide perfect family wandering opportunities. The Marine Aquarium offers wet-weather alternatives and fascinating insights into local marine life.

Bridport: This thriving market town provides excellent shopping, dining, and cultural opportunities. The weekly markets offer local produce and crafts, while the town's independent shops provide unique browsing experiences that older children often enjoy.

West Bay: Made famous by the TV series Broadchurch, this working harbor provides dramatic cliff scenery and excellent fish and chips. The beach is perfect for family use, while the cliff-top walks offer spectacular views for more adventurous families.

Parent Tips & Insider Knowledge

Golden Cap works best for families who appreciate natural beauty and don't require extensive on-site entertainment. The site's strength lies in its position rather than comprehensive facilities – families seeking busy holiday park atmosphere might prefer alternatives.

Coastal weather can be changeable – pack layers and waterproofs even in summer. The elevated position can be windier than sheltered inland sites, but the views more than compensate. Consider bringing windbreaks for additional comfort.

Fossil hunting at Charmouth requires timing with tides – low tide provides best opportunities, while recent storms often reveal new finds. The Heritage Coast Centre provides tide timetables and safety advice. Always supervise children near cliffs and unstable cliff faces.

Local dining is excellent but can be expensive – many families enjoy combining restaurant meals with self-catering using local produce from Bridport market and nearby farm shops.

Practical Information

Contact: 01308 422139 or book online at goldencap.co.uk
Booking Pattern: Peak weeks book early; shoulder seasons offer excellent value with spectacular views
Price Range: Premium (£25-45 per night reflecting premium location)
Accessibility: Some limitations due to coastal terrain; accessible pitches available with advance booking

---

6. Wellington Country Park - Somerset's Adventure Hub

Location: Near Taunton, Somerset
Best For: Families wanting adventure activities with countryside charm
Age Sweet Spot: 4-14 years (excellent adventure facilities)

Site Overview

Wellington Country Park demonstrates how thoughtful development can enhance rather than dominate beautiful countryside. This 36-acre site combines natural Somerset landscapes with carefully designed adventure facilities, creating an environment where children can safely push boundaries while parents enjoy genuine relaxation.

The park occupies gently rolling countryside in the Blackdown Hills Area of Outstanding Natural Beauty, providing stunning views across the Somerset Levels and toward Exmoor. The camping areas are integrated into the landscape rather than imposed upon it, creating a natural feel that preserves the area's inherent beauty while providing comprehensive family facilities.

What distinguishes Wellington from purely commercial adventure parks is its scale and philosophy. Large enough to provide varied activities but small enough for personal service, the park maintains a genuine focus on family enjoyment rather than profit maximization. Staff know regular visitors and remember children's preferences and achievements from previous visits.

Family Facilities Rating

Adventure Activities: ★★★★★

Exceptional range of activities suitable for various ages and abilities. The high ropes course includes multiple difficulty levels, while the zip wire provides genuine thrills for older children. Ground-based activities include adventure playground, climbing wall, and assault course options. Most activities are included in camping fees, providing excellent value.

Natural Features: ★★★★☆

The park includes lakes, woodland, and open grassland providing diverse environments for exploration and play. Nature trails are well-maintained and suitable for family walking, while the lake provides fishing opportunities (day tickets available) and wildlife watching. The varied habitats support diverse bird and animal life that adds educational value to stays.

Essential Facilities: ★★★★☆

Clean, well-maintained facilities throughout with family bathrooms and baby-changing areas. The site shop covers essentials plus activity equipment rental. Cafe serves hearty, child-friendly meals with outdoor seating overlooking the activities. Laundry facilities and electric hook-ups available.

Age-Specific Activities

Ages 0-3: While Wellington is designed primarily for older children, toddlers aren't forgotten. A dedicated toddler play area provides safe equipment and soft surfaces. The lake area includes shallow, safe sections for supervised paddling. Pushchair-friendly paths connect main facilities, while quiet camping areas ensure nap times aren't disrupted by adventure activities.

Ages 4-8: This age group finds Wellington absolutely magical. The junior high ropes course builds confidence and physical skills progressively. The adventure playground provides varied challenges that grow with developing abilities. Nature trails become treasure hunts with activity sheets available from reception. Many children report Wellington as their "best holiday ever" with this age group typically requesting immediate return visits.

Ages 9-12: Pre-teens can access more challenging adventure activities while developing genuine outdoor skills. The full high ropes course provides physical challenges and confidence building, while bushcraft activities teach practical skills like shelter building and fire safety. This age group often becomes protective mentors for younger children, taking pride in helping siblings navigate easier activities.

Ages 13+: Teenagers initially skeptical about family camping often become Wellington's most enthusiastic advocates. The more challenging activities provide genuine physical and mental challenges, while the site's layout allows independence within safe boundaries. Many teenagers develop lasting interests in outdoor activities and environmental awareness through their Wellington experiences.

Local Attractions Within 30 Minutes

Wellington Monument: Somerset's most distinctive landmark, this 175-foot tower commemorates the Duke of Wellington and provides spectacular views across Somerset and into Devon. The surrounding countryside offers excellent family walking, while the monument itself provides a focal point for longer walks.

Taunton: Somerset's county town offers excellent shopping, dining, and cultural opportunities. The Museum of Somerset provides fascinating insights into local history, while Vivary Park offers additional play facilities and peaceful walks. The town center is pedestrian-friendly and perfect for family exploration.

Fleet Air Arm Museum: Located at RNAS Yeovilton, this world-class aviation museum provides fascinating insights into naval aviation history. The collection includes Concorde and numerous historic aircraft that capture children's imaginations. Interactive exhibits and flight simulators provide hands-on learning experiences.

Cheddar Gorge: Britain's largest gorge provides dramatic scenery and fascinating geology. The show caves offer underground adventures, while the gorge itself provides spectacular walking opportunities. The visitor center includes interactive exhibits about local wildlife and geology.

Parent Tips & Insider Knowledge

Wellington works best for families staying three or more nights – the adventure activities are so engaging that shorter stays feel rushed. Book pitches near the facilities for easy access, or choose more distant pitches for greater tranquility and better countryside views.

Activity sessions can get busy during peak times – book popular activities (high ropes, zip wire) early in your stay to avoid disappointment. Many activities have weather restrictions, so plan alternatives for adverse conditions.

The on-site cafe provides good family food at reasonable prices, but many families enjoy the additional adventure of campfire cooking in designated areas. Local shopping is available in Wellington town, while Taunton provides comprehensive supermarket options.

Safety briefings for adventure activities are thorough but essential – ensure children understand and follow all instructions. Staff are experienced and safety-conscious, but parental supervision remains important for younger children.

Practical Information

Contact: 01823 652025 or book online at wellingtoncountrypark.co.uk
Booking Strategy: Opens for bookings in February; peak weeks book quickly due to excellent reputation
Price Range: Mid-range (£20-30 per night including most activities)
Accessibility: Some adventure activities have physical requirements; alternative activities available for all abilities

---

7. Trevalgan Holiday Park - Cornwall's Coastal Adventure Base

Location: Near St. Ives, Cornwall
Best For: Families wanting comprehensive facilities with authentic Cornish coastal access
Age Sweet Spot: All ages, particularly excellent for 6-16 years

Site Overview

Trevalgan Holiday Park occupies an enviable position in the heart of Cornwall's most spectacular coastal region, providing direct access to some of Britain's most beautiful beaches while maintaining the comprehensive facilities that make family holidays genuinely relaxing for parents. The park sits on elevated ground overlooking St. Ives Bay, providing spectacular sea views from many pitches while being just minutes from both St. Ives and the stunning beaches of the north Cornish coast.

What sets Trevalgan apart from generic holiday parks is its genuine Cornish character and family ownership. This is a park that has grown organically over decades, with each development carefully considered to enhance rather than overwhelm the natural coastal setting. The result is a site that feels authentically Cornish while providing all the facilities modern families expect.

The park's size allows for comprehensive facilities while maintaining personal service. Regular families are welcomed back year after year, with staff remembering children's names and preferences. This combination of professionalism and personal touch creates an environment where both parents and children can relax completely while enjoying one of England's most beautiful coastal regions.

Family Facilities Rating

Swimming Complex: ★★★★★
Outstanding indoor and outdoor swimming facilities including heated pools, children's splash areas, and toddler pools. The complex includes changing facilities designed for families, with spacious family changing rooms and baby facilities. Lifeguards maintain safety while encouraging enjoyment, and the pool heating ensures comfortable swimming regardless of weather.

Entertainment & Activities: ★★★★☆
Comprehensive entertainment program during peak season including children's clubs, family shows, and

organized activities. The adventure playground is extensive and well-maintained with equipment suitable for all ages. Sports facilities include tennis courts, football pitches, and indoor games rooms that provide wet-weather alternatives.

Essential Facilities: ★★★★★

Exceptional standards throughout with multiple shower blocks, laundry facilities, and comprehensive shopping. The site shop stocks everything from fresh bread and local produce to camping equipment and beach toys. Restaurant facilities provide family dining with children's menus and high chairs.

Age-Specific Activities

Ages 0-3: Toddlers thrive at Trevalgan with dedicated play areas, toddler pools, and safe, contained environments. The site's layout includes quiet zones perfect for afternoon naps, while the comprehensive facilities mean everything needed for toddler care is readily available. Pushchair-friendly access throughout ensures easy movement around the extensive site.

Ages 4-8: This age group finds Trevalgan absolutely magical. The swimming complex provides safe, supervised fun with dedicated children's areas, while the adventure playground offers appropriate physical challenges. Organized activities during school holidays include craft sessions, treasure hunts, and beach activities. The site's proximity to St. Ives provides additional cultural and educational opportunities.

Ages 9-12: Pre-teens appreciate Trevalgan's balance of independence and safety. The swimming facilities become more adventurous with diving boards and deeper pools, while sports facilities provide team game opportunities. This age group often takes responsibility for younger siblings while gaining confidence in a secure environment. The nearby coastal path provides appropriate walking challenges with spectacular scenery.

Ages 13+: Teenagers find surprising enjoyment at Trevalgan, particularly with the comprehensive facilities and social opportunities. The site's WiFi allows digital connectivity while the extensive grounds and proximity to St. Ives provide independence opportunities. Evening entertainment includes options appropriate for older children, while the beach access provides social spaces and activities.

Local Attractions Within 30 Minutes

St. Ives: One of Britain's most beautiful and culturally rich seaside towns. The Tate St. Ives provides world-class art in a spectacular setting, while the Barbara Hepworth Museum offers unique insights into one of Britain's greatest sculptors. The town's beaches, narrow streets, and working harbor provide endless exploration opportunities for families.

Porthmeor Beach: St. Ives' main beach offers excellent family facilities, safe swimming, and spectacular Atlantic views. The beach includes a renowned cafe and surf school, while the adjacent coastal path provides stunning walking opportunities. The beach is easily accessible from Trevalgan and provides a perfect day-trip destination.

Paradise Park: Cornwall's only wildlife sanctuary and JungleBarn indoor adventure area. The park combines wildlife conservation education with family entertainment, including bird of prey demonstrations, tropical bird collections, and extensive play facilities. The indoor areas provide excellent wet-weather alternatives.

Hayle RSPB Reserve: Excellent family-friendly nature reserve with level walking paths and bird-watching opportunities. The visitor center provides educational displays and refreshments, while the reserve supports diverse wildlife throughout the year. Perfect for quieter family activities and environmental education.

Parent Tips & Insider Knowledge

Trevalgan works excellently for week-long stays with comprehensive facilities meaning you rarely need to leave the park. However, the St. Ives location provides unlimited exploration opportunities for families wanting more adventurous holiday experiences.

Swimming pool sessions are popular during peak times – early morning or early evening provides more relaxed experiences. The outdoor pools are heated but weather-dependent for comfort. Indoor pools ensure swimming opportunities regardless of conditions.

St. Ives parking can be extremely challenging during peak season – the park provides shuttle services during busy periods, which are more convenient than driving independently. The coastal path provides spectacular walking access to St. Ives for more adventurous families.

Local dining is excellent but expensive – the park's restaurant provides good family food at reasonable prices. Self-catering using local produce from St. Ives markets and nearby farm shops provides authentic Cornish experiences while controlling costs.

Practical Information

Contact: 01736 797273 or book online at trevalgan.co.uk
Booking Timeline: Opens January for peak season bookings; popular weeks book within days
Price Range: Premium (£30-50 per night reflecting comprehensive facilities and prime location)
Accessibility: Excellent accessibility throughout with adapted pitches and facilities

---

8. River Dart Country Park - Dartmoor's Natural Adventure Playground

Location: South Devon, Dartmoor National Park
Best For: Families seeking authentic outdoor adventures in stunning natural settings
Age Sweet Spot: 5-15 years (outstanding for active children)

Site Overview

River Dart Country Park represents outdoor education and family adventure at its absolute best. This 90-acre site within Dartmoor National Park provides direct access to some of England's most spectacular river and woodland scenery while offering carefully designed activities that help children develop genuine outdoor skills and environmental awareness.

The park philosophy centers on authentic outdoor experiences rather than artificial entertainment. Children don't just play – they learn practical skills, develop environmental understanding, and build confidence through real outdoor challenges. The River Dart flows directly through the site, providing natural boundaries and endless opportunities for supervised water-based activities.

What makes this site exceptional for families is its educational approach combined with genuine adventure opportunities. Staff are qualified outdoor instructors rather than entertainers, meaning children receive proper guidance in developing outdoor skills while parents can be confident in comprehensive safety management.

Family Facilities Rating

Adventure Learning: ★★★★★

Unparalleled opportunities for children to develop genuine outdoor skills through expert instruction. High ropes courses, zip lines, raft building, and bushcraft activities provide progressive skill development. All activities emphasize safety while encouraging children to push personal boundaries and develop confidence.

Natural Environment: ★★★★★

The River Dart provides spectacular natural features including pools suitable for supervised swimming, shallow areas perfect for younger children, and dramatic river scenery throughout the site. Ancient woodland provides natural play areas and educational opportunities about local ecology and wildlife.

Educational Value: ★★★★★

Outstanding environmental education opportunities with qualified staff providing insights into Dartmoor's unique ecology, geology, and cultural heritage. Activity programs include wildlife identification, countryside skills, and conservation awareness that genuinely inspire children's long-term interest in environmental issues.

Basic Facilities: ★★★☆☆

Clean, functional facilities focusing on essentials rather than luxury. Shower blocks provide hot water and family bathrooms, while the site shop covers basic needs. The cafe serves hearty, wholesome food appropriate for active families, though options are limited.

Age-Specific Activities

Ages 0-3: While primarily designed for older children, toddlers can safely enjoy many aspects of the site. Shallow river areas provide supervised paddling opportunities, while the woodland setting offers endless natural play possibilities. Pushchair access is available for main paths, though much of the site requires more adventurous exploration.

Ages 4-8: This age group discovers outdoor skills they never knew they possessed. Junior high ropes courses build confidence progressively, while supervised raft-building activities combine creativity with practical learning. Nature trails become educational adventures with identification sheets and qualified guidance. Many children report developing lasting interests in outdoor activities and environmental awareness.

Ages 9-12: Pre-teens access more challenging activities while developing genuine outdoor competency. Bushcraft skills include shelter-building, fire safety, and wilderness awareness that provide practical knowledge and increased confidence. River activities become more adventurous with supervised swimming and advanced raft-building techniques.

Ages 13+: Teenagers often find River Dart Country Park transformative, developing skills and interests that influence long-term lifestyle choices. Advanced outdoor skills, leadership opportunities with younger children, and genuine physical challenges provide experiences often missing from typical teenage activities.

Local Attractions Within 30 Minutes

Dartmoor National Park: Unlimited exploration opportunities with dramatic tor formations, ancient settlements, and spectacular walking routes. The park provides excellent family walking with routes suitable for all abilities, while the unique landscape offers educational opportunities about geology, archaeology, and ecology.

Buckfastleigh: Historic market town with the famous Buckfast Abbey, working monastery that welcomes visitors. The abbey grounds include beautiful gardens, gift shops specializing in bee products, and peaceful walking areas. The South Devon Railway terminus provides additional attraction opportunities.

Totnes: Historic market town combining medieval architecture with contemporary culture. The castle provides excellent family exploration opportunities, while the town's independent shops and cafes offer browsing and refreshment opportunities that appeal to various age groups.

Dartington Hall: Historic estate with beautiful gardens, craft workshops, and cultural events. The grounds provide excellent family walking, while the various activities often include family-friendly workshops and performances.

Parent Tips & Insider Knowledge

River Dart works best for families staying minimum three nights to fully experience the activity range. Many activities have weather dependencies, so longer stays provide better opportunities to experience everything available.

Pack old clothes and waterproofs – children will get thoroughly muddy and wet through authentic outdoor experiences. The site has drying facilities, but backup clothing allows multiple adventures daily without comfort concerns.

Activity booking is essential during peak periods – popular activities like high ropes and raft building fill quickly. Staff provide excellent advice about age-appropriate challenges and can suggest activity sequences that build skills progressively.

The educational aspect appeals particularly to home-schooling families, though all children benefit from the qualified instruction and structured learning opportunities. Many families report children requesting books about outdoor skills and environmental topics after their stays.

Practical Information

Contact: 01364 652511 or email info@riverdart.co.uk
Booking Pattern: Accepts bookings from January; peak weeks book early due to limited capacity
Price Range: Mid-range (£22-35 per night including many activities)
Accessibility: Limited due to natural terrain; contact directly to discuss specific requirements

---

9. Tristram Camping - Authentic Cornish Farm Experience

Location: Polzeath, North Cornwall
Best For: Families seeking authentic farm life with spectacular coastal access
Age Sweet Spot: All ages, particularly magical for 4-12 years

Site Overview

Tristram Camping embodies everything wonderful about traditional Cornish farming culture while providing modern families with safe, comfortable camping experiences. This working farm has been in the same family for over a century, and their deep understanding of both agriculture and family needs creates something genuinely special on the dramatic North Cornwall coast.

The farm occupies spectacular clifftop position overlooking Polzeath Bay, providing direct access to one of Cornwall's finest family beaches while maintaining authentic working farm character. The camping areas are integrated into the farm's natural rhythms, meaning families experience real agricultural life rather than sanitized farm-themed entertainment.

What makes Tristram unique is its authenticity combined with genuine warmth toward families. This isn't farming designed for tourists – it's a real working farm that happens to welcome families with enormous expertise and enthusiasm. Children don't just see farm animals; they participate in agricultural life and develop understanding of food production, animal care, and environmental stewardship.

Family Facilities Rating

Farm Experience: ★★★★★
Exceptional authentic farm experiences with daily animal care activities, seasonal agricultural participation, and genuine learning opportunities about sustainable farming. Children can participate in egg collection,

animal feeding, and seasonal activities like harvesting. The farm includes traditional Cornish breeds providing educational opportunities about agricultural heritage and conservation.

Beach Access: ★★★★★

Direct access to Polzeath Beach via farm footpath – one of Cornwall's finest family beaches with excellent facilities, safe swimming, and spectacular coastal scenery. The walk takes approximately 10 minutes through farmland and provides perfect daily adventure for all ages.

Basic Facilities: ★★★☆☆

Clean, functional facilities focusing on essentials. Hot showers, family bathrooms, and basic laundry facilities meet practical needs without luxury appointments. The farm shop sells fresh produce from the farm alongside essential supplies.

Age-Specific Activities

Ages 0-3: Toddlers find endless fascination in authentic farm life. Daily animal care becomes major adventure, while the farm's gentle animals provide safe interaction opportunities. The protected coastal position provides natural safety while offering spectacular scenery and fresh air. Many toddlers develop particular attachments to specific farm animals.

Ages 4-8: This age group often considers Tristram their greatest holiday experience. Participating in real farm work provides genuine responsibility and pride, while learning about food production creates lasting awareness about agriculture and environment. The beach access provides perfect balance between farm adventures and coastal activities.

Ages 9-12: Pre-teens can take significant responsibility for animal care while developing agricultural knowledge and practical skills. The combination of farm work and coastal access provides perfect balance of responsibility and freedom. This age group often develops strong environmental awareness and interest in sustainable living.

Ages 13+: Teenagers initially skeptical about farm holidays often become passionate advocates. The authenticity appeals to developing social consciousness, while the combination of responsibility and coastal freedom provides ideal balance. Many teenagers report that farm experiences influence their perspectives on food, environment, and lifestyle choices.

Local Attractions Within 30 Minutes

Polzeath Beach: Directly accessible from the farm, this spectacular beach provides excellent family facilities, safe swimming, and famous surfing opportunities. Rock's Surf School offers lessons for all abilities, while the beach cafe provides good family dining with spectacular views.

Padstow: Historic fishing port combining working harbor with excellent dining and cultural attractions. The National Lobster Hatchery provides fascinating insights into marine conservation, while the town's narrow streets and harbor offer perfect family exploration opportunities.

Camel Trail: The Camel Valley cycle trail provides excellent family cycling opportunities with level, traffic-free routes and spectacular countryside scenery. Bike hire available in Padstow with child seats and tag-alongs for family groups.

Eden Project: World-famous environmental attraction combining education with spectacular botanical displays. The covered biomes provide excellent wet-weather alternatives, while the educational programs inspire environmental awareness and interest in plant science.

Parent Tips & Insider Knowledge

Farm experiences vary dramatically by season – spring provides lambing excitement, summer offers full agricultural activity, autumn includes harvest participation, and winter provides intimate experiences with reduced activity levels but greater animal interaction.

Wellington boots are absolutely essential – the farm provides authentic muddy experiences that require appropriate footwear. Pack clothes suitable for getting genuinely dirty and consider extra layers for changeable coastal weather.

The farm shop provides excellent local produce at reasonable prices – many families report eating exceptionally well by incorporating fresh farm products into camping meals. The farm's own eggs, milk, and vegetables provide authentic farm-to-table experiences.

Beach access timing should consider tides – low tide provides best rock pooling and beach exploration opportunities, while high tide offers optimal swimming conditions. Farm staff provide tide timetables and local knowledge about beach safety.

Practical Information

Contact: 01208 863727 or email bookings@tristramcamping.co.uk
Booking Timeline: Opens February for summer bookings; peak weeks book quickly
Price Range: Budget-friendly (£15-25 per night)
Accessibility: Limited access due to working farm environment; discuss specific requirements

---

10. Wowo - Premium Glamping with Spectacular Views

Location: South Devon Coast
Best For: Families wanting luxury camping with breathtaking coastal scenery
Age Sweet Spot: All ages, particularly appreciated by 8+ years

Site Overview

Wowo represents glamping at its most sophisticated, providing luxury accommodation in one of South Devon's most spectacular coastal positions. The site occupies elevated clifftop location with panoramic views across Start Bay, creating an environment where families can enjoy genuine luxury while maintaining authentic connection to coastal landscape and wildlife.

The accommodation consists of beautifully designed safari tents, each positioned to maximize privacy and spectacular sea views while providing comprehensive facilities for family comfort. What distinguishes Wowo from typical glamping sites is attention to detail in both accommodation design and site management – everything is designed to enhance rather than compete with the spectacular natural setting.

The site maintains exclusive atmosphere with limited accommodation, ensuring families can enjoy luxury and privacy while children can explore safely within contained, supervised environment. The combination of stunning location, thoughtful design, and comprehensive facilities creates genuinely memorable experiences for families seeking special coastal holidays.

Family Facilities Rating

Accommodation: ★★★★★

Outstanding safari tents with comfortable beds, proper bathrooms, and well-equipped kitchens. Each tent includes private deck with spectacular sea views, while interior design combines luxury with practical family needs. Heating and lighting ensure comfort in all weather conditions.

Natural Setting: ★★★★★

Unparalleled coastal position with direct access to secluded beaches and South West Coast Path. The clifftop location provides spectacular views while maintained safety barriers ensure children can explore safely. Natural play opportunities include rock pooling, coastal walking, and wildlife watching.

Privacy & Space: ★★★★★

Generous spacing between accommodations ensures privacy while the limited number of tents prevents overcrowding. Children can play safely while parents enjoy genuine relaxation in spectacular surroundings.

Facilities: ★★★★☆

High-quality facilities throughout with excellent bathrooms, well-equipped kitchens, and comfortable living spaces. Limited on-site shopping means advance planning necessary, though local suppliers provide delivery services.

Age-Specific Activities

Ages 0-3: Toddlers thrive in Wowo's safe, contained environment with spectacular natural features providing endless fascination. The private beach access allows safe seaside experiences, while the tent accommodation provides comfortable nap environments with sea views. Many toddlers develop lasting love of coastal environments through Wowo experiences.

Ages 4-8: This age group finds perfect balance of adventure and safety at Wowo. Rock pooling becomes daily obsession with identification charts provided, while the coastal setting provides natural play opportunities. The luxury accommodation allows parents to relax while children explore safely nearby.

Ages 9-12: Pre-teens appreciate Wowo's sophisticated atmosphere while accessing appropriate adventure opportunities. Coastal walking becomes more challenging with spectacular scenery, while rock pooling and beach activities develop environmental awareness and practical skills.

Ages 13+: Teenagers often find Wowo their favorite family holiday destination. The sophisticated accommodation and spectacular setting appeal to developing aesthetic appreciation, while the coastal location provides photography opportunities and social media content they're proud to share.

Local Attractions Within 30 Minutes

Start Point Lighthouse: Historic lighthouse providing guided tours and spectacular coastal views. The dramatic clifftop position offers excellent walking opportunities while the lighthouse itself provides interesting historical and maritime education.

Dartmouth: Historic naval town combining maritime heritage with contemporary culture. The Royal Naval College provides occasional tours, while the town's narrow streets, shops, and restaurants offer family-friendly exploration and dining opportunities.

Blackpool Sands: Award-winning beach providing excellent family facilities, safe swimming, and spectacular natural beauty. The beach includes good cafe facilities and water sports opportunities, while the surrounding coastal path provides additional walking options.

South Devon Railway: Steam railway providing scenic journey through Devon countryside. The vintage carriages and authentic steam experience appeals to all ages, while the route includes stops at interesting towns and villages.

Parent Tips & Insider Knowledge

Wowo represents significant investment but provides genuinely memorable experiences – many families report it as their best-ever holiday accommodation. Book well in advance as peak season availability disappears quickly.

The spectacular location can be weather-dependent – stunning conditions provide unforgettable experiences, while poor weather can limit outdoor activities. Consider shoulder season bookings for fewer crowds and often spectacular weather.

Local shopping requires planning – the nearest comprehensive shopping is 15 minutes away, though local suppliers provide delivery services. Many families enjoy the slower pace of meal planning using local produce and fish from nearby Dartmouth.

The coastal position provides spectacular sunset viewing – many families report spending more time outdoors than usual, watching weather patterns and wildlife from their private decks.

Practical Information

Contact: Book online at wowo.co.uk or phone 01803 770000

Booking Strategy: Opens January 1st for peak season; popular weeks book within hours

Price Range: Premium (£300-600 per night for family accommodation)

Accessibility: Limited due to coastal terrain and luxury tent design; contact directly for specific requirements

---

Regional Activities and Seasonal Considerations

Spring in the Southwest (March-May)

Spring transforms the Southwest into a landscape of possibility. This is lambing season on working farms, meaning sites like Halse Farm and Tristram provide incredible experiences watching new life emerge. The coastal paths burst into flower, creating stunning backdrops for family walks, while the weather begins to warm sufficiently for comfortable camping.

Spring camping requires flexible clothing – days can be gloriously warm while nights remain chilly. This season offers the perfect introduction to Southwest camping for families new to the region, providing spectacular scenery with fewer crowds and lower prices than peak summer.

Summer Peak Season (June-August)

Summer in the Southwest means full facilities, warmest weather, and busiest conditions. This is when all sites operate at full capacity, entertainment programs run daily, and beach conditions are optimal. However, it's also when advance booking becomes essential and prices reach their peak.

Families planning summer Southwest camping should book accommodations by February and prepare for busier conditions. The compensation comes in guaranteed warm weather, full facility operation, and the magical experience of Southwest summers that create lifelong family memories.

Autumn Adventures (September-November)

Autumn provides some of the Southwest's most spectacular camping experiences. Storm watching from clifftop sites becomes daily entertainment, while the changing landscape colors create perfect photography opportunities. Many sites remain open with reduced crowds but maintained facilities.

This season particularly appeals to families with older children who appreciate dramatic scenery and don't require extensive entertainment facilities. The combination of spectacular weather conditions, reduced crowds, and maintained facilities often provides the Southwest's best camping value.

Winter Retreats (December-February)

Limited sites remain open for winter camping, but those that do provide intimate experiences with dramatic coastal conditions and cozy evening atmospheres. This season appeals to experienced camping families seeking authentic outdoor experiences without summer crowds.

Winter Southwest camping requires comprehensive weather protection but rewards adventurous families with spectacular storm watching, intimate site atmospheres, and genuine connection to coastal landscapes in their most dramatic seasonal conditions.

Making the Most of Your Southwest Adventure

The Southwest's magic lies not just in individual sites but in the region's ability to provide diverse experiences within compact areas. Families can combine coastal adventures with moorland exploration, historic sites with natural beauty, and active pursuits with genuine relaxation.

The key to Southwest camping success involves matching site choice to family interests and energy levels. Sites like River Dart Country Park suit families seeking active adventures, while places like Wowo provide luxury relaxation with natural beauty. Understanding these differences ensures optimal site selection for your family's specific needs and interests.

Consider the Southwest's weather patterns when planning activities. Coastal conditions can change rapidly, but the region's comprehensive indoor facilities mean entertainment options remain available regardless of conditions. Many families report that Southwest weather variety adds to rather than detracts from holiday experiences.

Most importantly, allow time for spontaneous discovery. The Southwest rewards families who remain flexible and open to unexpected opportunities – whether that's an impromptu seal-watching trip, discovering a hidden cove, or simply spending an entire day building the most elaborate sandcastle your family has ever attempted.

The Southwest represents British family camping at its absolute best – combining spectacular natural beauty with comprehensive facilities, authentic cultural experiences with modern convenience, and adventure opportunities with genuine safety. These twelve sites provide entry points into this magical region, but the real adventure begins when your family steps outside the tent and starts exploring one of the world's most beautiful coastal regions.

Chapter 3: Southeast England - History, Gardens & Gentle Countryside

The Southeast of England offers families a perfect blend of gentle countryside, magnificent gardens, and living history that spans centuries. From Roman ruins to medieval castles, from world-famous gardens to charming market towns, this region provides an ideal introduction to camping for families with children of all ages. The landscape here is kinder than the dramatic moors of the Southwest - rolling hills, ancient woodlands, and meandering rivers create a peaceful backdrop for family adventures.

What makes Southeast England particularly special for family camping is its incredible density of attractions within short distances. You're never more than a quick drive from a castle to explore, a steam railway to ride, or a garden to wander through. The region's long history of welcoming visitors means facilities are generally excellent, roads are well-maintained, and there's always something to do when the weather turns.

The camping season here extends comfortably from Easter through October, with many sites offering heated facilities and indoor activities for shoulder season stays. Summer brings the famous English garden season into full bloom, while spring offers bluebell walks and baby animals, and autumn delivers spectacular colors in the region's many woodlands.

For families, Southeast England represents camping with a safety net - you're never far from civilization, medical facilities, or emergency supplies, yet you can still experience genuine countryside peace. The gentle terrain makes it perfect for families with pushchairs, elderly grandparents, or children just learning to walk longer distances.

1. Hill Cottage Farm Camping, Kent

Canterbury | 4.5/5 Stars | Open March-October

Nestled in the gentle Kent countryside just eight miles from the historic city of Canterbury, Hill Cottage Farm Camping offers families the perfect base for exploring England's ecclesiastical capital while enjoying traditional farm life. This 15-acre working farm campsite strikes an ideal balance between rural tranquility and cultural adventure.

The site occupies several gently sloping fields with mature hedge boundaries, providing natural windbreaks and privacy. Most pitches offer electrical hookup, and the newer touring field features hardstanding pitches perfect for motorhomes. What immediately strikes visiting families is the genuine warmth of hosts Sarah and Tom Fletcher, third-generation farmers who've been welcoming families for over twenty years.

Family Facilities Rating: 4.5/5

The facilities block, completely renovated in 2023, showcases family camping at its best. Separate family shower rooms include baby changing facilities and space for pushchairs, while the children's bathroom features lower sinks and child-sized toilets. The laundry room doubles as a games area on rainy days, complete with board games and children's books.

The farm shop stocks essentials plus local Kent produce - perfect for campfire cooking. Don't miss their fresh eggs (collected daily by the children if they wish) and homemade jam made from fruit grown on the farm. The small playground centers around a beautifully crafted wooden climbing frame, while the real attraction for many children is meeting Buttercup and Daisy, the resident Highland cattle, and the collection of rescue chickens.

Age-Specific Activities

Ages 0-3: The flat grass areas around the farmhouse provide perfect space for toddlers to toddle safely, while the shallow stream running through the site (well-fenced) offers gentle water play under supervision. Morning egg collection with farmer Tom has become a beloved ritual for many young visitors. The site's quiet country road access means minimal traffic concerns.

Ages 4-8: Adventure begins with the woodland walk trail Sarah has created around the site's boundary. Children receive a nature spotter's guide at check-in, encouraging them to identify local birds, trees, and wildflowers. The farm's collection of friendly animals - including rabbits, guinea pigs, and goats - provides endless entertainment. Evening campfire storytelling happens twice weekly during peak season.

Ages 9-12: Older children gravitate toward the mountain bike trail that connects to the nearby Crab and Winkle Way, a traffic-free cycle path following an old railway line to Canterbury. The site loans basic bikes and helmets. Tom offers junior farming sessions where children learn traditional skills like hedge laying and dry stone walling. The rope swing over the stream proves universally popular.

Ages 13+: WiFi reaches most pitches, crucial for teenage happiness. The site's location offers independence opportunities - the nearby village of Chartham has shops and cafes within walking distance, while Canterbury's attractions are easily accessible by bike for confident young cyclists. Evening wildlife photography workshops during summer months attract nature-loving teenagers.

Local Attractions Within 30 Minutes

Canterbury Cathedral stands as the obvious headline attraction, but approach it strategically with children. Book the family audio tour featuring stories and sound effects that bring the building's history alive for younger ears. The Cathedral Lodge's garden provides perfect picnic spots, while the Precincts offer space for children to run off energy.

Canterbury Tales attraction, despite tourist trap appearances, actually engages children brilliantly with its medieval storytelling experience. Budget two hours minimum. The nearby Westgate Towers offers spectacular city views and houses medieval prison cells that fascinate older children.

For contrast, Howletts Wild Animal Park (15 minutes away) provides world-class wildlife experiences. Their elephant and gorilla programs are internationally renowned, while the adventure playground ensures children burn energy between animal encounters. Entry costs reflect the park's conservation work, but family tickets offer reasonable value.

The Kent & East Sussex Railway at Tenterden runs vintage steam trains through beautiful countryside. Children love the Thomas the Tank Engine events, while parents appreciate the real ale available in the buffet car. Combine with visits to Tenterden's independent shops and cafes.

Avoid Canterbury on Saturdays unless you enjoy crowds. Wednesday mornings offer the most peaceful cathedral visits, while the Tales attraction is quietest first thing in the morning.

Parent Tips & Insider Knowledge

Request a pitch in the "top field" for the best views and morning sun, but avoid if you have very young children as it's furthest from facilities. The "stream field" offers the most adventure but can get muddy after rain.

Sarah's insider tip: Canterbury Park and Ride operates excellent value family tickets and eliminates city center parking stress. The buses run every ten minutes and children love the double-deckers.

For groceries, bypass Canterbury's expensive tourist shops. Instead, visit Chartham's village shop (ten minutes walk) for basics, or drive to Tesco in Sturry (five minutes) for major shopping. The farm shop's fresh bread arrives at 8:30 am - worth queuing for.

Book dinner at the Artichoke in Chartham for excellent pub food in a genuine village atmosphere. Children are genuinely welcomed (not just tolerated), and the play area in the garden means parents can finish their meals in peace.

Practical Information

- **Contact:** 01227 738925 | hillcottagefarmkent@gmail.com
- **Booking:** Essential during school holidays; online system opens January 1st
- **Price Range:** £18-25 per night for family pitch including electricity
- **Accessibility:** Level access to facilities; some pitches suitable for wheelchairs

---

2. Tanner Farm Park, Kent

Maidstone | 4.0/5 Stars | Open Year-Round

Located in the heart of the Garden of England, Tanner Farm Park demonstrates how modern family camping can work alongside traditional agriculture. This working fruit farm transforms into a comprehensive family destination during camping season, offering everything from pick-your-own fruit to adventure activities, all within easy reach of Kent's historic towns and gardens.

The 40-acre site spreads across gently undulating farmland, with camping areas nestled between established orchards and hop gardens. The setting feels authentically rural despite being just ten minutes from Maidstone's amenities. Modern facilities blend sensitively with traditional farm buildings, creating an atmosphere that's both practical and charming.

Family Facilities Rating: 4.0/5

The showpiece facility block, opened in 2022, features underfloor heating and family shower rooms that could grace a boutique hotel. Baby changing areas include complementary toiletries and disposable changing mats - small touches that demonstrate genuine family focus. The disabled access facilities exceed requirements, with roll-in showers and emergency assistance alarms.

The on-site farm shop has evolved into a destination in its own right, stocking everything from camping basics to gourmet local produce. Their fruit pies, made from farm-grown ingredients, have achieved legendary status among regular visitors. The site's restaurant serves hearty fare using farm ingredients, with children's portions that actually satisfy hungry young appetites rather than token offerings.

Adventure playground facilities include a large wooden fort, zip lines, and climbing walls suitable for various ages. The indoor soft play area ensures entertainment regardless of weather, while the adjacent games room features table tennis, pool, and vintage arcade games that parents remember from their own childhoods.

Age-Specific Activities

Ages 0-3: The dedicated toddler play area features age-appropriate equipment with safety surfaces and shade structures. Pushchair-friendly paths connect all main site areas, while the shallow paddling pool (supervised summer months only) provides safe water play. Morning tractor trailer rides around the farm prove universally popular with this age group.

Ages 4-8: Pick-your-own activities run from June through October, starting with strawberries and progressing through raspberries, blackcurrants, and finishing with apples and pears. Children receive collection baskets and learn about fruit growing during guided tours. The adventure playground's junior section includes a small climbing wall and rope bridges designed for developing confidence.

Ages 9-12: The site's mountain biking trail system offers gentle introductory routes through orchards and woodland. Bike hire includes helmets and basic maintenance instruction. During autumn, apple pressing demonstrations teach traditional skills, with children operating heritage equipment under supervision. The high ropes course (additional cost) provides supervised adventure for confident children.

Ages 13+: WiFi coverage extends across most camping areas, crucial for maintaining teenage happiness. The site offers work experience opportunities for interested young people - helping with fruit picking, animal care, and site maintenance. Evening activities during peak season include outdoor cinema screenings and live music events that appeal to older children while remaining family-friendly.

Local Attractions Within 30 Minutes

Leeds Castle, dubbed "the most beautiful castle in the world," justifies its reputation through spectacular island setting and family-friendly approach. The castle's audio tour includes special children's versions, while the grounds offer adventure playgrounds, a maze, and year-round events. Budget a full day visit, with picnic areas providing cost-effective meal solutions.

Sissinghurst Castle Garden represents English garden design at its finest. While potentially challenging for very young children due to gravel paths and delicate plantings, families with older children find inspiration in the garden rooms concept. The restaurant serves excellent lunches using garden produce, though prices reflect the location's prestige.

The Historic Dockyard Chatham brings maritime history alive through interactive exhibits and preserved warships. HMS Victory provides hands-on experience of naval life, while the rope-making demonstration fascinates children and adults equally. The site's size requires comfortable walking shoes, but various themed trails prevent overwhelming younger visitors.

For active families, Go Ape at Leeds Castle offers treetop adventures suitable for children over ten. The nearby Mote Park provides gentler outdoor activities including lake walks, mini golf, and seasonal events. The park's children's play areas rank among Kent's best, while the cafe serves reasonable prices compared to castle restaurants.

Parent Tips & Insider Knowledge

The orchard pitches offer the most character but can be windier than the main field. Pitch numbers 15-25 in the main camping field provide the best balance of facilities access and morning sun. Avoid pitches near the main road (numbers 1-8) due to early morning farm traffic.

Book restaurant tables at check-in, especially for weekend evenings. The breakfast service (8-10 am) offers excellent value and saves camping cooking hassle. Their full English breakfast includes black pudding made on-site - worth trying even for skeptical children.

Local shopping tip: Maidstone's Lockmeadow Centre provides comprehensive shopping with good parking, but Bearsted village (five minutes) offers charming alternatives including an excellent bakery and traditional butcher. The weekly farmers market in Maidstone (Saturdays) showcases regional produce.

For rainy day alternatives, visit the Museum of Kent Life (ten minutes) for indoor and covered outdoor activities. Their vintage fun fair and shire horses captivate children, while adults appreciate the authentic historical buildings relocated from across Kent.

Practical Information

- **Contact:** 01622 812218 | bookings@tannerfarmpark.co.uk
- **Booking:** Online booking preferred; phone for specific pitch requests
- **Price Range:** £22-30 per night for family pitch with electricity
- **Accessibility:** Excellent disabled access facilities; accessible pitches available

3. Wowo Camping, West Sussex

Chichester | 4.5/5 Stars | Open April-October

Hidden in the South Downs National Park, Wowo Camping redefines the family camping experience through its commitment to sustainable, back-to-nature adventures without sacrificing essential comforts. This eco-conscious site demonstrates that environmental responsibility and family fun work beautifully together, creating an atmosphere that feels more like a temporary village than a traditional campsite.

Set across 25 acres of mixed woodland and meadow, Wowo's individual camping areas feel like private forest clearings. The site's name derives from the Aboriginal word for "spiritual place," and there's definitely something special about this corner of Sussex. Ancient oak trees provide natural shelter, while wild meadows burst with seasonal wildflowers that children love exploring.

Family Facilities Rating: 4.5/5

The eco-toilet and shower blocks utilize sustainable technologies while maintaining cleanliness standards that impress even fastidious parents. Solar heating provides hot water, while rainwater harvesting supplies the facilities. Family shower rooms include space for multiple children and equipment storage, recognizing the realities of camping with young families.

The site's shop stocks local and organic produce alongside camping essentials, with prices that reflect quality rather than convenience store markup. Their coffee, roasted locally in Petersfield, has achieved legendary status among regular visitors. The camp kitchen provides covered cooking areas with gas rings and preparation space - invaluable during unsettled weather.

Wowo's approach to children's facilities emphasizes natural play over manufactured entertainment. The woodland adventure trail includes rope swings, balance beams, and climbing challenges built from sustainable materials. The communal fire pit areas, each surrounded by log seating, become social hubs where children from different families naturally intermingle.

Age-Specific Activities

Ages 0-3: The meadow areas provide safe spaces for toddlers to explore, with interesting textures from bark chips, grass, and woodland floors. The site maintains pushchair-accessible paths to main facilities while preserving natural terrain elsewhere. Morning wildlife spotting walks help young children develop observation skills while burning energy before breakfast.

Ages 4-8: Forest school activities run three times weekly during peak season, teaching traditional outdoor skills like whittling, fire-making (under supervision), and plant identification. Children construct dens using natural materials, participate in nature art projects, and learn basic outdoor cooking. The site's stream provides hours of entertainment through dam-building and pond-dipping activities.

Ages 9-12: Advanced outdoor skills workshops include map reading, basic first aid, and wildlife tracking. The site's mountain bike trails connect to the South Downs Way, offering progressively challenging routes for developing riders. Evening astronomy sessions take advantage of the area's Dark Sky status, with telescopes provided for planet and constellation observation.

Ages 13+: The site recognizes teenagers' different needs through designated areas with stronger WiFi signals and charging points. Photography workshops focus on nature and wildlife subjects, while older teenagers can participate in site conservation projects, learning about habitat management and sustainable living practices.

Local Attractions Within 30 Minutes

Chichester Cathedral offers family-friendly architecture tours and regular children's activities. The cathedral's modern Chagall window provides an accessible art appreciation opportunity, while the close's gardens offer space for children to decompress after indoor exploration. Free entry makes this an economical cultural experience.

Fishbourne Roman Palace showcases Britain's largest residential Roman building, with mosaics that captivate children through their colorful geometric patterns. The hands-on archaeology activities and Roman garden recreation bring history alive. Summer events include gladiator demonstrations and Roman cooking workshops that engage multiple age groups simultaneously.

South Downs National Park surrounds the site with walking opportunities ranging from gentle nature trails to challenging hill walks. The nearby Kingley Vale National Nature Reserve contains ancient yew forests and Bronze Age burial mounds that fascinate older children while providing excellent walking for adults. The visitor center offers family activity sheets and seasonal guided walks.

West Wittering Beach (20 minutes) provides classic English seaside experiences with sand dunes perfect for children's exploration. The beach's Blue Flag status indicates excellent water quality and safety standards. Rock pooling at low tide reveals crabs, anemones, and various marine life that captivate young naturalists.

Parent Tips & Insider Knowledge

Book well in advance - Wowo's reputation means summer weekends fill by February. Request pitches in the "Oak Clearing" for morning sun and wind protection, or "Meadow Edge" for easier access with young children. The "Deep Woods" pitches offer the most privacy but require confidence with woodland camping.

The site's communal evening meals (Wednesdays and Saturdays) provide opportunities to meet other families while experiencing locally sourced cuisine. Children often form lasting friendships during these relaxed gatherings. Book at arrival as spaces are limited.

Local shopping requires planning - the nearest major supermarket is in Chichester (15 minutes). However, the village of East Marden (10 minutes walk) has a community shop with basic supplies and excellent ice cream that children always remember. The Elsted Inn (5 minutes drive) serves outstanding gastropub food with genuine children's welcome.

For emergency supplies or forgotten essentials, the Tesco Express in Petersfield (15 minutes) stays open late, while Waitrose in Petersfield offers higher quality provisions for special camping meals.

Practical Information

- **Contact:** 01730 821244 | hello@wowo.co.uk
- **Booking:** Online only; waiting list operates for popular dates
- **Price Range:** £35-45 per night for family pitch (includes facilities access)
- **Accessibility:** Limited suitable pitches due to natural terrain; discuss requirements when booking

---

4. Blackberry Wood, East Sussex

Streat | 5.0/5 Stars | Open March-November

Blackberry Wood transcends traditional camping to create what feels like a children's adventure story come to life. This award-winning site in the South Downs demonstrates how imagination and careful planning can transform a simple camping experience into magical family memories. Every detail here considers children's perspectives, from the hobbit holes and tree houses available for overnight stays to the animals that wander freely around the site.

Spread across 15 acres of mixed woodland and meadow, Blackberry Wood feels more like a permanent settlement than a temporary camping site. Ancient oak and ash trees provide natural windbreaks, while the site's topography creates natural areas for different activities. The atmosphere combines outdoor adventure with fairy-tale enchantment that captivates children from the moment they arrive.

Family Facilities Rating: 5.0/5

The recently built facility blocks set new standards for family camping amenities. Heated throughout the season, they feature family bathrooms with roll-top baths perfect for muddy children after day-long adventures. The baby changing areas include complementary supplies and comfortable feeding chairs. Even the standard toilets accommodate families, with parent and child cubicles and step-stools for independence.

The site shop transcends typical camping provisions to stock quality outdoor gear, local produce, and carefully selected toys that enhance rather than compete with the natural environment. Their homemade bread, baked fresh each morning, has become legendary among regular visitors. The honesty shop system allows families to purchase items outside normal hours, reflecting the trust-based atmosphere that pervades the site.

Unique facilities include the communal kitchen with Aga cooking facilities, the reading room stocked with children's books, and the craft room where children can create nature art during unsettled weather. These spaces foster interaction between families while providing alternatives to tent living during extended stays.

Age-Specific Activities

Ages 0-3: The toddler meadow provides safe exploration space with interesting textures and gentle challenges. The site's Highland cattle, pigs, and chickens roam freely but remain gentle around small children. Morning animal feeding sessions become highlight experiences, with site staff ensuring safe interaction. The shallow stream includes constructed pools perfect for supervised water play.

Ages 4-8: This age group experiences Blackberry Wood at its full magic. Tree houses and shepherd's huts can be booked for special overnight experiences, while the woodland adventure trail includes rope bridges, zip lines, and climbing challenges. Forest school activities teach practical skills like fire-making and shelter construction. The site's treasure hunt changes weekly, encouraging exploration while developing problem-solving skills.

Ages 9-12: Advanced outdoor activities include mountain biking on site trails, fishing in the site's pond (equipment provided), and orienteering challenges. The high ropes course offers supervised adventure, while bushcraft workshops teach survival skills that fascinate this age group. Evening campfire sessions feature storytelling and traditional songs that create lasting memories.

Ages 13+: Recognizing teenage needs, the site provides WiFi in common areas and charging stations in the craft room. Photography workshops focus on wildlife and landscape subjects, taking advantage of the site's photogenic qualities. Older teenagers can participate in site maintenance projects, learning practical skills while contributing to the site's development.

Local Attractions Within 30 Minutes

Brighton's attractions provide urban contrast to rural camping. The i360 observation tower offers spectacular coastal views, while the pier's amusements entertain children of all ages. Brighton's independent shops and cafes create excellent browsing opportunities, though parking requires advance planning. The beach provides classic seaside experiences with pebbles that fascinate children accustomed to sandy beaches.

Ditchling Beacon, the South Downs' highest point accessible by car, offers panoramic views across Sussex and Kent. The walk to the summit is manageable for most children, while the Iron Age hill fort remains fascinate history-conscious families. Parking can be challenging on sunny weekends, but early morning visits avoid crowds while offering the best photographic light.

Sheffield Park Garden showcases English garden design through seasonal displays that photograph beautifully. The garden's lakes and waterfalls provide natural entertainment for children, while the woodland walks offer gentle exercise. The adjacent Bluebell Railway operates steam trains that captivate young railway enthusiasts. Combined tickets provide excellent value for full-day visits.

Ashdown Forest, inspiration for Winnie-the-Pooh stories, offers themed walks following Pooh Bear's adventures. The visitor center provides maps and activity sheets, while Poohsticks Bridge attracts international visitors but remains surprisingly accessible. The forest's heathland provides unique landscapes different from typical English countryside.

Parent Tips & Insider Knowledge

Book accommodation (tree houses, shepherd's huts) separately from camping pitches - they're extremely popular and require advance planning. Standard camping pitches in the "Dell" offer the most shelter, while "Top Field" provides the best views but can be windier. The "Orchard" area works best for families with very young children due to proximity to facilities.

The site's evening entertainment program varies by season but always includes at least one campfire evening weekly. Children often form natural friendships during these events, making them worth prioritizing over evening pub visits. The site provides marshmallows and campfire songs sheets.

Local shopping requires planning - Ditchling village (10 minutes) offers a small shop with essentials and excellent bakery, while Haywards Heath (15 minutes) provides comprehensive supermarket shopping. The farm shop at nearby Washbrooks Farm stocks exceptional local produce including rare breed meats perfect for camping cuisine.

For restaurant meals, book tables at The Bull in Ditchling for gastropub dining with children's options, or visit Plumpton College's restaurant (10 minutes) for excellent value meals using college-grown ingredients.

Practical Information

- **Contact:** 01273 890558 | enquiries@blackberrywood.com
- **Booking:** Online booking essential; phone for specific accommodation queries
- **Price Range:** £30-40 per night for family camping pitch; accommodation varies
- **Accessibility:** Some facilities accessible; woodland areas unsuitable for wheelchairs

---

5. Welsummer Camping, Hampshire

Alresford | 4.0/5 Stars | Open April-September

Nestled in the heart of Hampshire's chalk downland, Welsummer Camping offers families an authentic taste of English countryside life with easy access to historic Winchester and the Watercress Line steam railway. This working farm site demonstrates how traditional agriculture and modern family camping can complement each other beautifully, creating an atmosphere that's both educational and relaxing.

The 20-acre site spreads across gently rolling fields divided by traditional hedge boundaries that provide natural windbreaks and privacy. The River Arle meanders along one boundary, creating opportunities for supervised water activities while maintaining safe distances from camping areas. Ancient footpaths crossing the site connect to the extensive Hampshire countryside footpath network.

Family Facilities Rating: 4.0/5

The converted farm building housing the main facilities maintains rural character while providing modern amenities. Family shower rooms include space for equipment and multiple children, with powerful hot water systems that cope with peak demand. The laundry facilities include covered drying areas essential during unsettled weather periods.

The farm shop operates on an honesty system outside peak hours, stocking camping essentials alongside fresh produce from the farm and neighboring smallholdings. Their fresh eggs, collected daily from the farm's free-range flock, provide camping breakfast luxury at reasonable prices. The site's cafe serves hearty meals using locally sourced ingredients, with children's portions that actually satisfy growing appetites.

The children's play area centers around a traditional wooden playground with climbing frames and slides, but the real attraction is the farm's collection of rare breed animals. Children can participate in morning feeding routines and learn about traditional farming practices through hands-on experiences.

Age-Specific Activities

Ages 0-3: The farm's gentle animals, including miniature donkeys and friendly sheep, provide safe interaction opportunities under supervision. The shallow areas of the River Arle, accessed through designated points with safety barriers, offer water play during supervised family time. Pushchair-accessible paths connect major site areas while maintaining countryside authenticity.

Ages 4-8: Junior farming activities include egg collecting, animal feeding, and simple agricultural tasks that teach responsibility while providing entertainment. The site's woodland area features rope swings and natural climbing opportunities. Stream studies introduce basic ecology through pond dipping and wildlife observation, with identification sheets provided.

Ages 9-12: The South Downs Way passes directly through the site, offering walking opportunities ranging from short nature trails to longer expeditions for adventurous families. Mountain bike hire provides exploration options, with routes suitable for developing cyclists. Traditional craft workshops during school holidays teach skills like hedge laying and hurdle making.

Ages 13+: WiFi reaches most camping areas, maintaining teenage connectivity. The site's location offers independence opportunities - Alresford town center lies within walking distance, providing shops, cafes, and the famous Watercress Line railway station. Photography workshops focus on rural landscapes and wildlife subjects.

Local Attractions Within 30 Minutes

Winchester Cathedral represents one of England's finest Gothic buildings, with family-friendly tours that bring medieval history alive. The cathedral's crypt, often flooded, fascinates children while demonstrating ancient building challenges. The adjacent Great Hall houses the legendary Round Table, linking Arthurian legend with historical reality. Free entry to the hall makes this an economical cultural experience.

The Watercress Line steam railway operates from nearby Alresford, providing authentic steam train experiences through beautiful Hampshire countryside. Thomas the Tank Engine events prove extremely popular with young children, while the railway's museum entertains older children and adults. The buffet car serves traditional railway refreshments including excellent afternoon teas.

Marwell Zoo, consistently rated among England's finest zoos, focuses on conservation and education through impressive animal collections and interactive exhibits. The zoo's size requires comfortable walking shoes, but the various themed areas prevent overwhelming younger visitors. Annual membership provides excellent value for local families planning multiple visits.

Jane Austen's House Museum in Chawton offers literary pilgrimage opportunities for Austen enthusiasts, though younger children may find limited engagement. The village itself provides pleasant walking, while the nearby Chawton House Library hosts family-friendly events during summer months.

Parent Tips & Insider Knowledge

Request pitches in the "River Field" for the most scenic location and easy water access, though these can be cooler in early season. The "Top Field" offers better wind protection and morning sun. Pitch numbers 20-30 provide the best balance of facilities access and privacy.

The site's weekly barbecue evenings (Fridays during peak season) provide opportunities to meet other families while enjoying locally sourced food. Children naturally form friendships during these relaxed gatherings, often leading to shared activities throughout stays.

Local shopping convenience: Alresford's independent shops provide quality provisions, with the bakery earning particular recommendation. Waitrose in Winchester (15 minutes) offers comprehensive shopping with good parking. The Thursday farmers market in Winchester showcases regional specialties worth planning around.

For restaurant dining, The Globe on the Lake in Alresford serves excellent gastropub food with genuine family welcome. The nearby Hawkley Inn offers outstanding food in a traditional pub setting, though booking is essential during summer months.

Practical Information

- **Contact:** 01962 734312 | stay@welsummercamping.co.uk
- **Booking:** Online preferred; phone for specific pitch requests
- **Price Range:** £20-28 per night for family pitch including electricity
- **Accessibility:** Level access to main facilities; some riverside pitches unsuitable for wheelchairs

6. Southdown Camping, Surrey

Reigate | 4.0/5 Stars | Open May-October

Perched on the North Downs with panoramic views across the Surrey Weald, Southdown Camping offers families a perfect base for exploring London's green belt while maintaining genuine countryside atmosphere. This family-run site demonstrates how thoughtful management can create a peaceful retreat within easy reach of major attractions, making it ideal for families wanting to combine urban adventures with rural relaxation.

The site occupies terraced fields that follow the natural chalk downland contours, creating distinct camping areas with different characters. The elevated position provides spectacular sunset views while the mature beech and oak woodland offers shelter from prevailing winds. Despite being just 30 minutes from central London by train, the site maintains remarkably quiet atmosphere throughout most periods.

Family Facilities Rating: 4.0/5

The modern facilities block, completed in 2021, reflects careful design consideration for family needs. Underfloor heating ensures comfort during shoulder seasons, while the family bathrooms include roll-in showers and baby changing facilities with complementary supplies. The covered dish-washing areas with hot water make camping meal cleanup manageable even during unsettled weather.

The site shop stocks camping essentials plus carefully selected local products including Surrey Hills honey and locally baked bread. Their coffee, sourced from a Dorking roastery, has developed a following among regular visitors. The children's play area features natural materials and creative equipment that encourages imaginative play rather than simple entertainment.

The site's commitment to sustainability shows through solar heating, rainwater collection, and careful waste management systems that provide educational opportunities for environmentally conscious families. These features demonstrate responsible camping practices without compromising comfort or convenience.

Age-Specific Activities

Ages 0-3: The lower meadow provides safe exploration space with interesting textures and gentle slopes perfect for developing walking skills. The site's resident cats and occasional visiting farm animals from neighboring properties provide gentle animal interaction. Morning nature walks with pushchair-accessible routes help establish daily routines while introducing young children to countryside sights and sounds.

Ages 4-8: The woodland adventure trail includes natural obstacles, hidden treasures, and seasonal activities that change throughout the camping season. Traditional games equipment - cricket sets, rounders, football - is available for borrowing. The site organizes weekly treasure hunts that encourage exploration while developing problem-solving skills and observation abilities.

Ages 9-12: The North Downs Way passes adjacent to the site, offering walking opportunities ranging from short nature trails to challenging longer routes. Mountain bike trails through nearby woodland provide adventure for confident young cyclists. Evening wildlife watching sessions take advantage of the site's rural location and wildlife diversity.

Ages 13+: Strong WiFi coverage across most camping areas maintains teenage connectivity expectations. The site's proximity to Reigate and Dorking provides independence opportunities, with local buses offering transport to nearby towns for shopping and cafe culture. Photography workshops focus on landscape and wildlife subjects available around the site.

Local Attractions Within 30 Minutes

Box Hill, National Trust's most popular Surrey property, offers family-friendly walking trails with spectacular viewpoints and children's discovery activities. The visitor center provides maps, activity sheets, and seasonal event information. The challenging hill climb attracts cycling enthusiasts, but gentler paths accommodate families with varying fitness levels. The cafe serves excellent lunches with outdoor seating overlooking the Mole Valley.

Polesden Lacey showcases Edwardian country house life through magnificent interiors and extensive gardens. The house's collection includes artwork and furniture that bring the period alive, while the grounds offer excellent walking and picnicking opportunities. Children's activity trails and seasonal events provide age-appropriate engagement. The walled garden demonstrates traditional horticultural techniques still relevant today.

Leatherhead's swimming pool complex provides indoor entertainment during unsettled weather, while the town's shops and cafes offer urban variety. The nearby Givons Grove Light Railway operates miniature steam trains that fascinate young railway enthusiasts, particularly during special event weekends featuring Thomas the Tank Engine themes.

London attractions become accessible through the excellent rail links from nearby Reigate or Dorking stations. Day trips to museums, theaters, and tourist attractions become feasible, though advance planning for tickets and travel times is essential when camping with children.

Parent Tips & Insider Knowledge

The "Top Terrace" pitches offer the best views but can be windier during unsettled weather. The "Woodland Edge" pitches provide shelter and morning sun while maintaining privacy. Pitch numbers 15-25 in the middle terrace offer the best compromise between views, facilities access, and wind protection.

Local train services from Reigate provide direct access to London Victoria, but advance booking reduces costs significantly. Day travel cards offer good value for family groups planning multiple London attractions. Consider mid-week London visits to avoid weekend crowds and higher accommodation costs.

Shopping convenience: Reigate's high street provides comprehensive facilities including Marks & Spencer Food Hall for quality provisions. The Saturday farmers market showcases local Surrey produce. For major shopping, the Belfry Centre in Redhill offers comprehensive facilities with parking.

Restaurant recommendations include The Skimmington Castle in Reigate for family-friendly gastropub dining, or The Stepping Stones pub near Box Hill for traditional pub atmosphere with river views. Both welcome children genuinely rather than tolerating them.

Practical Information

- **Contact:** 01737 842548 | info@southdowncamping.co.uk
- **Booking:** Online booking preferred; phone for London event weekends
- **Price Range:** £25-35 per night for family pitch with electricity
- **Accessibility:** Sloping terrain limits wheelchair access; discuss

Chapter 4: London & Thames Valley - Urban Adventures & Royal Retreats

The Thames Valley region offers families a unique camping opportunity - the chance to explore one of the world's greatest cities while sleeping under canvas in peaceful countryside settings. This extraordinary combination means children can experience world-class museums, theaters, and cultural attractions during the day, then return to campfires and stargazing each evening. It's camping with a metropolitan twist that satisfies both urban adventure seekers and countryside lovers.

What makes this region particularly special for family camping is the remarkable transport infrastructure that connects rural campsites with central London in under an hour. The Thames itself provides a golden thread through the landscape, offering boat trips, riverside walks, and historic connections that span over a thousand years of English history. From Hampton Court's Tudor grandeur to Windsor Castle's royal majesty, families can literally camp in the shadow of palaces while maintaining all the freedom and flexibility that makes camping so appealing.

The region's royal connections run deep, creating opportunities for children to experience living history rather than simply reading about it. The stories here aren't confined to dusty textbooks - they unfold in magnificent palaces where kings and queens actually lived, worked, and shaped the nation. Yet between these grand set pieces lie gentle river meadows, ancient woodlands, and traditional market towns that provide perfect camping backdrops.

For families new to camping, the Thames Valley offers an ideal compromise. You're never far from urban amenities, medical facilities, or emergency services, yet you can experience genuine countryside peace. The relatively flat terrain along the Thames makes walking accessible for all ages, while the region's extensive public transport network means car-free days become not just possible but enjoyable adventures in themselves.

The camping season here extends comfortably from April through October, with many sites offering winter facilities for hardy families. Spring brings royal garden reopenings and perfect weather for outdoor exploring, while summer offers long days for maximizing London attractions combined with countryside evenings. Autumn provides spectacular colors along the Thames Path and harvest festivals in traditional market towns.

1. Thames Valley Camping, Berkshire

Reading | 4.5/5 Stars | Open March-November

Nestled in a bend of the River Thames just upstream from Reading, Thames Valley Camping offers families an exceptional base for exploring both London's attractions and the royal heritage of Berkshire. This family-run site occupies 20 acres of traditional river meadowland, where ancient pollarded willows create natural camping bays and the Thames provides a constantly changing backdrop of river traffic and wildlife.

The site's position couldn't be better for families wanting urban access with rural peace. Reading station, with its direct 30-minute trains to London Paddington, lies just fifteen minutes away by car or local bus, while Windsor Castle sits twenty minutes in the opposite direction. Yet step onto the site and London feels worlds away, with only the gentle sounds of river life and countryside tranquility.

What immediately strikes visitors is the site's respect for its riverside environment. Pitches are positioned to minimize impact on the flood plain while maximizing river views, and the traditional meadow management supports wildflower displays that peak in early summer. The site feels more like a temporary village than a commercial operation, with returning families creating a welcoming community atmosphere.

Family Facilities Rating: 4.5/5

The environmentally conscious facilities block demonstrates how sustainability and family comfort can work together beautifully. Solar heating provides reliable hot water while rainwater harvesting supplies washing facilities. Family shower rooms include space for multiple children and equipment storage, recognizing the realities of camping with various age groups.

The facilities' design incorporates natural ventilation and lighting that creates a pleasant atmosphere rather than the institutional feel common in larger sites. Baby changing areas include complementary supplies and comfortable feeding chairs, while the covered dish-washing areas provide shelter during Thames Valley's occasional downpours.

The site shop operates on environmental principles, stocking local produce from nearby farms alongside camping essentials. Their fresh bread, delivered daily from a Reading artisan bakery, has become legendary among regular visitors. The coffee, roasted locally in Henley-on-Thames, reflects the site's commitment to supporting regional businesses while providing quality that satisfies demanding adult palates.

Age-Specific Activities

Ages 0-3: The riverside meadows provide perfect spaces for toddlers to explore safely, with interesting textures from grass, wildflowers, and shallow stream edges (well-fenced from the main river). Morning wildlife walks help establish daily routines while introducing young children to river birds, water voles, and seasonal wildflowers. The site's quiet country road access means minimal traffic concerns for families with wandering toddlers.

Ages 4-8: River activities dominate this age group's experience, from supervised pond dipping that reveals freshwater wildlife to boat watching from the site's private Thames frontage. The nearby Thames Path provides easy cycling with traffic-free sections perfect for developing riders. Weekly treasure hunts encourage site exploration while teaching basic map reading and observation skills.

Ages 9-12: The Thames connection enables more adventurous activities including basic canoeing instruction (equipment available for hire from nearby Pangbourne) and longer cycling expeditions along the Thames Path toward Goring or Mapledurham. Evening wildlife watching takes advantage of the river's diverse ecosystem, with bat detecting equipment available from reception.

Ages 13+: The site's excellent transport connections provide independence opportunities for confident teenagers. Reading's shopping and cinema complexes become accessible, while London day trips can be managed independently by older teens. Strong mobile coverage and WiFi in common areas maintain connectivity expectations crucial for this age group.

Local Attractions Within 30 Minutes

Windsor Castle dominates the area's attractions, and rightly so. The world's oldest occupied castle continues serving as a working royal palace while welcoming families through exceptional public programs. The State Apartments showcase royal collections that span centuries, while St George's Chapel provides intimate royal history including recent royal weddings that children recognize from media coverage.

The castle's approach to family visitors sets standards other attractions struggle to match. Children's audio tours bring royal history alive through stories and sound effects, while seasonal events include medieval reenactments and royal ceremony demonstrations. The castle grounds provide space for children to release energy between indoor attractions, and the gift shop offers quality souvenirs that don't break family budgets.

Legoland Windsor, just five minutes from the castle, provides complementary experiences that satisfy children's needs for active engagement after cultural absorption. The park's educational approach to entertainment means children learn while playing, with attractions explaining engineering principles, environmental concepts, and creative problem-solving through interactive experiences.

The park operates efficiently for families, with clear age-appropriate zones and comprehensive facilities that handle peak capacity without overwhelming chaos. Advanced booking provides significant cost savings and queue-jumping benefits that transform busy days into manageable adventures.

Reading itself offers urban experiences that complement countryside camping. The Museum of Reading provides excellent local history exhibits, while Forbury Gardens offers Victorian park charm with excellent children's play facilities. The Oracle shopping center provides comprehensive retail therapy during unsettled weather, though parking can be expensive during peak periods.

Parent Tips & Insider Knowledge

Request riverside pitches (numbers 20-35) for the best Thames views and wildlife watching, but be prepared for occasional boat noise during busy summer weekends. The meadow pitches (40-60) offer more shelter and easier access for families with young children. Avoid pitches near the site entrance (1-10) due to late arrival disturbances.

London day trips work best when started early to avoid peak commuter periods and maximize attraction time. The 8:30 am train from Reading reaches London Paddington by 9:00 am, allowing first entry to popular attractions before crowds build. Return travel after 7:00 pm often provides quieter trains and better seating for tired children.

Windsor Castle booking strategy: Purchase tickets online for significant savings and priority entry. Wednesday mornings offer the quietest visiting conditions, while weekend State Apartment tours can involve lengthy queues. Combine castle visits with Windsor Great Park walks for free outdoor activities that provide excellent exercise after indoor cultural experiences.

Local shopping convenience: Reading's covered markets (Wednesdays and Saturdays) showcase regional produce and crafts at reasonable prices. For comprehensive grocery shopping, the Tesco Extra in Reading provides everything needed, while Waitrose in Windsor offers higher quality provisions at premium prices but excellent prepared foods for special camping meals.

Practical Information

- **Contact:** 0118 984 2088 | stay@thamesvalleycamping.co.uk
- **Booking:** Online booking preferred; phone for riverside pitch requests
- **Price Range:** £28-40 per night for family pitch including electricity
- **Accessibility:** Level riverside access; accessible facilities with some limitations due to flood plain requirements

---

2. Wellington Country Park Camping, Berkshire

Wokingham | 4.0/5 Stars | Open Year-Round

Set within the 350-acre Wellington Country Park estate, this unique camping site combines the convenience of comprehensive on-site activities with easy access to London and royal Windsor. The integration of camping with an established country park means families have immediate access to lakes, woodlands, adventure activities, and seasonal events while maintaining the independence that makes camping so appealing to families.

The camping area occupies level parkland beside ornamental lakes, with mature trees providing natural pitch boundaries and shade during summer months. The parkland setting creates a genteel atmosphere that feels more like staying on a grand country estate than typical camping, while the country park's facilities ensure entertainment regardless of weather conditions.

What sets Wellington apart is its approach to family camping as part of a broader countryside experience. The estate's history as a private residence means the buildings, gardens, and landscape were designed for leisure and enjoyment, creating an atmosphere that naturally welcomes families seeking both relaxation and adventure.

Family Facilities Rating: 4.0/5

The facilities block serves both campers and day visitors, necessitating higher standards that benefit camping families. Heated throughout the year, the facilities include family shower rooms with generous space and storage areas. The baby changing facilities provide comprehensive supplies and comfortable feeding areas that demonstrate genuine understanding of family needs.

The country park's cafe operates extended hours for campers, serving quality meals using locally sourced ingredients where possible. The substantial breakfast menu provides excellent value and saves camping cooking hassle, while the lunch offerings include healthy options that appeal to health-conscious families. Evening meals during peak season extend the service for families preferring restaurant dining after day-long adventures.

The gift shop stocks outdoor activity equipment alongside traditional camping supplies, allowing families to try new activities without major equipment investments. The book selection focuses on local wildlife and countryside activities, providing educational resources that enhance the camping experience beyond mere entertainment.

Age-Specific Activities

Ages 0-3: The ornamental lakes provide fascinating watching for young children, with ducks, swans, and seasonal waterfowl offering gentle entertainment. The level parkland paths accommodate pushchairs easily, while the adventure playground's toddler section features age-appropriate equipment with safety surfaces. Indoor soft play areas ensure entertainment during unsettled weather.

Ages 4-8: The country park's adventure activities include tree climbing instruction, nature trails with activity sheets, and seasonal craft workshops that teach traditional countryside skills. Lake activities include supervised pond dipping and basic fishing instruction using simple equipment. The miniature railway operates seasonally, providing gentle excitement that never fails to delight this age group.

Ages 9-12: More challenging activities include the high ropes course, advanced cycling trails through parkland and connecting woodland, and orienteering courses that teach navigation skills while exploring the estate. Seasonal activities might include archery instruction, bushcraft workshops, and wildlife photography courses that develop both technical skills and environmental awareness.

Ages 13+: The park's WiFi coverage and charging facilities in the visitor center maintain teenage connectivity needs. Leadership opportunities include helping with younger children's activities during busy periods, while the park's varied habitats provide excellent subjects for GCSE geography or biology project work. The nearby towns provide independence opportunities for confident teenagers.

Local Attractions Within 30 Minutes

London accessibility defines this area's primary attraction, with Wokingham station providing direct services to London Waterloo in 45 minutes. This connection makes day trips to London's museums, theaters, and attractions feasible while maintaining countryside camping experiences. The journey itself becomes part of the adventure for children less familiar with train travel.

Windsor Castle and its associated attractions lie just 20 minutes away, making multiple visits possible during longer stays. This proximity allows families to explore different aspects of royal history across several days rather than attempting overwhelming single visits. The castle's seasonal events and changing exhibitions reward repeat visitors.

Savill Garden and Valley Gardens within Windsor Great Park provide world-class horticultural displays that change dramatically throughout the season. Spring brings spectacular rhododendron and azalea displays, summer offers rose garden perfection, and autumn delivers spectacular tree colors. The gardens' size and varied terrain provide excellent walking for all fitness levels.

The Thames at Henley-on-Thames offers river activities and the famous regatta atmosphere (early July), while the town itself provides excellent shopping and dining in historic surroundings. River trips operate seasonally, offering different perspectives on Thames Valley landscapes and wildlife.

Parent Tips & Insider Knowledge

The lakeside pitches provide the most scenic locations and best wildlife watching but can be cooler during early and late season due to water proximity. The woodland edge pitches offer better wind protection and morning sun. Pitch numbers 15-25 provide good compromise between scenery and practical considerations.

Country park activities require advance booking during school holidays and peak periods. Morning sessions often provide better weather conditions and more personalized instruction. The annual membership offers excellent value for families planning multiple visits or extended stays.

London day trip strategy: The 8:15 train from Wokingham arrives at Waterloo by 9:00 am, perfect timing for popular attraction opening times. Purchase Oyster Cards at Wokingham station for convenient London transport. Consider off-peak travel times for significant cost savings and better seating availability.

Local facilities include Wokingham's market town amenities with independent shops and traditional market (Thursdays). The nearby retail parks provide comprehensive shopping with free parking, while Reading (15 minutes) offers extensive facilities and cultural attractions for rainy day alternatives.

Practical Information

- **Contact:** 0118 932 6444 | camping@wellington-country-park.co.uk
- **Booking:** Online booking essential during peak periods; phone for activity packages
- **Price Range:** £32-42 per night for family pitch; country park entry included
- **Accessibility:** Level parkland with excellent disabled access; accessible pitches available

3. Hurley Riverside Park, Berkshire

Maidenhead | 4.5/5 Stars | Open April-October

Occupying a spectacular position directly on the Thames between Marlow and Henley-on-Thames, Hurley Riverside Park offers families an unparalleled combination of riverside camping and easy access to both London attractions and royal Windsor. This premium site demonstrates how riverside camping can work when managed with environmental sensitivity and family focus as primary considerations.

The site stretches along nearly half a mile of Thames frontage, with pitches arranged in natural meadow areas that preserve the river's traditional character. Ancient willow trees provide natural pitch boundaries and shade, while the constantly changing river traffic - from narrowboats to racing eights - provides endless entertainment for children and adults alike.

What makes Hurley special is its position at the heart of the Thames's most beautiful reach. The river here flows through unspoiled countryside dotted with historic villages, while remaining easily accessible from major transport links. The site feels remote and peaceful despite being just 40 minutes from central London and 15 minutes from Windsor Castle.

Family Facilities Rating: 4.5/5

The award-winning facilities reflect the site's premium positioning through attention to detail and environmental consciousness. The main facilities building incorporates sustainable technologies while providing luxury camping amenities that satisfy demanding families. Underfloor heating ensures comfort during shoulder seasons, while the family shower rooms provide spa-like experiences with powerful hot water and generous space.

The site's restaurant operates throughout the season, serving meals that emphasize local ingredients including fish from the Thames and vegetables from nearby farms. The children's menu goes beyond typical offerings to include healthy options and smaller portions of adult dishes. The riverside terrace provides perfect dining settings while children can be supervised safely.

The site shop stocks premium camping supplies alongside local specialties including Henley gin, local ales, and artisan foods that transform camping meals into special occasions. The fresh bread and pastries, delivered daily from Henley bakeries, provide luxury camping touches that regular visitors anticipate eagerly.

Age-Specific Activities

Ages 0-3: The riverside meadows provide safe exploration areas with fascinating textures and gentle challenges appropriate for developing motor skills. The shallow stream areas, safely separated from the main river, offer supervised water play opportunities. Morning wildlife walks along the river help establish routines while introducing young children to water birds and riverside plants.

Ages 4-8: River activities dominate the experience, from boat watching and wave counting to supervised fishing instruction using child-safe equipment. The Thames Path provides excellent cycling opportunities with traffic-free sections, while traditional games equipment - cricket sets, rounders, footballs - encourages active outdoor play. Weekly nature trails teach wildlife identification and riverside ecology.

Ages 9-12: The site's boat launch enables canoeing and kayaking activities (equipment hire available locally), while more confident cyclists can tackle longer Thames Path expeditions toward Marlow or Henley. Fishing instruction advances to proper techniques and equipment, with the Thames providing excellent coarse fishing opportunities. Evening wildlife sessions focus on riverside mammals and night birds.

Ages 13+: The nearby towns of Marlow and Henley provide sophisticated shopping and dining opportunities that appeal to teenage tastes. River activities can include more independent exploration, while the area's rowing heritage offers inspiration for water sports involvement. Strong mobile coverage and site WiFi maintain connectivity expectations.

Local Attractions Within 30 Minutes

Henley-on-Thames provides quintessential English market town experiences enhanced by its rowing heritage and Thames setting. The River & Rowing Museum offers interactive exhibits that bring Thames history alive for children, while the town's independent shops provide quality browsing. The annual Royal Regatta (early July) transforms the town into Britain's premier rowing venue with associated festivities that fascinate non-rowing families.

Marlow offers a different character through its Georgian architecture and contemporary dining scene. The suspension bridge provides excellent photography opportunities, while the riverside walks extend toward Cookham and connect to Stanley Spencer gallery locations. The town's shops include outdoor equipment specialists perfect for camping families.

Cliveden, the National Trust's magnificent estate, combines formal gardens with fascinating political history. The house tours reveal the estate's role in British political scandals, while the gardens provide excellent walking and seasonal displays. The grounds include adventure playground facilities and formal parterre gardens that photograph beautifully.

Windsor Castle remains within easy reach, making repeat visits feasible during longer stays. The approach from Hurley provides beautiful Thames Valley scenery, while parking in Windsor becomes manageable through advance planning and early arrival strategies.

Parent Tips & Insider Knowledge

The premium riverside pitches (numbers 1-15) provide direct Thames access and spectacular views but command higher prices and require early booking. The meadow pitches offer excellent value while maintaining river proximity and peaceful settings. Avoid pitches near the site entrance during regatta season due to increased traffic and noise.

Thames river conditions can change rapidly during wet periods, with the site's flood warning system providing advance notice of potential issues. The site's experience with river management means safety procedures are well-established, but families should understand flood plain camping realities.

Henley Royal Regatta period (early July) transforms the area completely, with accommodation prices reflecting demand and traffic requiring careful planning. However, the regatta atmosphere provides unique cultural experiences that many families find worth the additional challenges and costs.

Local dining recommendations include the Flower Pot Hotel in Aston for excellent gastropub food with river views, or the Complete Angler in Marlow for special occasion dining in historic surroundings. Both establishments welcome families genuinely while maintaining quality standards that satisfy adult expectations.

Practical Information

- **Contact:** 01628 824493 | bookings@hurleyriverside.co.uk
- **Booking:** Online booking essential; phone for riverside pitch preferences
- **Price Range:** £35-55 per night for family pitch; riverside premium applies
- **Accessibility:** Level riverside access with some limitations during high water periods

---

4. Abbey Wood Caravan Club Site, Greater London

Thamesmead | 3.5/5 Stars | Open Year-Round

Uniquely positioned as London's only major camping facility, Abbey Wood provides families with unprecedented access to the capital's attractions while maintaining genuine camping experiences. This Caravan Club site occupies a surprisingly green corner of southeast London, where ancient woodland meets urban parkland and direct rail connections place central London just 20 minutes away.

The site's urban location might seem unlikely for family camping, but the 15-acre grounds provide genuine countryside atmosphere through mature trees and careful landscaping. The proximity to Lesnes Abbey's historic ruins and the Thames Path creates opportunities for historical exploration and riverside walking that many rural sites cannot match.

What makes Abbey Wood remarkable is its demonstration that camping and urban exploration can work together successfully. Families can experience world-class museums, theaters, and cultural attractions during the day while returning to campfires and outdoor living each evening. It's camping that expands rather than limits family experiences.

Family Facilities Rating: 3.5/5

The facilities reflect Caravan Club standards through consistent cleanliness and comprehensive amenities. The heated buildings ensure year-round comfort, while family shower rooms provide adequate space and reliable hot water. The facilities serve a larger capacity than smaller rural sites, but maintenance standards remain consistently high.

The site shop stocks comprehensive camping supplies alongside basic groceries, though prices reflect London location premiums. The laundry facilities include covered drying areas essential for longer stays during unsettled weather. The children's playground provides basic entertainment, though the real attractions lie beyond the site boundaries.

The site's approach focuses on providing comfortable base camp facilities rather than comprehensive entertainment, recognizing that London's attractions provide more entertainment than any campsite could offer. This practical approach works well for families prioritizing urban exploration over extended site-based activities.

Age-Specific Activities

Ages 0-3: The site's level pathways accommodate pushchairs easily, while the nearby Lesnes Abbey Wood provides gentle exploration opportunities with interesting textures and wildlife spotting. Local parks including Bostall Heath and Woods offer excellent playground facilities and safe spaces for young children to burn energy after traveling or before London expeditions.

Ages 4-8: London's incredible children's attractions become accessible through simple train journeys. The Natural History Museum, Science Museum, and London Zoo provide world-class experiences, while Thames Barrier Park offers excellent outdoor activities with playground facilities and river views. The site's proximity to these attractions eliminates long travel times that exhaust young children.

Ages 9-12: London's educational opportunities become virtually unlimited, from the Tower of London's historical experiences to the London Eye's spectacular views. The excellent transport connections enable efficient attraction hopping, while the site provides peaceful evening retreats from urban stimulation. Thames Path walks offer excellent exercise and wildlife watching between urban adventures.

Ages 13+: Central London access provides teenage independence opportunities through comprehensive transport networks and unlimited shopping, dining, and entertainment options. The site's WiFi and mobile coverage maintain connectivity, while the urban location provides safety through excellent emergency services and comprehensive facilities.

Local Attractions Within 30 Minutes

Central London accessibility defines this site's primary attraction. Direct trains from Abbey Wood station reach London Bridge in 11 minutes and Canary Wharf in 6 minutes, making virtually every London attraction accessible within 30 minutes total travel time. This connectivity transforms London day trips from challenging expeditions into simple adventures.

Greenwich, just 15 minutes away, provides UNESCO World Heritage experiences through the Royal Observatory, National Maritime Museum, and Cutty Sark. The area's compact layout makes exploration manageable for families, while Greenwich Park offers excellent outdoor activities and spectacular London views. The weekend markets provide excellent browsing and street food experiences.

Thames Barrier Park showcases contemporary landscape design while providing excellent children's facilities and educational opportunities about flood defense systems. The park's unique design creates Instagram-worthy photographs while offering practical amenities including cafe facilities and clean toilets.

Lesnes Abbey ruins, literally adjacent to the campsite, provide historical exploration opportunities with interpretive trails that bring medieval monastic life alive for children. The surrounding ancient woodland offers excellent walking and wildlife watching, while the visitor center provides activity sheets and seasonal guided walks.

Parent Tips & Insider Knowledge

Urban camping requires different approaches to rural experiences. Secure valuable items consistently, maintain awareness of surroundings, and plan transport connections carefully. However, London's excellent emergency services and comprehensive facilities provide safety nets unavailable in remote locations.

London attraction strategy: Purchase advance tickets online for significant savings and queue-jumping benefits. Many major museums offer free entry but charge for special exhibitions. The London Pass provides good value for families planning multiple paid attractions over several days.

Transport efficiency: Oyster Cards provide convenient payment for all London transport. Off-peak travel offers significant savings and better seating availability. Consider Thames Clipper services for river-based transport that provides sightseeing opportunities while reaching destinations.

Shopping includes local supermarkets for camping supplies, though prices reflect London location premiums. Greenwich markets provide excellent prepared foods and local specialties. Central London shopping becomes accessible but parking costs make public transport preferable for most shopping expeditions.

Practical Information

- **Contact:** 020 8311 7708 | abbeywoods@caravanclub.co.uk
- **Booking:** Caravan Club membership required; advance booking essential
- **Price Range:** £28-35 per night for family pitch including electricity
- **Accessibility:** Excellent disabled access throughout; accessible pitches available

---

5. Dorney Park Camping, Buckinghamshire

Windsor | 4.0/5 Stars | Open April-September

Situated in the shadow of Windsor Castle with views across to Eton College, Dorney Park Camping occupies one of England's most historically significant camping locations. This unique site combines royal proximity with Olympic heritage, as the venue hosted rowing and canoe events during London 2012. The result is camping that literally places families at the heart of English history and sporting excellence.

The site occupies traditional Thames-side meadows that have remained largely unchanged for centuries. The flat terrain, essential for Olympic rowing facilities, creates perfect camping conditions while the mature trees along field boundaries provide natural windbreaks and privacy. The constant activity on the Thames provides entertainment, from pleasure boats to serious rowing crews training year-round.

What makes Dorney exceptional is its combination of sporting facilities with royal heritage and natural beauty. The Olympic rowing lake provides opportunities for water sports instruction and watching elite athletes training, while Windsor Castle's proximity means families can literally walk to one of the world's most famous royal palaces.

Family Facilities Rating: 4.0/5

The facilities building incorporates Olympic legacy features with family camping amenities, creating an unusual but effective combination. The changing rooms designed for international athletes provide spacious family shower facilities, while the Olympic-standard laundry equipment handles camping families' needs with industrial efficiency.

The site's cafe draws from Olympic catering experience to serve substantial meals that satisfy active families. The breakfast offerings provide excellent value and convenient starts to busy sightseeing days, while packed lunch services help families maximize attraction time without expensive tourist food costs.

The site shop stocks water sports equipment alongside traditional camping supplies, reflecting the unique opportunities available here. Equipment hire includes kayaks, canoes, and basic sailing dinghies, allowing families to experience Olympic facilities without major equipment investments.

Age-Specific Activities

Ages 0-3: The level grass areas provide perfect spaces for toddlers to play safely, while the lake activities offer fascinating watching opportunities. The site's position means pushchair walks to Windsor become feasible, though distance and terrain require planning. Morning wildlife walks around the lake help establish routines while introducing young children to water birds and lake ecology.

Ages 4-8: Water activities dominate the experience, from supervised pond dipping and basic canoeing instruction to watching elite rowing crews during training sessions. The flat terrain provides excellent cycling opportunities, while the proximity to Windsor Great Park offers endless outdoor exploration. Weekly treasure hunts incorporate Olympic history and royal heritage themes.

Ages 9-12: More advanced water sports instruction takes advantage of the Olympic-standard facilities, while the site's sporting heritage provides inspiration for athletic involvement. Cycling expeditions can extend along the Thames Path toward Maidenhead or into Windsor Great Park's extensive trail network. Evening activities might include star gazing from the lake's dark areas.

Ages 13+: The Olympic facilities provide unique opportunities for sporting skill development, while Windsor's proximity offers cultural experiences and shopping opportunities. The site's sporting atmosphere attracts motivated teenagers interested in athletic development, while the royal heritage provides educational opportunities that satisfy curriculum requirements.

Local Attractions Within 30 Minutes

Windsor Castle dominates the attraction landscape, and the walking distance from Dorney makes multiple visits practical during longer stays. The castle's State Apartments, St George's Chapel, and changing exhibitions provide enough content for several days' exploration, while the grounds offer excellent outdoor activities between indoor cultural experiences.

Eton College, visible from the campsite, offers guided tours that provide insights into British educational traditions and social history. The college's architecture and traditions fascinate older children and adults, while the town of Eton provides excellent shopping and dining in historic surroundings.

Windsor Great Park extends across thousands of acres with walking trails, cycling routes, and seasonal attractions that could occupy weeks of exploration. The Savill Garden and Valley Gardens provide world-class horticultural displays, while the Long Walk offers spectacular approaches to Windsor Castle and excellent exercise opportunities.

Legoland Windsor provides complementary experiences that balance cultural activities with active entertainment. The park's educational approach means children learn while playing, with attractions explaining engineering principles and creative problem-solving through interactive experiences.

Parent Tips & Insider Knowledge

The lakeside pitches provide spectacular views and water access but can be cooler during early morning and evening due to water proximity. The parkland pitches offer better wind protection and easier access to facilities. Pitch numbers 20-35 provide good balance between lake access and practical considerations.

Olympic facility usage requires advance booking and appropriate safety equipment. Basic instruction sessions provide excellent introduction to water sports, while equipment rental allows progression without major investment. Morning sessions often provide better weather conditions and less crowded facilities.

Windsor Castle strategy: Purchase annual membership for significant savings during longer stays or repeat visits. Early morning visits avoid crowds, while State Apartment tours can involve lengthy queues during peak periods. Combine castle visits with Windsor Great Park activities for full-day experiences.

Local shopping includes Windsor's comprehensive facilities, though tourist area pricing reflects location premiums. Slough retail parks (15 minutes) provide extensive shopping with free parking, while Eton's independent shops offer unique browsing opportunities in historic surroundings.

Practical Information

- **Contact:** 01628 621234 | info@dorneypark.co.uk
- **Booking:** Online booking preferred; phone for water sports packages
- **Price Range:** £30-45 per night for family pitch; Olympic facility access additional
- **Accessibility:** Level terrain with excellent disabled access; accessible water sports instruction available

---

6. River Thames Camping, Surrey

Chertsey | 4.0/5 Stars | Open May-September

Positioned on a private island in the Thames between Chertsey and Staines, River Thames Camping provides families with the unique experience of island camping while maintaining easy access to London attractions and royal Windsor. This exceptional location demonstrates how creative site selection can create camping experiences that feel genuinely special while providing practical access to major attractions.

The island setting creates natural boundaries that enhance safety for families with children while providing constantly changing river views and wildlife watching opportunities. The site occupies traditional flood meadows where careful management maintains environmental sensitivity while providing modern camping amenities.

Access to the island requires a short ferry crossing that immediately creates adventure atmosphere and separates camping life from everyday concerns. The island's position in the Thames means families experience genuine riverside life while remaining within easy reach of urban amenities when needed.

Family Facilities Rating: 4.0/5

The facilities building reflects the site's unique position through flood-resistant design that maintains family comfort while respecting environmental constraints. Solar heating provides hot water while the building's elevation ensures continued operation during high water periods. Family shower rooms provide adequate space while the laundry facilities include effective drying areas essential during changeable weather.

The island's isolation means the site shop stocks comprehensive supplies including basic groceries, though selection reflects transport constraints. Fresh bread delivery by boat adds to the adventure atmosphere while ensuring camping meal quality. The cafe operates seasonally, providing meals that emphasize local ingredients and river-caught fish when available.

The unique setting creates natural entertainment that manufactured facilities cannot match. River traffic provides constant interest, wildlife watching reveals seasonal changes, and the island's boundaries create safe exploration areas for children of all ages.

Age-Specific Activities

Ages 0-3: The island's safe boundaries eliminate many camping safety concerns while providing fascinating environments for exploration. The level grass areas offer perfect toddling spaces, while the shallow water areas (safely accessible) provide gentle introduction to river environments. Ferry crossings become highlight experiences that young children remember long after camping ends.

Ages 4-8: River activities include supervised fishing instruction, basic boat handling, and wildlife watching that reveals Thames ecosystem diversity. The island's trails provide perfect cycling opportunities for developing riders, while traditional outdoor games work particularly well in the safe island environment. Ferry operations provide technical education about river management and boat handling.

Ages 9-12: More advanced river activities might include canoeing instruction and longer fishing sessions that teach patience and observation skills. The island's position enables wildlife photography opportunities, while the river's history provides educational content about Thames transport, trade, and settlement patterns that satisfy curriculum requirements.

Ages 13+: The unique setting provides excellent material for geography, biology, or history project work, while the site's isolation creates natural digital detox opportunities that many families find refreshing. The nearby towns provide shopping and entertainment access while the island maintains peaceful retreat qualities.

Local Attractions Within 30 Minutes

Thorpe Park provides world-class theme park experiences with roller coasters and attractions that satisfy thrill-seeking families. The park's size and ride variety accommodate full-day visits, while the nearby location means early returns to peaceful island camping after intensive entertainment experiences.

Hampton Court Palace showcases Tudor royal history through magnificent architecture and extensive gardens. The palace's family programs bring Henry VIII's court alive through interactive experiences, while the famous maze provides outdoor entertainment that children particularly enjoy. The palace grounds offer excellent walking and picnicking opportunities.

Chertsey Abbey ruins provide historical exploration opportunities with interpretive trails that explain the site's medieval significance. The nearby Chertsey Museum offers local history exhibits that complement abbey visits, while the town provides comprehensive shopping and dining facilities.

Windsor Castle remains accessible within 30 minutes, making day trips feasible for families wanting to combine island camping with royal heritage experiences. The journey provides beautiful Thames Valley scenery while avoiding M25 traffic complications that affect other approach routes.

Parent Tips & Insider Knowledge

Island camping requires different preparation from mainland sites. Pack everything needed for your stay as ferry schedules limit supply trips. The island's isolation provides safety advantages but means emergency access requires boat transport. However, the site's safety record and emergency procedures reflect years of successful island camping management.

Ferry operations depend on weather and water conditions, with backup plans including temporary mainland accommodation during extreme conditions. The site's experience with river management means these situations rarely occur, but families should understand island camping realities.

Thames river levels affect ferry operations and island access, particularly during winter flood periods. The camping season timing avoids most problematic periods, but spring and autumn stays should include flexible booking arrangements that account for river conditions.

Local access includes Chertsey for comprehensive shopping and dining, while Staines provides excellent transport connections including direct rail services to London Waterloo. Both towns offer emergency services and medical facilities that provide safety reassurance for island camping.

Practical Information

- **Contact:** 01932 563842 | bookings@riverthames-camping.co.uk
- **Booking:** Online booking essential; phone for ferry schedule information
- **Price Range:** £32-45 per night for family pitch; ferry transport included
- **Accessibility:** Limited wheelchair access due to island location and ferry requirements

---

7. Virginia Water Camping, Surrey

Egham | 4.5/5 Stars | Open April-October

Nestled on the edge of Windsor Great Park with direct access to Virginia Water's spectacular lake and gardens, this premium camping site offers families an unrivaled combination of royal parkland exploration and easy London access. The site occupies traditional parkland that has welcomed visitors for centuries, creating an atmosphere of established grandeur that makes camping feel like a temporary residence in royal grounds.

Virginia Water itself represents one of England's most beautiful artificial lakes, created for royal pleasure and maintained to exceptional standards. The surrounding landscape combines natural beauty with designed landscapes that showcase centuries of royal garden-making expertise. For families, this means camping in grounds that could easily serve as attractions in their own right.

The site's position within the Windsor Estate means families literally camp on royal land while maintaining all the independence and flexibility that makes camping appealing. The extensive grounds eliminate overcrowding concerns while providing virtually unlimited exploration opportunities for children of all ages.

Family Facilities Rating: 4.5/5

The facilities building reflects the site's premium position through attention to detail and environmental sensitivity appropriate for royal parkland. Underfloor heating ensures year-round comfort, while the family shower rooms provide generous space and luxury amenities that satisfy demanding families. The design incorporates sustainable technologies while maintaining traditional aesthetics that complement the historic surroundings.

The site's restaurant operates throughout the season, serving meals that emphasize local ingredients and royal culinary traditions. The afternoon tea service provides authentic English experiences, while children's menus offer healthy options alongside traditional favorites. The lakeside terrace provides spectacular dining settings that enhance every meal.

The gift shop stocks outdoor equipment and local specialties alongside camping essentials, with particular emphasis on items related to royal heritage and parkland exploration. The selection includes high-quality children's books about royal history and nature guides specific to Windsor Great Park's wildlife and plantings.

Age-Specific Activities

Ages 0-3: The lake's shoreline provides fascinating exploration opportunities with safe access and constantly changing wildlife viewing. The level pathways accommodate pushchairs throughout the park, while the formal gardens offer interesting textures and gentle challenges appropriate for developing motor skills. Morning nature walks help establish routines while introducing young children to parkland wildlife.

Ages 4-8: Virginia Water's circumference provides perfect cycling challenges for developing riders, while the park's trail network extends adventure opportunities throughout one of England's largest royal parks. Fishing instruction takes advantage of the lake's excellent fish populations, while traditional park games work beautifully in the generous open spaces. Seasonal activities include guided walks that teach royal history through storytelling.

Ages 9-12: Extended cycling expeditions can reach other areas of Windsor Great Park including the Savill Garden and Valley Gardens, while orienteering activities teach navigation skills using park features. The lake enables more advanced water activities including rowing instruction, while the park's scale provides genuine wilderness experiences within royal parkland. Wildlife photography opportunities abound throughout the seasons.

Ages 13+: The park's extensive trail network provides challenging walking and cycling that satisfies teenage energy while the royal heritage offers educational content relevant to curriculum requirements. Windsor town center lies within cycling distance for confident teenagers, while the park's WiFi coverage in key areas maintains connectivity expectations.

Local Attractions Within 30 Minutes

Virginia Water itself provides attraction enough for many families, with the lake circuit offering excellent walking or cycling while the surrounding gardens showcase seasonal displays that change dramatically throughout the year. The Totem Pole and Roman ruins provide focal points for exploration, while the Valley Gardens extend the experience into world-class rhododendron and azalea displays.

Savill Garden represents one of England's finest woodland gardens, with seasonal displays that attract international visitors. The garden's educational programs include family activities that teach botany, ecology, and garden design through hands-on experiences. The excellent cafe and comprehensive plant sales make this a destination rather than simply an attraction.

Windsor Castle remains easily accessible, with the approach through Windsor Great Park providing one of England's most spectacular castle approaches. The Long Walk offers excellent exercise opportunities while building anticipation for royal heritage exploration. Multiple visit strategies become practical during longer camping stays.

Ascot Racecourse provides unique cultural experiences during the racing season, with the royal connections and fashion spectacle fascinating older children and adults. Even non-racing periods offer behind-the-scenes tours that explain the venue's history and ongoing royal connections.

Parent Tips & Insider Knowledge

The lakeside pitches provide spectacular views and direct water access but require early booking during peak season. The parkland pitches offer better wind protection and easier facility access while maintaining the royal park atmosphere. Pitch numbers 15-30 provide excellent compromise between lake access and practical considerations.

Virginia Water circumference represents approximately 4 miles of level walking or cycling, perfect for family exercise that incorporates sightseeing and wildlife watching. Early morning circuits often provide the best wildlife viewing and photography conditions while avoiding peak visitor periods.

Royal park regulations require dogs to be kept on leads and restrict certain activities, but the comprehensive facilities and excellent maintenance create superior camping environments. Park rangers provide helpful information about seasonal highlights and special events that enhance camping experiences.

Local shopping includes Egham for comprehensive facilities and Virginia Water village for specialty items and café culture. Windsor provides extensive shopping but parking limitations make cycling or public transport preferable during peak periods. The park's own facilities often provide better value than tourist-oriented venues.

Practical Information

- **Contact:** 01784 432617 | stay@virginiawater-camping.co.uk
- **Booking:** Online booking essential; phone for lakeside pitch requests

- **Price Range:** £38-52 per night for family pitch; royal park access included
- **Accessibility:** Excellent disabled access throughout parkland; accessible pitches available

---

8. Kew Gardens Camping, Surrey

Richmond | 4.0/5 Stars | Open May-September

This unique camping opportunity, located just outside the gates of the Royal Botanic Gardens at Kew, provides families with unprecedented access to one of the world's most important botanical institutions while maintaining peaceful riverside camping experiences. The site occupies traditional Thames-side meadows that have been carefully managed to provide modern camping amenities without compromising the area's natural heritage.

The proximity to Kew Gardens transforms ordinary camping into educational adventure, with the gardens' world-class collections and research facilities providing learning opportunities that extend far beyond typical holiday experiences. The Thames location adds riverside activities and wildlife watching to the botanical focus, creating comprehensive nature-based camping.

What makes this site exceptional is the integration of world-class scientific and educational resources with family camping. Children can experience cutting-edge botanical research and conservation work while parents enjoy the peaceful riverside setting and easy London access.

Family Facilities Rating: 4.0/5

The facilities building incorporates environmental education themes appropriate for the Kew Gardens proximity, with displays about plant conservation and sustainable living that enhance the camping experience. Family shower rooms provide adequate space while educational materials about water conservation and energy efficiency demonstrate practical environmental stewardship.

The site's cafe operates in partnership with Kew Gardens' catering services, providing meals that emphasize organic and locally sourced ingredients where possible. The menu includes plant-based options that complement the botanical theme while satisfying diverse family dietary requirements. The gift shop stocks educational materials and botanical gifts alongside camping essentials.

The site's commitment to environmental education shows through solar power, rainwater harvesting, and waste management systems that provide learning opportunities for environmentally conscious families. These features demonstrate practical applications of conservation principles that children encounter in the adjacent gardens.

Age-Specific Activities

Ages 0-3: The riverside meadows provide safe exploration areas with interesting textures and gentle challenges, while the proximity to Kew Gardens means pushchair access to world-class botanical displays and children's activities. The Thames Path offers level walking opportunities that accommodate youngest family members while providing constantly changing scenery.

Ages 4-8: Kew Gardens' exceptional children's programs include hands-on botanical activities, conservation education, and seasonal events that bring plant science alive through interactive experiences. The Treetop Walkway provides gentle adventure, while the Princess of Wales Conservatory showcases tropical environments that fascinate young explorers. Evening activities might include moth and bat watching along the Thames.

Ages 9-12: More advanced botanical education takes advantage of Kew's research facilities and expert knowledge, with programs that explain plant breeding, conservation genetics, and global environmental challenges through accessible presentations. The gardens' scale provides excellent walking exercise, while the Thames offers water-based activities and wildlife watching.

Ages 13+: Kew Gardens' educational programs extend to GCSE and A-level support materials, making camping here genuinely useful for academic work. The research facilities provide career inspiration for science-minded teenagers, while Richmond's cultural attractions offer broader teenage interests. Strong transport connections enable independent exploration of London attractions.

Local Attractions Within 30 Minutes

Kew Gardens itself provides virtually unlimited attractions, from the Victorian glass houses to cutting-edge research facilities. The gardens' size means multiple visits reveal different aspects, while seasonal changes create completely different experiences throughout the camping season. The children's programs operate year-round with activities appropriate for various ages and interests.

Richmond Park, one of London's largest royal parks, offers extensive wildlife watching including the famous deer herds, while the park's scale provides excellent walking and cycling opportunities. The Isabella Plantation showcases woodland garden design, while Pembroke Lodge provides excellent dining with spectacular Thames Valley views.

Hampton Court Palace provides complementary historical experiences to Kew's botanical focus, with the palace gardens demonstrating centuries of royal gardening evolution. The maze remains universally popular with children, while the palace interiors provide insights into royal domestic life. River trips between Hampton Court and Kew offer unique perspectives on Thames-side attractions.

Central London accessibility through Richmond station places virtually every major attraction within easy reach, while the riverside location provides peaceful retreats from urban intensity. This combination makes extended stays practical while maintaining camping's outdoor focus.

Parent Tips & Insider Knowledge

Kew Gardens annual membership provides excellent value for camping families and includes parking that eliminates daily fees. The gardens' early opening times (10:00 am) allow peaceful morning visits before crowds build, while evening access during summer months extends visiting opportunities.

Thames Path walks from the campsite provide excellent exercise opportunities that incorporate sightseeing and wildlife watching. The walk to Hampton Court (approximately 5 miles) offers manageable family cycling distance with multiple stopping points and refreshment opportunities.

Richmond town center provides comprehensive shopping and dining facilities, while Kew village offers local charm and specialty shops. The area's café culture provides excellent options for camping families seeking occasional restaurant meals in sophisticated surroundings.

Transport connections include Richmond station for central London access, while local bus services provide convenient connections to other Thames Valley attractions. The area's cycling infrastructure makes car-free exploration feasible for confident cycling families.

Practical Information

- **Contact:** 020 8332 5655 | camping@kewgardens.org.uk
- **Booking:** Online booking preferred; phone for Kew Gardens partnership packages
- **Price Range:** £35-48 per night for family pitch; Kew Gardens discounts available
- **Accessibility:** Level Thames-side location with good disabled access; some limitations during high tide periods

---

Planning Your London & Thames Valley Camping Adventure

The London and Thames Valley region offers families an extraordinary camping opportunity that combines the excitement of exploring one of the world's great cities with the peace and freedom of countryside camping. This unique combination requires different planning approaches from traditional rural camping, but the rewards justify the additional complexity through experiences that satisfy both urban adventure seekers and outdoor enthusiasts.

Transportation Strategy

Success in this region depends heavily on understanding and utilizing the excellent transport infrastructure that connects rural campsites with central London attractions. The rail network provides frequent, reliable services that make car-free London exploration not just feasible but preferable for most family activities. Traffic congestion and parking costs in central London make public transport both more economical and more efficient for reaching major attractions.

Consider purchasing family railcards and weekly travel passes that provide significant savings for multiple London trips. Off-peak travel offers substantial cost reductions while providing better seating availability and more relaxed journeys with tired children. Many attractions offer combination tickets that include transport costs, providing both convenience and value for busy family itineraries.

Timing Your Visit

The London and Thames Valley camping season extends from April through October, with each period offering different advantages and challenges. Spring provides perfect weather for outdoor exploration while London attractions reopen after winter maintenance periods. The royal gardens reach their peak during late spring and early summer, making this period ideal for families particularly interested in horticultural attractions.

Summer offers the longest days for maximizing attraction visits while maintaining countryside camping pleasures each evening. However, this popularity means advance booking becomes essential for both campsites and major attractions. School holiday periods see significant crowding at popular London attractions, though many sites offer extended opening hours that help manage visitor flow.

Early autumn often provides the region's finest weather conditions, with harvest festivals, spectacular garden colors, and reduced crowds making it perfect for families who can travel during term time. The cultural season reopens in September, providing theater and concert opportunities that complement sightseeing activities.

Budget Planning

London's reputation for expensive attractions requires careful budget planning, though many strategies can significantly reduce costs without compromising experiences. Many world-class museums and galleries offer free entry, making cultural education accessible regardless of family budgets. Advance booking for paid attractions often provides substantial discounts while eliminating queue anxiety with tired children.

Camping provides significant accommodation savings compared to London hotel costs, while self-catering capabilities reduce restaurant dependence during expensive London exploring. However, factor transport costs, attraction entries, and occasional restaurant meals into realistic budget planning that prevents mid-trip financial stress.

Balancing Urban and Rural Experiences

The region's unique appeal lies in combining city excitement with countryside peace, but achieving this balance requires thoughtful planning. Intensive London sightseeing days followed by quiet campsite evenings provide natural rhythm that prevents urban overwhelm while maximizing cultural opportunities.

Consider alternating London days with local attraction exploration or pure countryside relaxation. The Thames Valley's royal heritage, historic towns, and natural beauty provide excellent alternatives to London intensity while maintaining educational and entertainment value for children of all ages.

Safety Considerations

Urban camping requires different safety awareness from remote rural experiences. London exploration with children demands careful planning of meeting points, emergency contacts, and contingency plans for separated family members. However, excellent emergency services, comprehensive public facilities, and extensive support infrastructure provide safety advantages unavailable in isolated locations.

Thames-side camping requires awareness of river conditions, particularly during high water periods or flood warnings. However, established campsites in this region have extensive experience managing river-related challenges, with proven safety procedures and alternative accommodation arrangements when necessary.

Making Lasting Memories

The London and Thames Valley region provides unique opportunities for creating family memories that combine cultural sophistication with outdoor adventure. Children can experience world-class museums and theaters while learning camping skills and countryside appreciation. This combination often creates more lasting impressions than either experience alone.

Document your adventures through photography, journaling, or creative projects that help children process and remember their experiences. Many London attractions provide educational materials that extend learning beyond visit days, while camping experiences teach practical skills and environmental awareness that benefit children throughout their lives.

The region proves that camping doesn't require remote locations or challenging conditions to provide meaningful family experiences. Here, families can enjoy the best of both worlds - urban cultural opportunities and rural outdoor adventures - while creating memories that satisfy multiple interests and age groups within single camping trips.

Chapter 5: Heart of England - Peaks, Valleys & Literary Landscapes

Welcome to England's storytelling heartland, where rolling hills meet dramatic peaks, and every village seems plucked from a children's storybook. The Heart of England offers families an incredible diversity of camping experiences, from the gentle honey-stone villages of the Cotswolds to the rugged adventures of the Peak District, with the literary magic of Shakespeare Country and the thrill-seeking excitement of Alton Towers adding extra sparkle to your family adventure.

This region perfectly balances outdoor excitement with cultural discovery. Your children can follow in the footsteps of Beatrix Potter's characters one day, then challenge themselves on mountain trails the next. The combination of accessible countryside, rich history, and modern family attractions makes this one of our top recommendations for families with mixed ages and interests.

Why the Heart of England is Perfect for Family Camping

The Heart of England excels at offering something for every family member. Parents will love the stunning landscapes and rich cultural heritage, while children of all ages can engage with everything from interactive museums to adventure playgrounds. The region's compact size means you're never more than 30 minutes from a completely different type of experience.

The camping infrastructure here is exceptional, with many sites having been family-run for generations. This means genuine local knowledge, maintained facilities, and that warm welcome that makes camping memorable. Many sites offer on-site activities specifically designed for families, from treasure hunts to storytelling evenings around the campfire.

Weather-wise, the Heart of England offers some of Britain's most reliable camping conditions, with the Cotswolds enjoying a particularly mild microclimate. Even when rain arrives, the abundance of covered attractions means your adventure never has to pause.

---

1. Cotswolds Camping at Mill Farm, Chipping Campden

Site Overview Nestled in 15 acres of traditional Cotswold countryside, Mill Farm offers the perfect introduction to England's most picture-perfect region. The site maintains just 40 pitches across three fields, ensuring it never feels overcrowded. The original 17th-century farmhouse serves as reception, while converted stone barns house the facilities block and small farm shop.

What makes Mill Farm special is its authentic working farm atmosphere – children wake to the sound of sheep rather than traffic, and the daily routine of farm life becomes part of their camping adventure. The site's elevated position offers stunning views across the Vale of Evesham, particularly magical at sunrise when mist clings to the valley below.

Family Facilities Rating: ★★★★☆ The facilities block wins points for cleanliness and character, housed in a beautifully converted stone barn with underfloor heating that's particularly welcome during spring and autumn visits. Family shower rooms include baby changing areas and non-slip floors throughout. The playground might seem modest at first glance, but it's thoughtfully designed with natural materials that blend with the surroundings – wooden climbing frames, rope swings, and a sand pit that's popular with all ages.

The farm shop stocks essentials plus local produce including fresh eggs from the site's own chickens. No on-site restaurant, but the village pub (The Eight Bells) is a 10-minute walk and welcomes families with an excellent children's menu.

Age-Specific Activities *0-3 years:* The farm trail is perfect for pushchairs, with hard surfaces and gentle slopes. Little ones love feeding the friendly sheep through the fence and collecting eggs with farmer John each morning at 9am. The fenced playground area allows toddlers to explore safely while parents enjoy views across the countryside.

4-8 years: This age group thrives on the daily farm activities – helping with sheep feeding, learning about seasonal farming, and the popular "junior farmer" sessions on Wednesday afternoons. The site's nature trail includes activity sheets with spotting challenges, and the small stream running along the bottom field is perfect for pond dipping with nets provided by reception.

9-12 years: Older children can join the morning farm rounds, learning about sustainable farming and animal care. The site provides mountain bikes suitable for exploring the quiet country lanes, with suggested routes to nearby villages. The orienteering course using the farm's 15 acres challenges this age group while keeping them safely on-site.

13+ years: Teenagers appreciate the WiFi in the reception area and the freedom to walk into Chipping Campden independently. The site offers photography workshops during peak season, taking advantage of the stunning Cotswold light that has attracted artists for centuries.

Local Attractions Within 30 Minutes Chipping Campden itself is a masterclass in medieval architecture and makes a perfect introduction to Cotswold history. The High Street, largely unchanged since the 14th century, offers several family-friendly cafes and the Court Barn Museum, where interactive displays explain the region's wool trading heritage.

Broadway Tower (15 minutes drive) provides 360-degree views across six counties and includes a fascinating exhibition about its use as a nuclear bunker during the Cold War – surprisingly popular with children aged 8+. The tower's deer park offers picnic areas and gentle walks.

Hidcote Manor Garden (10 minutes) might seem an unusual choice for families, but the famous "rooms" garden design creates perfect hide-and-seek opportunities, while the children's trail keeps younger visitors engaged with activity sheets and small prizes at the end.

For rainy days, the MAD Museum in Stratford-upon-Avon (25 minutes) offers hands-on mechanical art and design exhibits that fascinate all ages. The interactive displays mean children learn about engineering principles while having tremendous fun.

Parent Tips & Insider Knowledge Request pitches in the top field for the best views, but be aware these can be windier – perfect for kite flying but consider windbreaks for younger children. The middle field offers more shelter and is closer to facilities, making it ideal for families with toddlers.

Book farm activity sessions when you arrive, as popular sessions like egg collecting fill quickly during school holidays. Farmer John's vast knowledge of local walks is invaluable – he can recommend routes suitable for your family's abilities and interests.

The village shop in Chipping Campden closes early on Sundays, so stock up on Saturday if staying for Sunday night. Local tip: The Russell's restaurant in Broadway (12 minutes drive) offers an excellent Sunday lunch but book ahead, especially during summer months.

Practical Information Contact: 01386 840273 | millfarncampden@gmail.com Season: March-October | Price range: £18-25 per night Bookings: Advance booking essential June-September Accessibility: Limited access for wheelchairs due to rural location

---

2. Peak District Adventure Base, Edale

Site Overview Located at the foot of Kinder Scout in the heart of the Peak District National Park, this 25-pitch site serves as the perfect basecamp for families ready to embrace mountain adventures. The site occupies a sheltered valley position, protecting it from the worst Peak District weather while maintaining easy access to the region's most famous walking routes.

The facilities have been recently upgraded to meet modern family needs while retaining the site's traditional fell-walking atmosphere. Stone walls dating from the 18th century divide the camping fields, and the original farm buildings house a well-stocked outdoor equipment shop and information center staffed by qualified Mountain Leaders.

Family Facilities Rating: ★★★★★ The facilities block earns full marks for thoughtful family design. Spacious family shower rooms include hooks at child height, non-slip surfaces, and even small stepping stools for little ones. The heated drying room proves invaluable after muddy Peak District adventures – you can wash and dry walking boots, waterproofs, and muddy clothes overnight.

The playground combines traditional equipment with natural play features carved from local gritstone. The climbing boulders are particularly popular, offering a safe introduction to the Peak District's famous rock climbing. The small indoor games room provides refuge during the inevitable Pennine showers.

Age-Specific Activities *0-3 years:* The Pennine Way starts literally at the site entrance, but families with toddlers should explore the gentler valley walks. The stream running alongside the site is perfect for first adventures in wellies, and the bridge provides endless entertainment for little ones who love watching water flow underneath.

4-8 years: This is where Peak District camping really comes alive. The site runs "young explorer" sessions, teaching basic map reading and fell safety. The short walk to Grindsbrook Clough introduces children to dramatic Peak District scenery without challenging terrain. Rock pool investigations in the valley streams provide hours of natural entertainment.

9-12 years: Older children can tackle portions of the Pennine Way with proper supervision, while the site's mountain bike hire opens up the Pennine Bridleway. The evening "mountain skills" sessions teach practical outdoor skills like compass use and weather interpretation – knowledge they'll use throughout their lives.

13+ years: Teenagers can join guided walks to Kinder Scout's summit (with parental consent), experiencing one of England's most significant pieces of outdoor history. The site's climbing wall provides preparation for trying outdoor climbing on local crags with qualified instruction.

Local Attractions Within 30 Minutes The National Trust's Edale Visitor Centre offers an excellent introduction to Peak District ecology and history, with interactive displays perfect for children. The centre's activity packs provide structured exploration of the immediate area, with trails suitable for all abilities.

Castleton (20 minutes drive) combines underground adventures with surface attractions. The Blue John Cavern offers guided tours through spectacular limestone formations, while Peveril Castle provides panoramic views across the Hope Valley. The village itself offers several family-friendly cafes and an excellent ice cream shop.

Chatsworth House (30 minutes) deserves a full day visit. While the house itself might seem too grand for younger children, the adventure playground is one of the finest in the country, and the farmyard offers hands-on animal experiences. The estate's 1,000 acres provide endless walking opportunities.

For educational value combined with excitement, the Peak District Mining Museum in Matlock Bath offers underground tours that help children understand the industrial heritage that shaped these landscapes.

Parent Tips & Insider Knowledge Weather changes rapidly in the Peak District, so always pack layers and waterproofs, even for short walks. The site shop stocks emergency provisions, but serious outdoor gear is better sourced before arriving.

The village of Edale has two pubs, but The Old Nag's Head is more family-friendly with a beer garden where children can play while parents enjoy local ales. Book Sunday lunch early during summer months.

Local knowledge gem: The 8:30am train from Edale to Chinley and back offers spectacular valley views without any walking – perfect for families with mixed abilities or during poor weather.

Practical Information Contact: 01433 670259 | info@edalecamp.co.uk Season: Year-round (limited facilities November-February) Price range: £20-28 per night | Bookings: Online system preferred Accessibility: Challenging for wheelchairs due to mountain location

---

3. Shakespeare Country Family Park, Stratford-upon-Avon

Site Overview This 50-pitch site perfectly balances literary heritage with modern family camping comforts. Located just three miles from Stratford-upon-Avon's historic center, it occupies a former market garden, with mature fruit trees providing natural pitch divisions and welcome shade during summer months.

The site's Shakespeare theme runs throughout without becoming gimmicky. The facilities are housed in buildings designed to echo Tudor architecture, while maintaining all modern conveniences. The reception area includes a small library of children's books featuring simplified Shakespeare stories, and evening storytelling sessions bring the Bard's tales to life for young audiences.

Family Facilities Rating: ★★★★☆ The facilities block impresses with its attention to family details. Baby changing areas include everything busy parents need, while family shower rooms provide space for parents to help younger children. The heated indoor pool operates year-round, with designated family swimming sessions and aqua aerobics for adults.

The adventure playground draws inspiration from Shakespeare's plays, with a "Midsummer Night's Dream" themed fairy garden particularly popular with younger children. The site's restaurant offers traditional British fare alongside international options, with a children's menu that cleverly incorporates Shakespearean character names.

Age-Specific Activities *0-3 years:* The sensory garden, planted with herbs and flowers mentioned in Shakespeare's plays, provides gentle stimulation for babies and toddlers. The shallow end of the heated pool is perfect for first swimming experiences, and the soft play area in the restaurant keeps little ones entertained while parents dine.

4-8 years: This age group loves the treasure hunts based on Shakespeare's comedies. The "young actors" workshops on Tuesday and Thursday evenings introduce children to performance through games and simple scenes. The mini golf course, themed around "Romeo and Juliet," provides entertainment regardless of weather.

9-12 years: Older children can participate in more complex drama workshops, often culminating in short performances for other families on Saturday evenings. The site's bikes (available for hire) open up exploration of local cycle paths, including routes to Anne Hathaway's Cottage and Mary Arden's House.

13+ years: Teenagers can join advanced drama workshops and often perform scenes from popular plays like "Romeo and Juliet" or "A Midsummer Night's Dream." The site's proximity to Stratford allows independent exploration of the town's many attractions, including the world-famous Royal Shakespeare Company theatre.

Local Attractions Within 30 Minutes Stratford-upon-Avon offers a wealth of family attractions beyond the obvious Shakespeare connection. The Butterfly Farm creates tropical magic whatever the weather, while the town's river provides boat trips and swan watching opportunities that children find endlessly fascinating.

The five Shakespeare houses (Shakespeare's Birthplace, Anne Hathaway's Cottage, Mary Arden's House, Hall's Croft, and New Place) offer different experiences for different ages. Mary Arden's House, with its working Tudor farm, proves most engaging for younger children, while older ones prefer the interactive displays at Shakespeare's Birthplace.

Warwick Castle (15 minutes) provides medieval excitement with daily shows, falconry displays, and interactive exhibits. The castle's "Horrible Histories" maze and the Kingmaker exhibition offer education disguised as entertainment.

For modern thrills, Hatton Country World (20 minutes) combines farm experiences with adventure play, including go-karting and quad biking for older children.

Parent Tips & Insider Knowledge Book evening drama sessions early – they're incredibly popular and spaces are limited. The performances on Saturday evenings create a real community atmosphere, with families gathering on the small amphitheatre area.

Stratford can be expensive for dining, but the site's restaurant offers good value and saves the hassle of driving into town. However, the Windmill Inn (10 minutes walk) serves excellent family meals in a beautiful historic setting.

The park and ride system into Stratford works well for families – it's cheaper than town center parking and eliminates the stress of navigating historic streets with modern cars.

Practical Information Contact: 01789 292312 | bookings@shakespearecamp.co.uk Season: Year-round | Price range: £25-35 per night Bookings: Online booking system with good availability Accessibility: Excellent wheelchair access throughout site

---

4. Chatsworth Estate Camping, Bakewell

Site Overview Camping within the grounds of one of England's greatest stately homes feels like a privilege, and this 35-pitch site delivers that experience beautifully. Set in parkland designed by Capability Brown, the site offers incredible views of Chatsworth House while maintaining the peaceful atmosphere that makes camping so special.

The pitches are spaciously arranged across gently sloping meadows, with mature trees providing natural windbreaks and privacy. The site operates seasonally, opening when the weather is most favorable for camping and closing before winter weather becomes challenging. This seasonal approach means facilities and service remain at consistently high standards.

Family Facilities Rating: ★★★★★ The facilities have been designed to complement the estate's grandeur while serving practical family needs. The shower block, built from local Peak District stone, includes underfloor heating and spacious family rooms with everything needed for families with young children.

What sets this site apart is access to Chatsworth's facilities. Campers receive discounted entry to the house and gardens, plus access to the estate's farm shop and restaurant. The children's playground, while maintaining estate elegance, offers exciting play opportunities with natural materials and challenging equipment suitable for various ages.

Age-Specific Activities *0-3 years:* The flat paths around the immediate camping area are perfect for pushchairs and first walking adventures. The nearby stream provides gentle water play, while the peaceful atmosphere makes this an ideal location for families seeking relaxation with very young children.

4-8 years: The estate's farmyard provides hands-on animal experiences, from feeding sheep to collecting eggs. The children's treasure trail through the formal gardens combines education with excitement, and the adventure playground includes equipment specifically designed for this age group.

9-12 years: Older children can explore the estate's 1,000 acres more independently, with cycle paths and walking trails offering various difficulty levels. The house itself becomes more interesting to this age group, particularly the sculpture gallery and the painted hall.

13+ years: Teenagers appreciate the estate's art collection and can join specialized tours focusing on historical intrigue or artistic techniques. The nearby market town of Bakewell offers independent exploration opportunities, famous for its original Bakewell pudding.

Local Attractions Within 30 Minutes Bakewell (10 minutes) provides traditional market town charm with numerous tea shops, antique stores, and the original Bakewell pudding shop. The Monday market creates authentic atmosphere, while the Old House Museum offers insights into Peak District life through the centuries.

Haddon Hall (15 minutes) provides a more intimate historic house experience than Chatsworth, with medieval and Tudor architecture that children find easier to relate to than grand Georgian rooms. The terraced gardens offer hide-and-seek opportunities and stunning valley views.

The Peak District's numerous hiking trails are easily accessible, with routes suitable for all abilities clearly marked from the estate. Monsal Trail, following an old railway line, provides safe cycling and walking with spectacular viaduct views.

Parent Tips & Insider Knowledge The estate's restaurant offers high-quality dining but can be expensive for families. The farm shop provides excellent picnic ingredients, and eating outdoors among Capability Brown's parkland creates memorable family meals.

Visit Chatsworth House early in your stay to avoid disappointment – popular exhibitions can become crowded, and you'll want to return to explore areas that particularly interest your children.

Book the estate's seasonal activities (lambing, harvest festivals, Christmas events) when making camping reservations, as these fill quickly and add significant value to your visit.

Practical Information Contact: 01246 565300 | camping@chatsworth.org Season: April-October | Price range: £30-40 per night Bookings: Advance booking essential, online system Accessibility: Good access, with adapted facilities available

---

5. Alton Towers Resort Camping, Staffordshire

Site Overview For families seeking the ultimate combination of outdoor adventure and theme park thrills, this resort camping offers direct access to one of Britain's most famous attractions. The 200-pitch site spreads across several fields adjacent to Alton Towers theme park, with different areas catering to various camping styles and family needs.

The site operates with theme park efficiency while maintaining camping's relaxed atmosphere. Sound barriers minimize noise from the park, though the distant screams of excitement from roller coasters add to the anticipation. The facilities have been designed to handle large numbers while maintaining cleanliness and functionality.

Family Facilities Rating: ★★★★☆ The scale of facilities impresses, with multiple shower blocks ensuring queues never become problematic. Family rooms include all necessary amenities, while the central washing and drying facilities prove invaluable after theme park adventures in unpredictable weather.

The site's splash zone provides cooling relief during summer visits, while indoor areas offer shelter during rainy periods. The main advantage lies in early park access for campers, often allowing an hour's head start before day visitors arrive.

Age-Specific Activities *0-3 years:* While Alton Towers might seem inappropriate for very young children, the CBeebies Land area provides perfect introduction to theme park excitement. Gentle rides based on familiar characters, combined with indoor and outdoor play areas, create magical experiences without overwhelming little ones.

4-8 years: This age group finds Alton Towers absolutely magical. Beyond CBeebies Land, Mutiny Bay and The Gardens provide adventure without extreme thrills. The camping experience adds outdoor skills to theme park excitement, with evening campfire activities provided by resort staff.

9-12 years: Older children can access most attractions while still enjoying camping's social aspects. Evening activities on site include treasure hunts, outdoor games, and movie screenings, allowing friendships with other camping families while parents enjoy well-earned relaxation.

13+ years: Teenagers experience Alton Towers' most extreme rides while appreciating camping's independence and social opportunities. Evening entertainment often continues later for this age group, with organized activities that let teenagers socialize while remaining safely supervised.

Local Attractions Within 30 Minutes While Alton Towers dominates, the surrounding area offers attractions for non-theme park days. The Churnet Valley Railway provides gentle steam train experiences through beautiful countryside, perfect for recovering from theme park excitement.

Uttoxeter Racecourse (20 minutes) offers family race days with picnic areas and children's activities, providing completely different entertainment. The market town itself offers traditional shopping and dining opportunities.

For cultural contrast, Stafford Castle (25 minutes) provides historical exploration with panoramic views across the county. The visitor center offers interactive displays about medieval life, while the castle ruins provide exploration opportunities for all ages.

Parent Tips & Insider Knowledge Stay multiple nights to truly benefit from early park access and to justify the premium camping prices. Single-day visits rarely provide value for money given the site's costs.

Pack layers and waterproofs regardless of weather forecasts – theme parks are exposed, and queuing outdoors requires appropriate clothing. The on-site shop stocks essentials but at premium prices.

Use the resort's meal plans carefully – they can provide good value but limit dining flexibility. The camping area's BBQ facilities often provide better family meals and social opportunities with other campers.

Practical Information Contact: 0871 663 4060 | camping@altontowers.com Season: March-November | Price range: £35-55 per night Bookings: Package deals with park entry available online Accessibility: Good facilities with adapted options throughout

---

6. Forest of Dean Family Escape, Gloucestershire

Site Overview Hidden within ancient woodland that once supplied oak for Nelson's fleet, this 45-pitch site offers families the chance to camp among some of England's oldest trees. The Forest of Dean's unique landscape, with its mixture of broad-leaved and coniferous forest, creates a magical environment where children can experience genuine wilderness while remaining safely within a managed environment.

The site occupies a clearing that provides open sky for stargazing while maintaining the forest's protective canopy. Original foresters' cottages house the facilities, and the reception area includes a small museum explaining the forest's remarkable history from Roman times to the present day.

Family Facilities Rating: ★★★★☆ The facilities blend seamlessly with the forest environment, using local materials and traditional building techniques. The shower blocks maintain modern standards while feeling authentically rustic. Family rooms include space for muddy boots and outdoor clothes, essential given the forest's muddy paths.

The natural playground uses fallen trees, rope courses, and cleared areas to create adventure opportunities that change with the seasons. The covered outdoor classroom provides space for the site's excellent environmental education programs, popular with school groups and families alike.

Age-Specific Activities *0-3 years:* The forest paths offer perfect pushchair routes with gentle gradients and hard surfaces. Little ones love the sensory experiences – different textures underfoot, varying light levels, and the sounds of forest life. The small fenced area near reception provides safe outdoor play.

4-8 years: This age group thrives in forest environments. Daily "nature detective" sessions teach woodland identification skills, while the adventure course provides challenging but safe climbing opportunities. Evening badger watches (seasonal) create magical wildlife encounters.

9-12 years: Older children can participate in "forest skills" workshops, learning traditional crafts like charcoal making and wood carving. The mountain bike trails offer various difficulty levels, with bike hire available on-site. Night walks with qualified guides reveal the forest's nocturnal activities.

13+ years: Teenagers can join advanced outdoor skills courses, including navigation, wildlife tracking, and survival techniques. The forest's cycle network provides independence while maintaining safety, with challenging routes for experienced young cyclists.

Local Attractions Within 30 Minutes The Forest of Dean offers numerous family attractions within easy reach. Puzzlewood, with its maze of paths and bridges through ancient woodland, inspired J.R.R. Tolkien and provides adventure for all ages. The sculpture trail combines art appreciation with forest walking.

Clearwell Caves offer underground adventures, with tours suitable for various ages and abilities. The deep cave tours challenge older children while short tours accommodate families with younger members. The adjacent castle provides historical context and tea room comfort.

The Dean Forest Railway operates steam trains through beautiful countryside, with special events throughout the year including "teddy bear specials" and Thomas the Tank Engine days that delight younger visitors.

For rainy day alternatives, the National Birds of Prey Centre provides close encounters with magnificent raptors, while flying demonstrations continue in most weather conditions.

Parent Tips & Insider Knowledge The forest can be muddy year-round, so wellington boots are essential for all family members. The site shop stocks basic provisions, but serious food shopping is better done in nearby Coleford before arriving.

Book wildlife watching sessions early – they're popular and group sizes are limited for safety and effectiveness. The evening badger watches require patience but often provide unforgettable family memories.

Local tip: The Speech House Hotel, a historic inn in the forest center, offers excellent family meals in atmospheric surroundings. The adjacent lake provides easy walking and waterfowl watching.

Practical Information Contact: 01594 833057 | info@deanforestcamp.co.uk Season: March-October | Price range: £22-30 per night Bookings: Phone booking preferred for activity packages Accessibility: Limited due to forest location, but adapted facilities available

---

7. Malvern Hills Walking Base, Worcestershire

Site Overview Positioned at the foot of the Malvern Hills, this intimate 20-pitch site caters specifically to families who love walking and outdoor adventures. The ancient hills, inspiration for Elgar's music and Tolkien's landscapes, provide a dramatic backdrop to camping that feels more like Wales or the Lake District despite being in the English Midlands.

The site maintains a peaceful atmosphere with widely spaced pitches and strict quiet hours that ensure everyone enjoys restorative sleep after active days. The converted Victorian water station houses facilities that blend period charm with modern convenience, while the small shop stocks local produce and walking supplies.

Family Facilities Rating: ★★★★☆ The facilities prioritize functionality for active families. Spacious drying rooms prove invaluable after Malvern Hills adventures, while gear washing facilities handle muddy boots and clothing. Family shower rooms include seating and hooks at various heights, acknowledging different family members' needs.

The playground focuses on natural materials and challenging equipment that develops coordination and confidence. The covered picnic area provides social space when weather interrupts outdoor plans, while the small library includes guidebooks and local interest material.

Age-Specific Activities *0-3 years:* The gentler slopes around the site base provide perfect first hill walking experiences. The small stream offers safe water play, while the peaceful atmosphere makes this ideal for families seeking relaxation with very young children. Pushchair-friendly paths lead to the first viewpoints.

4-8 years: This age group can tackle easier hills with proper support, experiencing the achievement of reaching summits and enjoying panoramic views. The site runs "young mountaineers" sessions, teaching basic safety and navigation skills through games and short expeditions.

9-12 years: Older children can attempt more challenging peaks, with routes to Worcester Beacon and North Hill providing genuine mountain experiences despite modest heights. Evening astronomy sessions take advantage of dark sky conditions, weather permitting.

13+ years: Teenagers can join guided walks covering the entire ridge, learning about local geology, history, and wildlife. The hills' literary connections provide educational opportunities, while photography workshops take advantage of spectacular lighting conditions.

Local Attractions Within 30 Minutes Great Malvern town offers Victorian spa heritage with family-friendly attractions including the Malvern Museum and the Priory Church with its magnificent medieval stained glass. The town's independent shops and cafes provide rainy day alternatives.

Worcester Cathedral (20 minutes) combines historical significance with family activities. The medieval crypt and Victorian graves fascinate children, while the cathedral's height provides impressive views across the Severn Valley. The adjacent museum offers interactive displays about local history.

The Three Counties Showground hosts events throughout the year, from agricultural shows to craft fairs, providing insight into rural life. Even without specific events, the permanent farming displays and children's playground make worthwhile visits.

For educational value, the Worcester Porcelain Museum offers hands-on pottery workshops alongside displays of famous ceramics, combining local industrial heritage with creative activities.

Parent Tips & Insider Knowledge Weather changes rapidly on the hills, so layers and waterproofs are essential even for short walks. The site's weather station provides accurate local forecasts, often different from general regional predictions.

The nearby Abbey Hotel offers excellent family dining with spectacular views, but book ahead during summer months. The pub welcomes muddy walkers and provides hearty meals perfect after hill walking.

Local knowledge: The Worcestershire Beacon path can be challenging for inexperienced walkers. Start with British Camp (easier parking and gentler approach) to gauge your family's capabilities before attempting longer routes.

Practical Information Contact: 01684 540154 | malverncamp@outlook.com Season: April-October | Price range: £20-28 per night Bookings: Phone reservations with deposit required Accessibility: Challenging due to hilly terrain, limited adapted facilities

---

8. Cotswold Water Park Family Adventure, Gloucestershire

Site Overview Built around a series of flooded gravel pits that have become Britain's largest water park, this 80-pitch site offers families water-based adventures combined with Cotswold countryside charm. The site occupies a peninsula jutting into one of the larger lakes, providing water access from multiple directions while maintaining safe, shallow areas perfect for children.

The facilities reflect the site's water focus, with excellent changing rooms, equipment storage, and boat launching areas. The reception includes a small museum about the area's transformation from gravel extraction to recreational paradise, helping children understand environmental restoration.

Family Facilities Rating: ★★★★★ The facilities excel in supporting water-based activities. Large family changing areas include non-slip surfaces and space for water sports equipment. The heated indoor pool operates year-round, providing swimming opportunities regardless of weather conditions.

The adventure playground includes water play features alongside traditional equipment, while the site's beach area provides safe lake access with lifeguard supervision during peak season. The restaurant offers meals designed to refuel active families, with healthy options alongside traditional favorites.

Age-Specific Activities *0-3 years:* The shallow, sandy beach areas provide perfect introduction to lake swimming, while the heated indoor pool offers more controlled aquatic experiences. The gentle nature trails around the immediate site provide pushchair-friendly walking with wildlife spotting opportunities.

4-8 years: This age group loves the water confidence courses run by qualified instructors. Kayaking lessons in sheltered bays build skills safely, while the site's pedal boats provide family adventures. Evening pond dipping reveals lake wildlife, combining education with excitement.

9-12 years: Older children can advance to windsurfing and sailing lessons, with equipment sized appropriately. The mountain bike trails around the various lakes provide traffic-free cycling with varying difficulty levels. Fishing lessons teach patience alongside practical skills.

13+ years: Teenagers can pursue water sports more seriously, with advanced sailing and windsurfing instruction available. The site's social areas provide meeting opportunities with other young people, while the nearby Cotswold towns offer independent exploration possibilities.

Local Attractions Within 30 Minutes Cirencester (15 minutes), known as the capital of the Cotswolds, offers Roman history alongside modern shopping. The Corinium Museum provides interactive displays about Roman Britain, while the town's parks and river walks offer gentle family activities.

Cricklade (10 minutes) provides a more intimate Cotswold town experience, with the Thames Path beginning here offering easy riverside walking. The town's historic buildings and small shops create authentic market town atmosphere.

For contrast, Swindon's STEAM Museum (20 minutes) celebrates Britain's railway heritage with interactive displays and preserved locomotives that fascinate transport enthusiasts of all ages.

The nearby Cotswold Wildlife Park (25 minutes) combines traditional zoo experiences with beautiful parkland, offering educational opportunities alongside entertainment.

Parent Tips & Insider Knowledge The lakes can be surprisingly deep away from designated swimming areas – supervise children carefully and respect safety boundaries. The site's safety briefings are mandatory and provide valuable local knowledge about conditions and hazards.

Water temperatures remain cool even in summer, so wetsuits are advisable for extended swimming or water sports. The site shop stocks basic equipment, but serious water sports gear is better sourced elsewhere.

Book water sports lessons early – they're popular and group sizes are limited. The site's flexibility allows rescheduling if weather makes activities unsafe, but advance booking ensures availability.

Practical Information Contact: 01285 861459 | bookings@cotswoldwaterpark.com Season: Year-round | Price range: £28-40 per night Bookings: Online system with activity packages available Accessibility: Good access with adapted water sports equipment

---

9. Warwick Castle Camping Meadows

Site Overview Camping in the shadow of Britain's finest medieval castle creates instant excitement for families. This 60-pitch site occupies meadowland within the castle's outer grounds, providing unique access to one of England's most spectacular historical attractions while maintaining the peaceful atmosphere essential for good camping.

The site operates seasonally, coinciding with the castle's main season and optimal camping weather. Medieval-themed facilities blend historical atmosphere with modern convenience, while the proximity to castle attractions means evening entertainment often includes falconry displays and medieval tournaments visible from the camping area.

Family Facilities Rating: ★★★★☆ The facilities creatively incorporate medieval themes without sacrificing functionality. The main shower block, designed to echo castle architecture, includes excellent family facilities with space for castle visit preparation. The medieval-themed playground provides adventure opportunities that complement castle visits.

Direct castle access for campers eliminates parking fees and queuing, while early morning access allows exploration before day visitors arrive. The site's restaurant serves hearty medieval-inspired meals alongside modern family favorites.

Age-Specific Activities *0-3 years:* While the castle itself might seem intimidating for very young children, the peacocks roaming the grounds provide natural entertainment, and the gentle walks around the camping meadows offer safe exploration. The site's medieval playground includes equipment suitable for toddlers.

4-8 years: This age group finds Warwick Castle absolutely magical. The castle's shows and attractions are designed with families in mind, from the "Horrible Histories" maze to the trebuchet demonstrations. Evening storytelling sessions around the campfire often feature tales of knights and princesses.

9-12 years: Older children can participate in the castle's interactive experiences more fully, including archery lessons and medieval craft workshops. The site runs "young knights" training sessions, teaching medieval games and skills in the camping meadows.

13+ years: Teenagers appreciate the castle's more sophisticated historical presentations and can join specialized tours focusing on medieval warfare or daily life. The site's evening entertainment often includes medieval music and dancing lessons.

Local Attractions Within 30 Minutes Stratford-upon-Avon (15 minutes) provides Shakespearean experiences, while Leamington Spa offers Victorian elegance with excellent parks and shopping. The combination of medieval and Tudor history within easy reach creates comprehensive historical education.

Kenilworth Castle (10 minutes) offers a more ruined but atmospheric castle experience, with Elizabethan gardens that provide gentler exploration opportunities. The English Heritage interpretation helps children understand how castles evolved over centuries.

For modern family attractions, Hatton Country World (20 minutes) combines farm experiences with adventure activities including go-karting and crazy golf, providing variety from historical attractions.

Parent Tips & Insider Knowledge Castle visits can be overwhelming for younger children – plan shorter visits and use the camping meadows as a retreat when needed. The peacocks are beautiful but can be aggressive during breeding season, so supervise children around them.

The castle's restaurants are expensive and crowded during peak times. The site's BBQ facilities and nearby pubs offer better value and more relaxed family dining. The case & Crown in Warwick serves excellent traditional meals.

Book the castle's special events (medieval tournaments, Christmas celebrations) when making camping reservations, as these add significant value but fill quickly.

Practical Information Contact: 01926 406610 | camping@warwick-castle.com Season: April-October | Price range: £32-45 per night Bookings: Package deals with castle entry highly recommended Accessibility: Good access with castle providing adapted tours

---

10. Bredon Hill Panoramic Camping, Worcestershire

Site Overview Perched on the lower slopes of Bredon Hill, this 25-pitch site offers some of the most spectacular views in the Heart of England. The elevated position provides panoramic vistas across the Vale of Evesham and towards the Malvern Hills, creating sunset views that regularly stop conversations mid-sentence.

The site maintains an intimate atmosphere with widely spaced pitches, many offering private views across the countryside. The converted Victorian farm buildings house facilities that combine period charm with modern functionality, while the working farm atmosphere adds authentic rural experiences.

Family Facilities Rating: ★★★★★ The facilities focus on quality over quantity, with spotless shower blocks and well-maintained family rooms. The farm shop stocks local produce including vegetables grown on-site, while the small cafe serves meals made from ingredients sourced within 10 miles.

The playground uses natural materials and incorporates the sloping site cleverly, with different levels providing various play opportunities. The covered outdoor area proves invaluable when weather interrupts outdoor plans.

Age-Specific Activities *0-3 years:* The gentle slopes around the site provide perfect first hill walking, while the farm animals offer close encounters with sheep, chickens, and the friendly farm cat. The peaceful atmosphere makes this ideal for families seeking relaxation.

4-8 years: Daily farm activities include egg collecting and animal feeding, while the hill walks reveal spectacular views and seasonal wildflowers. The site runs nature identification sessions, helping children recognize local wildlife and plants.

9-12 years: Older children can attempt the walk to Bredon Hill's summit, with its ancient hill fort and panoramic views. The site's geocaching course provides modern treasure hunting using GPS technology.

13+ years: Teenagers can join photography workshops taking advantage of the spectacular lighting conditions, while the nearby market towns offer independent exploration opportunities.

Local Attractions Within 30 Minutes Evesham (15 minutes) provides market town charm with the added attraction of the Almonry Museum, housed in a 14th-century building. The town's riverside walks and parks offer gentle family activities, while the weekly market provides authentic local atmosphere.

Tewkesbury (20 minutes) combines medieval architecture with modern family attractions. The abbey church impresses with its massive Norman architecture, while the medieval streets provide exploration opportunities. The annual medieval festival transforms the town into a living history experience.

Pershore Abbey (18 minutes) offers a more intimate religious building experience, with beautiful gardens and peaceful atmosphere perfect for quiet family time. The town's Victorian architecture and independent shops provide pleasant browsing.

Parent Tips & Insider Knowledge The elevated position means weather can change quickly – pack layers even for short walks. The views are spectacular in clear conditions but the site can feel exposed during windy weather.

The nearby Fleece Inn in Bretforton, owned by the National Trust, serves excellent traditional meals in an authentic medieval setting. Children love the ancient building's atmosphere and the pub's fascinating historical features.

Local tip: The walk to Bredon Hill's summit is moderate but rewarding. Start early morning for the best light and fewer people, returning for a late breakfast at the site's cafe.

Practical Information Contact: 01386 881381 | info@bredonhillcamp.co.uk Season: March-October | Price range: £24-32 per night Bookings: Phone preferred, advance booking essential in summer Accessibility: Limited due to hilly location

---

11. Ironbridge Gorge Heritage Camping, Shropshire

Site Overview Camping within walking distance of the birthplace of the Industrial Revolution provides families with unique educational opportunities. This 40-pitch site occupies a former ironworks yard, with some original buildings converted to house facilities and a small museum explaining the area's world-changing significance.

The site's location in the Severn Gorge creates a sheltered microclimate while providing easy access to the famous Iron Bridge and associated museums. The industrial heritage theme runs throughout the site without becoming overwhelming, creating educational value alongside camping enjoyment.

Family Facilities Rating: ★★★★★ The facilities cleverly incorporate industrial heritage elements while providing excellent modern amenities. The shower blocks, housed in converted forge buildings, maintain original architectural features while offering family-friendly facilities including baby changing areas and accessible options.

The playground includes equipment inspired by industrial themes – pulleys, wheels, and mechanical elements that children can operate safely. The covered workshop area hosts craft sessions where children can try traditional skills like pottery and metalworking under expert supervision.

Age-Specific Activities *0-3 years:* The flat paths along the River Severn provide perfect pushchair routes, while the industrial museum's hands-on displays fascinate even very young children. The peaceful riverside location offers gentle introduction to industrial heritage.

4-8 years: This age group loves the working demonstrations at nearby museums, from Victorian tile making to traditional iron forging. The site runs "young inventors" workshops where children create simple machines using basic materials.

9-12 years: Older children can understand the revolutionary significance of the Iron Bridge and participate in more complex workshop activities. The Tar Tunnel provides underground adventure with historical significance, while the Museum of the Gorge offers interactive displays about industrial development.

13+ years: Teenagers can engage with the serious historical significance of the area, understanding how the Industrial Revolution began here and spread worldwide. Advanced workshops in traditional crafts provide hands-on historical education.

Local Attractions Within 30 Minutes The Ironbridge Gorge Museums represent one of Britain's finest museum complexes, with ten different attractions telling the story of industrial development. The Iron Bridge itself provides the iconic focal point, while Blists Hill Victorian Town offers immersive historical experience.

Coalbrookdale Museum of Iron tells the foundry story that began the Industrial Revolution, with working demonstrations that fascinate all ages. The Jackfield Tile Museum shows industrial craft development, with workshops where families can create their own tiles.

Shrewsbury (25 minutes) provides medieval contrast to industrial heritage, with the castle, abbey, and medieval streets offering different historical perspectives. The town's parks and river walks provide gentle family activities.

Parent Tips & Insider Knowledge The museum passport provides excellent value for families planning multiple visits, while individual attractions can be overwhelming for younger children. Plan shorter visits with playground breaks between museums.

The nearby White Hart Inn offers excellent traditional meals with historical atmosphere, while the museum cafes provide convenient refreshment during sightseeing. Book Sunday lunch early during summer months.

Industrial sites can involve walking on uneven surfaces and near water – supervise children carefully and wear appropriate footwear. The museums provide excellent educational materials for different ages.

Practical Information Contact: 01952 433424 | heritage@ironbridgecamp.co.uk Season: Year-round (limited facilities November-February) Price range: £26-35 per night | Bookings: Online with museum packages Accessibility: Good access with adapted facilities throughout

---

12. Black Mountains Border Camping, Herefordshire

Site Overview Positioned where England meets Wales, this 30-pitch site offers families dramatic mountain scenery combined with gentle valley camping. The Black Mountains provide a spectacular backdrop while the site itself occupies a sheltered valley position protected from harsh weather.

The border location creates unique opportunities to experience both English and Welsh culture within a single camping holiday. The site celebrates this heritage with evening entertainment that might include Welsh male voice choirs, traditional Morris dancing, or storytelling sessions featuring legends from both cultures.

Family Facilities Rating: ★★★★☆ The facilities reflect the site's border heritage, with buildings that incorporate both English and Welsh architectural traditions. Family shower rooms provide excellent amenities, while the drying room proves essential after mountain adventures in changeable weather.

The playground includes challenging equipment suitable for developing mountain skills, with climbing frames and balance beams that prepare children for hillwalking adventures. The indoor activity area provides craft sessions featuring traditional skills from both cultures.

Age-Specific Activities *0-3 years:* The sheltered valley location provides safe outdoor exploration, while the gentle stream offers water play opportunities. The peaceful atmosphere and stunning mountain views create a relaxing environment for families with young children.

4-8 years: This age group can tackle easier hill walks with spectacular views, while the site's "mountain skills for beginners" sessions teach basic safety and navigation through games and short expeditions. Evening storytelling features legends of the Black Mountains.

9-12 years: Older children can attempt more challenging peaks with proper supervision, experiencing genuine mountain walking. The site's mountain bike trails provide traffic-free cycling, while evening astronomy sessions take advantage of dark sky conditions.

13+ years: Teenagers can join guided walks to higher summits, learning about mountain safety and navigation. The border location provides opportunities to explore both English market towns and Welsh villages independently.

Local Attractions Within 30 Minutes Hay-on-Wye (20 minutes) combines literary fame with market town charm. The town's numerous bookshops fascinate older children and adults, while the River Wye provides gentle walking and occasional canoeing opportunities.

Llanthony Priory (15 minutes) offers atmospheric ruins in a spectacular valley setting, with walking trails suitable for various abilities. The nearby pub, built into the priory ruins, provides unique dining experiences with historical atmosphere.

Abergavenny (25 minutes) provides Welsh market town experience with the added attraction of excellent museums and the annual food festival (if timing coincides). The town's position makes it an excellent base for exploring both the Brecon Beacons and the Black Mountains.

Parent Tips & Insider Knowledge Mountain weather changes rapidly – always pack waterproofs and warm layers even for short walks. The site's weather monitoring equipment provides accurate local forecasts often different from regional predictions.

The border location means some attractions use different currencies and may have different opening hours. Check requirements before visiting Welsh attractions, though most accept English currency.

Local knowledge: The Gospel Pass road is spectacular but challenging for nervous drivers. The alternative route via Abergavenny takes longer but provides easier driving with equally beautiful scenery.

Practical Information Contact: 01873 890241 | info@blackmountainscamp.co.uk Season: April-October | Price range: £22-30 per night Bookings: Phone booking preferred for mountain activity packages Accessibility: Limited due to mountain location

---

Regional Weather Patterns & Seasonal Considerations

The Heart of England enjoys some of Britain's most favorable camping weather, with the Cotswolds benefiting from a particularly mild microclimate. However, the region's diversity means weather can vary significantly between locations.

Spring Camping (March-May): Perfect for avoiding crowds while enjoying mild weather and spectacular wildflower displays. The literary gardens are at their finest, while lamb feeding adds extra farm attraction. Pack layers as temperatures can vary significantly between valley and hill locations.

Summer Camping (June-August): Peak season brings crowds but also the most reliable weather and longest days. Theme parks operate full programs, while outdoor activities continue until late evening.

Book accommodations well in advance and expect premium pricing.

Autumn Camping (September-November): Outstanding value with fewer crowds, spectacular autumn colors, and harvest festival atmosphere. Many attractions offer special programs, while comfortable temperatures make this ideal for active families. Weather becomes more variable from October onwards.

Winter Options: Limited but rewarding, with Christmas markets, cozy pub atmospheres, and winter walking opportunities. Only selected sites remain open, but heated facilities and festive programs create magical experiences for hardy families.

Budget Planning for Heart of England Camping

The Heart of England offers excellent value for money, particularly outside peak summer months. Family-run sites typically provide the best value, while resort-style camping commands premium prices but includes extensive facilities.

Cost-Saving Strategies:

- Book early for summer discounts, or choose shoulder season for significant savings
- Utilize site restaurants and shops during peak times when local alternatives may be crowded and expensive
- Take advantage of attraction package deals offered by many sites
- Consider longer stays to benefit from weekly rates and reduce travel costs

Budget Expectations:

- Basic family sites: £18-25 per night
- Mid-range sites with good facilities: £25-35 per night
- Premium resort-style sites: £35-55 per night
- Add 20-30% for peak summer weeks
- Factor attraction entry costs: £10-25 per person for major sites

The Heart of England perfectly balances outdoor adventure with cultural enrichment, creating camping experiences that educate and entertain in equal measure. Whether your family seeks literary inspiration, mountain adventures, or theme park thrills, this region provides the perfect backdrop for creating lasting memories while exploring England's rich heritage and stunning landscapes.

Chapter 6: Eastern England - Wide Skies, Gentle Rivers & Seaside Fun

Eastern England unfolds like a children's storybook, with its endless horizons, meandering rivers, and cheerful seaside resorts that seem frozen in time. This is camping country par excellence – where families can wake up to spectacular sunrises over the North Sea, spend lazy afternoons punting along the Norfolk Broads, and fall asleep to the gentle lapping of waves on sandy beaches. From the medieval streets of Norwich to the Victorian charm of Great Yarmouth, Eastern England offers that perfect blend of outdoor adventure and gentle exploration that makes family camping holidays truly magical.

The region's geography is wonderfully child-friendly. The landscape rarely rises above gentle hills, making it ideal for families with pushchairs, wobbly cyclists, and little legs that tire easily. The Norfolk Broads create Britain's largest protected wetland, offering unique boating experiences where even the youngest family members can safely help navigate shallow waterways. Meanwhile, the coastline stretches for hundreds of miles, providing endless opportunities for sandcastle architects, shell collectors, and aspiring marine biologists.

What sets Eastern England apart for camping families is its remarkable diversity within manageable distances. You might start your day watching seals at Blakeney Point, enjoy a medieval feast in a Norfolk castle by lunchtime, and end with fish and chips on a traditional seaside pier – all within a 30-mile radius. The region's relatively dry climate (it's one of Britain's sunniest areas) means camping is particularly rewarding here, with long summer evenings perfect for campfire storytelling and outdoor games.

The camping infrastructure in Eastern England has evolved beautifully to serve families. Many sites have embraced the region's maritime heritage, offering everything from boat trips to sailing lessons, while others focus on the area's rich wildlife, with nature trails and bird-watching hides integrated into the camping experience. The best sites understand that successful family camping requires variety – the ability to switch between active adventures and quiet contemplation, between educational experiences and pure fun.

1. Whitlingham Broad Campsite, Norfolk

Location: Trowse, Norwich, NR14 8TR
Best for: Water sports enthusiasts and nature-loving families

Nestled beside one of Norfolk's most beautiful broads, Whitlingham offers that rare combination of wild natural beauty and family-friendly facilities just minutes from a cathedral city. The site sits on the edge of Whitlingham Country Park, where 80 acres of reclaimed gravel pits have created a water sports paradise surrounded by reed beds and ancient woodlands.

Family Facilities Rating: 9/10

The playground here is exceptional – a nautical-themed adventure area that captures the imagination while challenging different age groups appropriately. Toddlers have their own safe sailing ship with gentle slides and climbing nets, while older children can tackle the impressive rope climbing frame designed like a lighthouse. The toilet blocks are spotlessly maintained with dedicated family bathrooms featuring baby-changing facilities and step-stools for little ones.

The on-site shop stocks everything from forgotten camping essentials to locally-made treats, while the café serves hearty breakfasts that fuel adventure-packed days. What makes this place special is the outdoor activity centre, offering everything from kayaking to archery, with qualified instructors who genuinely understand how to engage children of different ages safely.

Age-Specific Activities

0-3 years: The site's paved paths are perfect for pushchairs, leading to a dedicated toddler area beside the water where little ones can safely paddle under supervision. The sensory garden features plants that encourage touch and smell exploration, while the duck-feeding platform (with approved food available from reception) provides endless entertainment for the youngest family members.

4-8 years: This age group will be in heaven with the beginner-friendly sailing courses and supervised pond dipping sessions. The nature trail includes child-friendly interpretation boards featuring cartoon characters that guide young explorers through different habitats. Weekly treasure hunts combine physical activity with environmental education, and the outdoor craft sessions let children create art using natural materials found around the broad.

9-12 years: Adventure seekers can progress to proper kayaking and windsurfing lessons, while the high ropes course (with safety harnesses) provides supervised thrills. The site offers orienteering courses of varying difficulty, and the fishing lake has designated child-friendly areas with equipment hire available. Evening activities include supervised campfire sessions with marshmallow toasting and ghost stories.

13+ years: Teenagers appreciate the excellent mobile phone coverage and the dedicated teen activity area with basketball courts. They can earn certificates in water sports activities and participate in conservation projects, giving them a sense of achievement beyond just having fun. The site's proximity to Norwich means day trips to shopping centres and cinemas are easily arranged.

Local Attractions Within 30 Minutes

Norwich Cathedral and Castle provide fascinating history lessons brought to life through interactive exhibitions designed for families. The cathedral's spectacular tower climb is suitable for children over 8, offering breathtaking views across the Norfolk countryside. The castle's medieval galleries include hands-on activities where children can try on replica armour and learn about castle life.

BeWILDerwood, just 20 minutes away, is an award-winning outdoor adventure park set in beautiful woodland. This isn't your typical theme park – it's based on local children's books and features treehouses, zip wires, and boat trips through mysterious marshes. The park is designed for imaginative play, encouraging children to become part of the story rather than passive consumers of entertainment.

Pettitts Adventure Park offers more traditional theme park excitement with rides suitable for all ages, from gentle trains for toddlers to roller coasters for thrill-seekers. The park also features a fantastic zoo with regular feeding sessions and educational talks that captivate young animal lovers.

For gentler entertainment, Plantation Garden in Norwich provides a secret Victorian garden perfect for picnics and peaceful exploration. The nearby Sainsbury Centre for Visual Arts offers free admission and frequently hosts family workshops combining art appreciation with hands-on creativity.

Parent Tips & Insider Knowledge

Book pitches 15-25 for the best broad views without sacrificing convenience to facilities. The site gets busy during school holidays, but weekends in late spring and early autumn offer the perfect balance of good weather and reasonable crowds.

The on-site restaurant serves excellent Sunday roasts, but booking is essential during peak season. For budget-conscious families, the nearby Morrison's supermarket (10 minutes by car) offers competitive prices for camping supplies. The site's boat hire service provides great value for families wanting to explore the broader waterway network.

Consider bringing bicycles – the network of quiet lanes around Whitlingham provides safe cycling for families, and the site offers secure bicycle storage. The nearby Wherryman's Way walking route is pushchair-friendly and features several pubs with family gardens, perfect for lunch stops.

Practical Information
Contact: 01603 622049
Booking tips: Reserve water sports activities when booking your pitch
Price range: ££-£££
Accessibility: Excellent paths and disabled facilities throughout

---

2. Hill Cottage Farm Camping, Suffolk

Location: Stanfield, Diss, IP21 4PY
Best for: Families seeking authentic farm experiences and rural tranquility

This working farm campsite represents everything wonderful about Suffolk countryside – rolling fields dotted with ancient oak trees, traditional red-brick farmhouses, and the kind of peaceful atmosphere that instantly slows down the family pace. Hill Cottage Farm has been welcoming camping families for over two decades, and their experience shows in every thoughtfully planned detail.

Family Facilities Rating: 8/10

The facilities here embrace the farm setting beautifully. The converted barn housing the toilet blocks maintains rustic charm while providing thoroughly modern amenities, including heated floors that are particularly appreciated during cooler months. The playground equipment is crafted from sustainable timber, creating adventure opportunities that blend seamlessly with the rural environment.

The farm shop is a treasure trove of local produce, from freshly laid eggs to home-made jams, while the tea room serves traditional Suffolk fare with a modern twist. What children remember most, though, is the daily animal feeding sessions where they can help care for sheep, pigs, chickens, and the farm's gentle horses.

Age-Specific Activities

0-3 years: The dedicated baby animal area provides safe, supervised interaction with kid goats, lambs, and rabbits. Pushchair-friendly farm trails include sensory stations where toddlers can touch different textures (bark, wool, smooth pebbles) while learning about farm life. The shallow paddling area uses natural stream water and is surrounded by soft grass perfect for crawling explorers.

4-8 years: Children this age can participate in proper farm chores, collecting eggs each morning and helping with animal feeding under farmer supervision. The purpose-built adventure playground features a fantastic tree house complex connected by rope bridges, while the nature trail includes child-friendly identification challenges. Weekly barn dances teach traditional Suffolk folk dances that get the whole family laughing and moving.

9-12 years: The farm offers junior farmer programs where children learn genuine agricultural skills, from basic animal husbandry to understanding crop rotation. Mountain bike trails of varying difficulty wind through the farm's woodland areas, while the fishing lake provides peaceful opportunities to develop patience and observation skills. The site's geocaching trail combines technology with outdoor exploration.

13+ years: Teenagers can participate in conservation projects, learning about sustainable farming practices and environmental stewardship. The farm offers work experience opportunities during longer stays, giving young people insights into agricultural careers. Evening activities include astronomy sessions taking advantage of the area's dark skies, perfect for teaching constellation identification.

Local Attractions Within 30 Minutes

Diss town provides charming market town exploration with its attractive mere (natural lake) offering boat trips and swan feeding opportunities. The town's museum organizes family-friendly treasure hunts that combine local history with outdoor adventure, while the weekly market introduces children to traditional trading concepts.

Africa Alive! at Lowestoft (25 minutes) offers an exceptional zoo experience focusing on African wildlife conservation. The park's walkthrough exhibits allow close encounters with lemurs and meerkats, while the educational programs teach children about wildlife protection through engaging, hands-on activities.

The Bressingham Steam and Gardens provides triple attractions – magnificent gardens perfect for peaceful family walks, steam train rides that thrill all ages, and a collection of vintage fire engines that fascinate young vehicle enthusiasts. The site includes adventure playgrounds and picnic areas that make for perfect day-long family expeditions.

For cultural enrichment, the nearby village of Long Melford features one of England's finest Tudor mansions, Melford Hall, where children can experience life in an Elizabethan household through interactive displays and costumed guides who bring history to vibrant life.

Parent Tips & Insider Knowledge

The farm's most peaceful pitches are numbers 40-50, offering privacy while remaining close enough to facilities for convenience with young children. Book the farm tour when you arrive – it's free but provides invaluable insights into rural life that enhance the entire camping experience.

The on-site farm shop offers excellent value for families, with free-range meat, seasonal vegetables, and homemade preserves at prices competitive with supermarkets. The nearby village pub, The Crown, welcomes families and serves traditional Suffolk dishes including the famous Suffolk lamb.

Timing visits around lambing season (March-April) creates magical experiences for children, but book well in advance as this is the site's most popular period. The farm provides Wellington boots for children participating in animal care activities, but bringing extra socks is always wise.

Practical Information
Contact: 01379 854999
Booking tips: Request farm activity timetables when booking
Price range: ££
Accessibility: Farm trails suitable for sturdy pushchairs; facilities fully accessible

---

3. Heacham Beach Holiday Park, Norfolk

Location: Heacham, King's Lynn, PE31 7HX
Best for: Traditional seaside holidays with modern family amenities

Positioned directly behind one of Norfolk's finest sandy beaches, Heacham represents the perfect evolution of British seaside camping – maintaining traditional charm while embracing modern family needs. The park stretches along the coastline, offering accommodations from traditional tent pitches to luxury static caravans, but it's the location that makes this place truly special for families seeking classic beach holidays.

Family Facilities Rating: 9/10

The indoor swimming complex provides weather insurance for family holidays, featuring pools suitable for every age group from baby splash areas to teen-friendly flume slides. The pool area includes a dedicated teaching pool where swimming lessons are available, along with comfortable viewing areas for supervising parents.

The entertainment complex rivals professional venues, with daily children's clubs organized by age group and evening family shows that actually entertain adults as well as children. The multiple playground areas are strategically positioned throughout the park, ensuring no family accommodation is far from safe play opportunities.

Dining options range from the main restaurant serving traditional British fare to takeaway outlets offering everything from fish and chips to international cuisine. The supermarket on-site stocks everything families need, from sun cream to barbecue supplies, at reasonable prices.

Age-Specific Activities

0-3 years: The toddler splash zone provides safe water play with tiny slides and fountain features, while the soft play area offers rainy day alternatives. Beach access via pushchair-friendly boardwalks makes seaside exploration effortless, and the regular Punch and Judy shows capture the imagination of even the youngest audience members.

4-8 years: The kids' clubs operate morning and afternoon sessions with qualified childcare professionals, offering everything from treasure hunts to craft workshops. The adventure playground features a fantastic pirate ship climbing frame, while the mini golf course provides gentle competition perfect for developing coordination skills. Beach activities include supervised donkey rides and sandcastle competitions with genuine prizes.

9-12 years: The sports facilities include tennis courts, football pitches, and table tennis areas where tournaments create friendly competition between families. The amusement arcade features modern games alongside classic seaside entertainment, while the beach activities expand to include bodyboarding lessons and rock pooling expeditions guided by local marine biologists.

13+ years: The teen zone includes pool tables, video games, and WiFi areas where young people can maintain social connections. The park organizes teen discos and sports competitions, while the proximity to Hunstanton provides shopping and cinema opportunities. Beach volleyball courts and water sports equipment hire offer more active entertainment options.

Local Attractions Within 30 Minutes

Hunstanton's unique cliffs provide geological interest alongside traditional seaside pleasures. The town's sea life sanctuary offers close encounters with seals and other marine creatures, while the cliff-top walks provide spectacular coastal views suitable for families with older children.

The nearby Sandringham Estate, when open to public, provides insights into royal country life through magnificent gardens and fascinating museums. The estate's visitor centre includes interactive exhibitions designed to engage children with royal history and countryside management.

Castle Acre Priory, though ruined, captures children's imagination through excellent audio guides featuring medieval characters. The village itself provides perfect examples of traditional English rural architecture, while the nearby river offers gentle canoeing opportunities for families seeking water-based adventures.

For rainy day alternatives, the True's Yard Fisherfolk Museum in King's Lynn brings maritime history to life through reconstructed cottages showing how fishing families lived. The interactive displays and dress-up opportunities make history tangible for young learners.

Parent Tips & Insider Knowledge

Choose beach-facing pitches for the ultimate seaside experience, but be prepared for slightly higher costs and earlier booking requirements. The park's entertainment peaks during school holidays but continues year-round, making shoulder season visits particularly good value.

The on-site laundry facilities are comprehensive, essential for beach holidays where sandy, salty clothes are inevitable. The park shop stocks high-quality sun protection products, but supermarket prices in nearby Hunstanton offer better value for bulk purchases.

Beach safety is excellent, with lifeguard coverage during peak season and clear information about tide times and swimming conditions. The park provides beach equipment hire, including windbreaks and deck chairs, which can be more convenient than bringing your own.

Practical Information
Contact: 01485 571113
Booking tips: Beach-view pitches book up quickly for summer season
Price range: £££
Accessibility: Beach access via boardwalks; comprehensive disabled facilities

---

4. Manor Park Holiday Village, Essex

Location: Hunstanton Road, Heacham, PE31 7HX
Best for: Multi-generational families seeking comprehensive entertainment

Manor Park represents the evolution of family holiday parks, combining traditional camping opportunities with resort-style amenities that ensure everyone from grandparents to teenagers finds their perfect holiday experience. Set in 50 acres of landscaped grounds, the park balances natural beauty with carefully planned entertainment facilities.

Family Facilities Rating: 9/10

The swimming complex includes indoor and outdoor pools, with the outdoor area featuring a lazy river that provides gentle fun for all ages. The indoor facility ensures year-round swimming opportunities, while the poolside café offers healthy snacks and refreshments without the premium prices often found at similar facilities.

The children's entertainment program operates throughout the holiday season with age-appropriate activities running simultaneously, allowing parents to relax while knowing their children are safely engaged. The teen zone provides space for older children to socialize independently while remaining within the secure park environment.

Dining facilities include a family restaurant with children's menus that go beyond typical nuggets and chips, offering healthy options that actually appeal to young palates. The takeaway outlets provide convenient meal solutions for families preferring to eat at their accommodation.

Age-Specific Activities

0-3 years: The purpose-built soft play area provides safe exploration opportunities regardless of weather, while the toddler pool features gentle water play equipment. The park's pushchair-friendly paths connect all facilities, and the baby changing rooms are equipped to professional standards with complementary supplies available.

4-8 years: The adventure playground features multiple zones including a junior assault course that builds confidence through age-appropriate challenges. The kids' club offers structured activities including nature walks, craft sessions, and games that encourage both creativity and social interaction. The mini railway provides gentle excitement while teaching basic transportation concepts.

9-12 years: Sports facilities include basketball courts, football areas, and organized tournaments that teach teamwork and fair play. The park's geocaching trail combines technology with outdoor exploration, while the fishing lake offers peaceful activities that develop patience and observation skills. Weekly talent shows provide opportunities for children to showcase abilities and build confidence.

13+ years: The teen entertainment program includes discos, gaming tournaments, and social activities designed to help young people make holiday friendships. The sports bar provides supervised space for older children, while the park's WiFi coverage ensures they can maintain social connections. Adventure activities include high ropes courses and climbing walls suitable for this age group.

Local Attractions Within 30 Minutes

Southend-on-Sea provides classic seaside entertainment with the world's longest pleasure pier offering traditional amusements alongside modern attractions. The Adventure Island theme park features rides suitable for all ages, from gentle carousels to thrilling roller coasters, while the nearby beaches provide traditional bucket-and-spade opportunities.

The historic town of Colchester offers England's oldest recorded town, with a castle that brings Roman and medieval history to life through interactive exhibitions. The castle's virtual reality experiences allow children to witness historical events, while the surrounding park provides space for picnics and outdoor games.

RHS Garden Hyde Hall demonstrates how gardens can be both beautiful and educational, with children's trails that teach plant identification and seasonal changes. The garden's events program includes family workshops where children can learn practical gardening skills while creating takeaway projects.

For wildlife enthusiasts, the nearby RSPB reserves offer bird watching opportunities that fascinate children when supported by knowledgeable guides. The reserves provide hide facilities where families can observe wildlife without disturbance, while the visitor centres offer interactive displays explaining ecosystem relationships.

Parent Tips & Insider Knowledge

The park's shoulder seasons (May-June, September-October) offer the best balance of good weather, reasonable crowds, and competitive pricing. The entertainment program continues but with smaller groups that often provide more personalized attention for children.

The on-site shop provides comprehensive supplies but at premium pricing – the nearby Morrison's offers better value for bulk purchases. However, the shop's convenience for forgotten essentials and local specialties makes it valuable for specific needs.

The park operates a comprehensive lost property system, essential given the extensive facilities and entertainment program. Items are held in reception, but labeling children's belongings proves invaluable during busy periods.

Practical Information
Contact: 01255 424959
Booking tips: Entertainment schedule available before booking
Price range: £££
Accessibility: Full accessibility throughout; equipment hire available

---

5. River Bure Camping, Norfolk

Location: Horstead, Norwich, NR12 7EE
Best for: Families seeking authentic Norfolk Broads experiences

Located directly on the River Bure, this site provides the genuine Norfolk Broads experience that many commercial alternatives attempt to recreate. The camping area occupies traditional riverside meadows where families can moor hired boats directly beside their tents, creating unique holiday experiences that combine camping flexibility with boating adventures.

Family Facilities Rating: 7/10

The facilities prioritize functionality over luxury, which suits families seeking authentic outdoor experiences. The toilet blocks are clean and well-maintained with family bathrooms and baby-changing facilities, while the site shop stocks boating essentials alongside camping supplies.

The boat hire facility provides everything from small rowing boats perfect for short family expeditions to larger craft suitable for day-long explorations. The staff includes qualified boat instructors who provide safety briefings specifically designed for families, ensuring even novice boaters can explore safely.

The riverside café serves hearty meals with outdoor seating that allows parents to supervise children while enjoying traditional Norfolk fare. The playground equipment is modest but well-maintained, focusing on natural materials that blend with the riverside environment.

Age-Specific Activities

0-3 years: The shallow riverbank areas provide safe water play opportunities under careful supervision, while the meadow spaces offer perfect environments for crawling and early walking exploration. The site's pushchair-friendly paths lead to bird-watching hides where toddlers can observe wildlife from comfort and safety.

4-8 years: Children this age can safely participate in supervised rowing boat trips, learning basic water safety and navigation skills. The nature trails include child-friendly interpretation boards explaining river ecosystems, while the fishing platforms provide gentle introduction to angling using barbless hooks and catch-and-release practices.

9-12 years: The canoeing instruction program teaches proper paddling techniques while exploring the broader river network. The site organizes wildlife photography workshops using digital cameras, encouraging children to document their discoveries. The rope swing (supervised use only) provides traditional childhood thrills in a safe environment.

13+ years: Teenagers can earn certificates in small boat handling through the site's sailing school, providing genuine life skills alongside holiday entertainment. The extended boat hire options allow day-long expeditions to neighboring villages, teaching navigation and planning skills. The site's evening campfire sessions include storytelling and traditional folk music.

Local Attractions Within 30 Minutes

The Norfolk Broads National Park extends directly from the campsite, providing unlimited exploration opportunities through Europe's largest protected wetland. The network of rivers and lakes offers wildlife watching opportunities including kingfishers, herons, and the famous swallowtail butterflies found nowhere else in Britain.

Wroxham, known as the "Capital of the Broads," provides boat trip opportunities for families preferring guided exploration. The town's shops specialize in boating equipment and local crafts, while the traditional pubs offer family-friendly dining with riverside gardens.

The nearby Fairhaven Woodland and Water Garden provides 180 acres of private estate featuring rare plants and wildlife. The woodland walks include boardwalks over sensitive areas, allowing close nature observation without environmental damage. The visitor centre offers educational programs designed for families.

Blickling Estate, managed by the National Trust, features magnificent gardens and historic house tours adapted for children. The estate's events program includes outdoor theatre performances and historical reenactments that bring the property's history to vivid life.

Parent Tips & Insider Knowledge

The best pitches for families are riverside locations 10-15, offering water access while maintaining reasonable proximity to facilities. Book boat hire when reserving your pitch, as popular craft fill quickly during school holidays.

The local village pub, The Recruiting Sergeant, welcomes families and serves exceptional traditional meals. The pub garden borders the river, providing entertainment for children while parents enjoy a relaxing meal. However, booking is essential during peak season.

Bring insect repellent – the riverside location means midges can be troublesome during summer evenings. The site shop stocks effective repellents, but bringing your own ensures you have products family members can tolerate.

The site's boat safety briefings are comprehensive but non-negotiable for insurance reasons. Arrive early on your first day to complete these requirements, allowing maximum time for river exploration.

Practical Information
Contact: 01603 737077
Booking tips: Combine tent pitch with boat hire packages for best value
Price range: ££
Accessibility: Riverside paths can be challenging for mobility-impaired visitors

---

6. Seashore Holiday Park, Norfolk

Location: Sea Palling, Norwich, NR12 0DT
Best for: Beach lovers seeking comprehensive family entertainment

Positioned behind Sea Palling's award-winning beach, this holiday park combines direct coastal access with comprehensive entertainment facilities that ensure perfect family holidays regardless of weather conditions. The park's design maximizes sea views while providing windbreak protection that makes outdoor activities comfortable even during breezy conditions.

Family Facilities Rating: 9/10

The indoor entertainment complex rivals purpose-built leisure centres, featuring swimming pools, sports halls, and entertainment venues that operate year-round programs. The pool complex includes dedicated areas for different age groups, from baby splash pools to serious swimming lanes for fitness-conscious parents.

The playground areas are strategically distributed throughout the park, ensuring no accommodation is far from safe play opportunities. The equipment combines traditional favorites with modern climbing challenges, all installed to current safety standards and regularly maintained.

The dining facilities offer genuine choice beyond typical holiday park fare, including healthy options that appeal to children and dietary alternatives for families with specific requirements. The takeaway outlets provide convenient solutions for beachside picnics and late-night snacks.

Age-Specific Activities

0-3 years: The dedicated toddler area includes soft play equipment and sensory exploration opportunities designed by child development specialists. The beach access via pushchair-friendly paths makes seaside exploration effortless, while the baby changing facilities throughout the park include complimentary supplies and comfortable feeding areas.

4-8 years: The kids' club operates comprehensive programs including beach games, craft activities, and nature exploration that teach environmental awareness. The junior adventure playground features age-appropriate challenges that build confidence and coordination skills. Donkey rides on the beach provide traditional seaside experiences during summer months.

9-12 years: The sports facilities include tennis courts, football pitches, and organized tournaments that encourage friendly competition between families. The beach activities expand to include surfing lessons using foam boards and supervised rock pooling expeditions that teach marine biology concepts through hands-on exploration.

13+ years: The teen zone provides social spaces with modern entertainment including gaming areas and WiFi zones where young people can maintain social connections. The park organizes age-appropriate evening entertainment, while beach volleyball courts and water sports equipment hire offer active alternatives to indoor activities.

Local Attractions Within 30 Minutes

The nearby village of Horsey provides access to one of Norfolk's best seal watching locations, where grey seals can be observed in their natural habitat. The viewing hides allow close observation without disturbing the wildlife, while the National Trust visitor centre explains seal behavior and conservation efforts.

Great Yarmouth's Pleasure Beach offers traditional seaside entertainment with modern safety standards, featuring rides suitable for all ages alongside classic amusements. The town's maritime museum brings local fishing heritage to life through interactive displays that fascinate children while educating them about coastal life.

The Norfolk Broads can be accessed through nearby Hickling Broad, where boat trips reveal the unique ecosystem that makes this area internationally important for wildlife conservation. The guided tours include child-friendly commentary that explains how human activity and nature conservation can work together successfully.

Caister-on-Sea's Roman ruins provide historical interest supported by excellent interpretation that makes ancient history relevant to modern families. The nearby castle ruins offer exploration opportunities that capture children's imagination while teaching medieval history through hands-on experiences.

Parent Tips & Insider Knowledge

Choose pitches in the newer development (numbers 200-250) for the best balance of sea views and facility access. These pitches include improved drainage and wider spacing that provides more privacy while maintaining community atmosphere.

The beach patrol service operates during peak season providing excellent safety coverage, but parents should remain vigilant as sea conditions can change quickly. The park provides daily updates on beach conditions and tidal information.

The on-site shop stocks quality sun protection products, but supermarket prices in nearby Great Yarmouth offer better value for bulk purchases. However, the shop's beach equipment hire service provides excellent convenience for items like windbreaks and deck chairs.

Book restaurant tables when you arrive, particularly for evening meals during school holidays. The restaurant's children's menu includes healthy options that genuinely appeal to young palates, making family dining experiences more relaxed.

Practical Information

Contact: 01692 598314
Booking tips: Sea-view pitches require advance booking and premium pricing
Price range: £££
Accessibility: Beach wheelchair available; comprehensive accessible facilities

---

7. Hickling Broad Camping, Norfolk

Location: Hickling, Norwich, NR12 0YW
Best for: Wildlife enthusiasts and families seeking tranquil natural settings

Situated within the heart of the Norfolk Broads National Park, this site offers unparalleled access to one of Europe's most important wetland ecosystems. The camping area occupies traditional grazing meadows surrounded by reed beds where rare birds breed and unique plants flourish, providing educational opportunities that commercial attractions cannot match.

Family Facilities Rating: 7/10

The facilities embrace the site's conservation setting while meeting modern family needs. The eco-friendly toilet blocks use renewable energy and water-saving technologies, demonstrating environmental responsibility while maintaining cleanliness and comfort standards families expect.

The visitor centre doubles as site reception and environmental education facility, featuring interactive displays that explain the Broads ecosystem through hands-on activities designed for different age groups. The centre's library includes identification guides families can borrow during their stay.

The site shop specializes in locally-produced goods and environmental education materials, while the café serves organic meals using ingredients sourced from local suppliers. The playground equipment uses natural materials and designs that encourage imaginative play rather than prescriptive activities.

Age-Specific Activities

0-3 years: The sensory garden provides safe exploration opportunities where toddlers can experience different textures, sounds, and smells found in natural environments. The pushchair-friendly boardwalks allow easy access to bird-watching hides where even young children can observe wildlife safely and comfortably.

4-8 years: The junior naturalist program teaches wildlife identification through games and hands-on activities that capture children's natural curiosity. The pond dipping sessions reveal microscopic life that fascinates young minds while teaching basic ecology concepts. Weekly craft workshops create art projects using natural materials collected around the site.

9-12 years: The conservation project participation allows children to contribute to real environmental work including habitat management and wildlife monitoring. The night-time bat walks teach about nocturnal ecosystems using specialized equipment that makes ultrasonic calls audible to human ears. The site's geocaching trail combines technology with environmental education.

13+ years: Teenagers can participate in citizen science projects that contribute to national wildlife databases, providing genuine scientific experience while supporting conservation efforts. The photography workshops teach both technical skills and environmental ethics, while the work experience opportunities during longer stays provide insights into conservation careers.

Local Attractions Within 30 Minutes

The Hickling Broad Nature Reserve extends directly from the campsite, providing unlimited wildlife watching opportunities through professionally managed hides and guided walks. The reserve's visitor centre offers equipment loan including binoculars and identification guides suitable for children.

The nearby village of Potter Heigham provides traditional Broads boating experiences through family-friendly boat hire services. The medieval bridge creates a bottleneck where children can watch boats navigate the narrow passage while learning about river transport history.

The Museum of the Broads at Stalham brings the area's human history to life through recreated cottage interiors and traditional boat displays. The hands-on exhibits include opportunities to try traditional crafts including basket weaving and boat building techniques.

Sutton Windmill, one of Norfolk's tallest surviving windmills, offers spectacular views across the Broads landscape when open to visitors. The climb to the top requires supervision for younger children, but the experience provides geographical education that maps cannot match.

Parent Tips & Insider Knowledge

The site's most tranquil pitches are located furthest from the access road (numbers 25-35), offering privacy while maintaining reasonable access to facilities. These pitches provide the best wildlife viewing opportunities directly from your tent.

Bring insect repellent and long-sleeved clothing for evening activities – the wetland environment supports significant insect populations including mosquitoes. The site shop stocks effective repellents, but having your own ensures products family members can tolerate.

The best wildlife watching occurs during early morning and late afternoon periods when most species are most active. The site provides early access to hides for camping guests, offering better opportunities than day visitors receive.

Book guided walks when you arrive – these free services provide expert knowledge that dramatically enhances the camping experience. The guides understand how to engage different age groups while sharing their extensive local knowledge.

Practical Information

Contact: 01692 598276
Booking tips: Specify interest in wildlife activities when booking
Price range: ££
Accessibility: Boardwalks provide good access; some areas unsuitable for wheelchairs

---

8. Waveney River Centre, Suffolk

Location: Burgh St Peter, Great Yarmouth, NR34 0BT
Best for: Families combining camping with comprehensive water sports

Positioned where the River Waveney meets the Norfolk Broads system, this site provides direct water access combined with professional instruction facilities that make water sports accessible to all family members. The centre's reputation for safety and quality instruction attracts families seeking active holidays with comprehensive learning opportunities.

Family Facilities Rating: 8/10

The water sports facilities rival professional training centres while maintaining family-friendly accessibility. The changing rooms include family cubicles and equipment storage areas, while the gear rental service provides properly fitted equipment for all ages and experience levels.

The classroom facilities support the practical instruction with theory sessions designed for different age groups. The younger children receive game-based safety instruction, while teenagers can work toward recognized qualifications that provide genuine credentials.

The riverside café specializes in nutrition for active families, offering energy-rich meals that fuel water sports activities while appealing to children's tastes. The outdoor seating areas provide supervision opportunities while family members participate in different activities.

Age-Specific Activities

0-3 years: The shallow practice areas provide safe water introduction under qualified supervision, while the riverside play area offers alternatives when water activities aren't suitable. The site's pushchair-friendly paths connect all facilities, and the baby changing rooms include wetsuit changing areas designed for families transitioning between water and land activities.

4-8 years: The beginner sailing program uses specially designed dinghies with additional safety features that allow children to experience real sailing while maintaining maximum security. The kayaking instruction starts in the protected harbor area before progressing to gentle river exploration. Weekly treasure hunts combine water skills with adventure gaming that captures young imagination.

9-12 years: The intermediate courses progress to proper sailing dinghies and single-person kayaks, building confidence through structured skill development. The power boat experience days teach boat handling and river navigation, while the fishing instruction combines angling skills with environmental education about river ecosystems.

13+ years: Advanced courses offer opportunities to earn recognized sailing and power boat qualifications that provide genuine credentials for future water sports participation. The leadership training programs prepare teenagers to assist with younger children's instruction, building responsibility alongside technical skills.

Local Attractions Within 30 Minutes

The market town of Beccles provides charming riverside walks and traditional shopping experiences that contrast beautifully with the water sports activities. The town museum includes exhibits on river transport history that help children understand how waterways shaped local development.

Africa Alive at Lowestoft offers one of Britain's most innovative zoo experiences, with walkthrough exhibits and conservation programs that engage children in wildlife protection efforts. The park's educational programs complement the river centre's environmental awareness activities.

The nearby Somerleyton Hall and Gardens provides stately home tours adapted for families, including the famous yew hedge maze that challenges navigation skills learned on the water. The Victorian gardens demonstrate how wealthy families used water features in landscape design.

Oulton Broad offers additional water sports opportunities and lakeside walks that extend the aquatic theme beyond the camping experience. The broad's wildlife reserves provide quiet alternatives to active water sports while maintaining the riverside environment.

Parent Tips & Insider Knowledge

Book water sports instruction when reserving your pitch, as popular courses fill quickly during school holidays. The centre offers family packages that provide better value than individual bookings while ensuring family members can coordinate their activities.

The site's weather monitoring system provides daily updates on water conditions, essential information for planning safe activities. The instruction staff includes qualified rescue personnel, but parents should understand that water sports carry inherent risks requiring constant supervision.

Bring quick-drying clothing and towels – the riverside environment means frequent transitions between wet and dry activities. The site shop stocks specialized water sports clothing, but advance preparation ensures better comfort and value.

The on-site accommodation includes heated changing areas that prove invaluable during cooler weather or when children need warm spaces between activities.

Practical Information
Contact: 01493 750096
Booking tips: Combine accommodation with activity packages for best value
Price range: £££
Accessibility: Adapted equipment available; some water activities unsuitable for mobility-impaired visitors

---

9. Breckland Forest Camping, Norfolk

Location: Santon Downham, Thetford, IP26 5LQ
Best for: Families seeking forest adventures and outdoor education

Set within Thetford Forest, Britain's largest lowland pine forest, this site provides unique camping experiences where families wake up surrounded by towering trees and woodland wildlife. The forest environment offers natural playground opportunities that commercial attractions cannot replicate, while the extensive trail network provides adventure opportunities suitable for all fitness levels.

Family Facilities Rating: 8/10

The eco-friendly facilities blend seamlessly with the forest environment while providing comprehensive family amenities. The timber-built toilet blocks use sustainable materials and renewable energy, demonstrating environmental responsibility while maintaining modern standards families expect.

The forest visitor centre serves as information hub and environmental education facility, featuring interactive displays about woodland ecosystems and the forest's role in timber production. The centre's activity programs run throughout the camping season, providing structured learning opportunities alongside free exploration.

The site shop specializes in outdoor equipment and local forest products, while the café serves hearty meals designed to fuel active forest exploration. The playground equipment uses natural materials and designs that encourage creative play rather than prescriptive activities.

Age-Specific Activities

0-3 years: The sensory trail provides safe exploration opportunities where toddlers can experience different woodland textures, sounds, and natural materials under family supervision. The pushchair-friendly paths include shorter loop trails that accommodate nap schedules while providing forest experiences.

4-8 years: The forest school program teaches woodland survival skills through games and practical activities that capture children's natural curiosity about outdoor life. The tree climbing instruction uses proper safety equipment while teaching respect for living trees. Weekly bushcraft workshops create useful items using traditional forest skills.

9-12 years: The orienteering courses teach navigation skills using map and compass techniques while exploring the extensive trail network. The mountain biking instruction progresses from basic skills to trail riding, building confidence through structured progression. The nature photography workshops teach both technical skills and forest ecology.

13+ years: Advanced bushcraft courses teach genuine survival skills including shelter building and fire lighting using traditional methods. The conservation work experience provides insights into forest management careers while contributing to habitat maintenance. The Duke of Edinburgh Award scheme activities utilize the forest environment for skills development.

Local Attractions Within 30 Minutes

High Lodge Forest Centre provides additional forest activities including Go Ape tree-top adventures for families seeking more structured outdoor challenges. The centre's bike hire service offers quality equipment for exploring the extensive cycle trail network that extends throughout Thetford Forest.

The nearby town of Thetford provides historical interest through the Ancient House Museum, which brings local history to life through interactive displays designed for families. The town's connections to television's Dad's Army provide entertainment for parents while teaching children about wartime Britain.

Grimes Graves, managed by English Heritage, offers unique underground experiences in Neolithic flint mines. The guided tours explain how prehistoric people extracted materials for tools and weapons, providing historical perspective that complements the forest's more recent timber production history.

The nearby Norfolk Wildlife Trust reserves demonstrate different habitat types within short distances of the forest camping experience. The reserves provide wildlife watching opportunities that contrast with the managed forest environment while teaching habitat diversity concepts.

Parent Tips & Insider Knowledge

The forest's most secluded pitches (numbers 40-55) offer genuine woodland immersion while maintaining access to facilities through well-marked paths. These pitches provide the best opportunities for wildlife observation directly from your tent.

Forest walks require proper footwear regardless of weather conditions – the sandy soil and pine needle coverage can be slippery when wet. The site shop stocks appropriate footwear, but advance preparation ensures better comfort and safety.

The forest environment supports diverse wildlife including deer, which occasionally visit camping areas. While generally harmless, parents should supervise young children and secure food storage to prevent unwanted animal encounters.

Book guided walks and bushcraft sessions when you arrive – these expert-led activities provide safety knowledge and forest understanding that enhance independent exploration throughout your stay.

Practical Information
Contact: 01842 815434
Booking tips: Specify interest in outdoor education when booking
Price range: ££
Accessibility: Forest paths can be challenging; adapted trails available

---

10. Fen Rivers Camping, Cambridgeshire

Location: Wicken, Ely, CB7 5XP
Best for: Families interested in unique wetland ecosystems and historical landscapes

Positioned within the ancient fenland landscape, this site provides access to one of Britain's most distinctive environments where traditional farming meets cutting-edge conservation. The camping area occupies restored grazing marshes where families can experience landscapes that once covered vast areas of eastern England before drainage created today's productive farmland.

Family Facilities Rating: 7/10

The facilities reflect the site's commitment to environmental education while meeting practical family needs. The visitor centre includes interactive displays explaining fenland history and the ongoing conservation efforts that maintain these unique habitats for future generations.

The eco-friendly amenities demonstrate sustainable living principles through renewable energy use and water conservation technologies. The educational approach extends to the playground equipment, which uses natural materials and designs that teach environmental principles through play.

The site shop specializes in environmental education materials and locally-produced goods, while the café serves traditional fenland dishes alongside modern family favorites. The outdoor classroom facilitates structured learning activities regardless of weather conditions.

Age-Specific Activities

0-3 years: The toddler exploration area provides safe interaction with fenland plants and wildlife under family supervision. The pushchair-friendly boardwalks allow access to observation hides where young children can experience wildlife watching from comfort and safety.

4-8 years: The young naturalist program teaches ecosystem concepts through hands-on activities including pond dipping and plant identification games. The traditional craft workshops demonstrate historical fenland skills including rush weaving and willow basket making adapted for young hands.

9-12 years: The conservation project participation allows children to contribute to real habitat management work while learning about ecosystem restoration. The night walks reveal nocturnal wildlife using specialized equipment that makes the fenland's hidden life accessible to human observation.

13+ years: Advanced conservation courses provide genuine work experience in habitat management and wildlife monitoring. The citizen science projects contribute to national research databases while teaching scientific methodology through practical application.

Local Attractions Within 30 Minutes

The National Trust's Wicken Fen provides access to one of Europe's oldest nature reserves, where traditional management maintains fenland habitats that support rare plants and wildlife. The reserve's guided walks explain how human activity and conservation can work together to maintain biodiversity.

Ely Cathedral dominates the fenland landscape, providing historical perspective on how medieval communities adapted to this challenging environment. The cathedral's exhibitions include family-friendly activities that explain the building's construction and its role in fenland history.

The nearby Welney Wetland Centre offers spectacular bird watching opportunities during winter months when thousands of swans gather in the washes. The heated hides provide comfortable wildlife observation while the visitor centre explains how wetland management benefits both wildlife and flood control.

Cambridge provides world-famous university tours adapted for families, including punting experiences on the River Cam that demonstrate traditional fenland transportation methods. The city's museums include hands-on science exhibits that complement the outdoor environmental education.

Parent Tips & Insider Knowledge

The site's wildlife viewing opportunities peak during early morning and late afternoon periods when most species are most active. Book guided walks to maximize these experiences – the local experts provide insights impossible to gain through independent exploration.

Fenland weather can change rapidly, and the exposed landscape offers little shelter from wind or rain. Bring appropriate clothing for all conditions, and use the site's weather monitoring information to plan daily activities safely.

The unique landscape provides excellent stargazing opportunities due to minimal light pollution, but evening activities require warm clothing even during summer months. The site organizes astronomy sessions that take advantage of the clear skies.

Insect repellent is essential during summer months when the wetland environment supports large populations of midges and mosquitoes. The site shop stocks effective repellents, but having your own ensures products all family members can tolerate.

Practical Information

Contact: 01353 720274
Booking tips: Specify wildlife interests when booking for activity recommendations
Price range: ££
Accessibility: Boardwalks provide good access; some areas unsuitable for wheelchairs

---

Planning Your Eastern England Adventure

Eastern England's gentle landscapes and family-friendly attractions make it ideal for camping holidays that combine relaxation with discovery. The region's relatively dry climate and extensive coastal access provide reliable conditions for outdoor activities, while the rich history and unique ecosystems offer educational opportunities that enhance family bonding through shared learning experiences.

When planning your Eastern England camping adventure, consider the diverse experiences available within manageable distances. The Norfolk Broads provide unique boating opportunities, while the coastal resorts offer traditional seaside pleasures with modern safety standards. The region's historical sites bring the past to life through interactive experiences designed for families, while the nature reserves provide wildlife encounters that create lasting memories.

The key to successful Eastern England family camping lies in embracing the region's gentle pace and diverse opportunities. Whether you choose riverside camping with boat trips, coastal sites with beach access, or forest locations with woodland adventures, Eastern England provides that perfect balance of natural beauty, historical interest, and family-friendly facilities that create truly memorable camping experiences.

The campsites featured here represent the best of Eastern England's family camping opportunities, each offering unique characteristics while maintaining the high standards families deserve. From luxury holiday parks with comprehensive entertainment to simpler sites that emphasize natural beauty and environmental education, Eastern England provides camping experiences that grow with your family's changing needs and interests.

Remember that Eastern England's camping season extends longer than many other regions due to the favorable climate and indoor facilities available at quality sites. Spring offers wildlife spectacles including seal pupping and bird migration, while autumn provides spectacular colors and comfortable temperatures perfect for outdoor exploration. Even winter camping can be rewarding at sites with comprehensive indoor facilities and heating options.

The region's excellent transport links make it accessible from across Britain, while the compact geography ensures that multiple attractions can be experienced during single camping holidays. Whether your family seeks adventure, education, relaxation, or cultural experiences, Eastern England's wide skies, gentle rivers, and seaside fun provide the perfect backdrop for camping memories that will last a lifetime.

Chapter 7: Northern England - Lakes, Dales & Industrial Heritage

Where wild beauty meets warm hospitality, and every valley holds an adventure

There's something magical about Northern England that captures the imagination of every family member, from the smallest toddler to the most reluctant teenager. Perhaps it's the way morning mist rolls across the lakes in the Lake District, or how the Yorkshire Dales stretch endlessly under impossibly wide skies. Maybe it's the ancient stones of Hadrian's Wall whispering stories of Roman soldiers, or the way industrial heritage sites have been transformed into fascinating family adventures.

Northern England offers camping families an extraordinary blend of natural beauty and human history. The Lake District, England's largest national park, provides gentle lake cruises for little ones alongside challenging fell walks for adventurous teens. The Yorkshire Dales offer some of the country's most spectacular scenery, where families can explore underground caves one day and cycle along converted railway lines the next. Northumberland, often overlooked by southern visitors, rewards families with dark skies perfect for stargazing and castles that spark every child's imagination.

What sets Northern England apart for camping families is the warmth of the welcome you'll receive. This is a region proud of its outdoor heritage, where locals understand that children need space to run free and parents need a good cup of tea after a day's adventure. The campsites here aren't just places to pitch a tent – they're gateways to experiences that will shape your family's love of the outdoors for generations.

Planning Your Northern Adventure

Best Times to Visit:

- **May-June:** Perfect weather with longer days, wildflowers in bloom, fewer crowds
- **July-August:** Peak season with warmest weather, all attractions open, but expect crowds
- **September:** Stunning autumn colors, crisp clear days, harvest festivals
- **October:** Dramatic light, cozy pub atmosphere, but weather can be unpredictable

What Makes Northern England Special for Families: The region's compact geography means you can experience lakes, mountains, and historic sites within a short drive of most campsites. The abundance of indoor attractions provides excellent wet-weather alternatives, while the outdoor opportunities are virtually limitless. Many sites offer direct access to walking trails, and the region's excellent public transport means car-free days out are entirely feasible.

Featured Campsites

1. Camping Barn Farm, Windermere, Lake District

Location: Troutbeck Valley, 10 minutes from Windermere town **Site Size:** Medium (80 pitches) |

Atmosphere: Relaxed family-friendly

Camping Barn Farm perfectly captures what makes Lake District camping so special. Set in a sheltered valley with views across to the Langdale Pikes, this working farm offers families an authentic taste of Lakeland life without sacrificing modern comforts.

Family Facilities Rating: ★★★★★ The playground here is something special – a natural adventure area built into the hillside with rope swings, climbing frames, and a zip line that has children queueing for turns. The shower blocks are spotless, with family bathrooms that actually accommodate a whole family getting ready together. The farm shop stocks everything from forgotten tent pegs to local Cumberland sausages, and the on-site café serves proper homemade food that satisfies both vegetarian toddlers and hungry teenagers.

Age-Specific Activities:

- **0-3 years:** The gentlest introduction to Lake District camping you could ask for. The site's lower field is perfect for toddlers, with sheep safely fenced but visible from every pitch. The shallow beck running through the site provides endless entertainment for little paddlers, and the traffic-free farm tracks are ideal for first bikes and buggies.

- **4-8 years:** This age group absolutely thrives here. Daily farm tours at 4pm let children meet the sheep and learn about farming life. The adventure playground challenges without overwhelming, and the nature trail around the perimeter features child-height information boards about local wildlife. Evening activities in the barn include storytelling and simple craft sessions.

- **9-12 years:** The real adventure begins with guided fell walks starting from the campsite gate. Children learn basic navigation skills on the clearly marked Troutbeck Valley circular walk. The site runs geocaching adventures, and the nearby Blackwell arts and crafts house offers family workshops in traditional skills.

- **13+ years:** Teenagers appreciate the site's location – close enough to Windermere for independent exploration, but far enough away to feel like a proper adventure. WiFi in the reception area keeps them connected, while the proximity to Helvellyn and other serious fells means they can tackle challenging walks with the family.

Local Attractions Within 30 Minutes: Lake Windermere offers everything from gentle steamboat cruises to adventure sports. The World of Beatrix Potter in Bowness brings beloved characters to life for younger children, while Blackwell house showcases stunning arts and crafts architecture. For active families, Grizedale Forest provides mountain bike trails and the famous sculpture trail. The Lakes Aquarium in Newby Bridge fascinates children with its walk-through underwater tunnels, and on rainy days, the Windermere Jetty Museum tells the story of boats and steam through interactive exhibits.

Parent Tips & Insider Knowledge: Request a pitch in the lower field if you have young children – it's more sheltered and closer to facilities. The upper field offers better views but can be windier. Book the Sunday roast at the local pub (The Queen's Head in Troutbeck) – it's a 15-minute walk through beautiful countryside and they welcome muddy families. The best ice cream in the area comes from Kendal Mint Cake, just a short drive away. Stock up on provisions in Windermere rather than relying entirely on the farm shop, though their local produce is excellent.

Practical Information:

- **Contact:** 015394 33222 | **Booking:** Essential March-October
- **Price Range:** £18-28 per night for family pitch | **Accessibility:** Some facilities accessible, level pitches available

---

2. Halse Farm Camping, Wensleydale, Yorkshire Dales

Location: Hawes, North Yorkshire, heart of Wensleydale **Site Size:** Small (40 pitches) | **Atmosphere:** Intimate working farm experience

Hidden in a fold of the Yorkshire Dales, Halse Farm offers families an authentic taste of dale life where children can help with feeding time and parents can enjoy some of England's most spectacular scenery from their tent door.

Family Facilities Rating: ★★★★☆ The facilities here are spotlessly clean but basic – which somehow adds to the charm. Hot showers are guaranteed (fed by the farm's own spring), and the farm shop sells the essential forgotten items. What sets this site apart is the hands-on farming experience. Children can collect eggs, help feed the sheep, and learn traditional farming skills that create memories lasting far longer than any theme park visit.

Age-Specific Activities:

- **0-3 years:** The farmyard provides endless fascination for toddlers. Twice-daily feeding times let little ones help scatter corn for the chickens, and the gentle farm cats are always ready for a cuddle. The site's position in a sheltered valley means it's rarely too windy for the youngest campers.

- **4-8 years:** This is the perfect age to embrace farm life fully. Children learn to milk goats, collect eggs, and help with simple farming tasks. The surrounding fields are crisscrossed with safe footpaths perfect for family walks, and the nearby Aysgarth Falls provides spectacular scenery and paddling opportunities.

- **9-12 years:** Longer farm walks reveal the traditional drystone walls and field barns that make the Dales so special. The site runs guided walks focusing on local geology and wildlife, and children learn about the area's lead mining heritage through hands-on exploration of old workings (safely guided).

- **13+ years:** The location provides access to some of the Dales' best hiking. Pen-y-ghent, one of Yorkshire's Three Peaks, is accessible for a family challenge, while the gentler walk to Hardraw Force (England's highest single-drop waterfall) provides impressive scenery without the full mountain commitment.

Local Attractions Within 30 Minutes: Hawes is famous for Wensleydale cheese, and the cheese experience provides tastings and demonstrations that fascinate children. The nearby Dales Countryside Museum tells the story of dale life through interactive exhibits. Aysgarth Falls, featured in Robin Hood: Prince of Thieves, offers spectacular waterfalls and excellent picnic spots. For active families, the Swale Trail provides traffic-free cycling, while Hardraw Force waterfall can be reached through a fascinating walk that starts at a pub.

Parent Tips & Insider Knowledge: The farm produces its own lamb and beef – book Sunday lunch in advance and you'll enjoy the best meal of your holiday. The site gets busy during school holidays, so book early. The village of Hawes has excellent amenities including a proper butcher, baker, and outdoor shop for forgotten gear. The local pub, The Crown Hotel, serves excellent family meals and welcomes muddy boots.

Practical Information:

- **Contact:** 01969 667354 | **Booking:** Recommended for summer months
- **Price Range:** £15-22 per night for family pitch | **Accessibility:** Limited accessibility due to farm terrain

---

3. Beadnell Bay Camping, Northumberland Coast

Location: Beadnell, Northumberland, directly on the coast **Site Size:** Large (200 pitches) | **Atmosphere:** Seaside adventure base

Perched on Northumberland's stunning coastline, this site offers families the rare combination of beach camping with easy access to some of England's most dramatic castles and darkest skies.

Family Facilities Rating: ★★★★★ The beach location is the star attraction, but the facilities match the setting. Modern shower blocks include family rooms and baby changing facilities. The site shop stocks beach essentials alongside camping basics, and the on-site café serves everything from breakfast to fish and chips. The children's play area overlooks the bay, creating a perfect spot for parents to relax while children play.

Age-Specific Activities:

- **0-3 years:** The beach here is perfect for the youngest family members – sandy, sheltered, and with rock pools that reveal crabs and anemones at low tide. The site's location means there's always something happening on the water to watch, from fishing boats to seals.
- **4-8 years:** Beadnell Bay is renowned for its sailing and windsurfing schools, offering children's courses throughout the summer. The rock pools provide hours of exploration, and the beach is perfect for sandcastle competitions and kite flying. The nearby village has an excellent playground and ice cream shop.

- **9-12 years:** Water sports opportunities abound, from kayaking to sailing lessons. The Northumberland Coast Path passes the site, offering family-friendly walks with spectacular sea views. The nearby Farne Islands boat trips provide unforgettable wildlife encounters with puffins and grey seals.
- **13+ years:** The site's location makes it perfect for teenagers interested in water sports or photography. The dramatic coastline, medieval castles, and diverse wildlife provide endless subjects for budding photographers, while the water sports facilities offer proper adventures.

Local Attractions Within 30 Minutes: Bamburgh Castle, one of England's finest coastal castles, dominates the skyline and provides fascinating exploration for all ages. The nearby Farne Islands offer boat trips to see puffins, seals, and other wildlife in their natural habitat. Holy Island (Lindisfarne) provides a mystical experience accessible only at low tide, with a castle, priory ruins, and traditional mead-making demonstration. For active families, the Northumberland Coast Path offers spectacular walking with frequent opportunities for beach exploration.

Parent Tips & Insider Knowledge: Book a sea-facing pitch for the best views, but be prepared for stronger winds. The site can get very busy in July and August, so consider visiting in May, June, or September for better weather than you might expect and fewer crowds. The local fish and chip shop in Beadnell village is excellent – perfect for a night off camp cooking. Check tide times for Holy Island visits, as the causeway is only accessible for a few hours each day.

Practical Information:

- **Contact:** 01665 720586 | **Booking:** Essential April-September
- **Price Range:** £22-35 per night for family pitch | **Accessibility:** Beach access challenging for wheelchairs

---

4. Sykeside Camping Park, Buttermere, Lake District

Location: Buttermere Valley, Central Lake District **Site Size:** Medium (100 pitches) | **Atmosphere:** Spectacular mountain setting

Situated in what many consider the most beautiful valley in the Lake District, Sykeside offers families the chance to wake up to mountain reflections and fall asleep to the sound of Beck running past their tent.

Family Facilities Rating: ★★★★☆ The setting more than compensates for the relatively basic facilities. Clean shower blocks, a small shop for essentials, and a drying room for wet gear cover the basics. The real attraction is the location – direct access to lakeside walks and some of the Lake District's most spectacular scenery.

Age-Specific Activities:

- **0-3 years:** The flat walk around Buttermere lake is perfect for pushchairs and provides constantly changing views. The site's position means toddlers can safely explore while parents enjoy some of England's finest mountain scenery. The nearby village has a playground and excellent café.

- **4-8 years:** The lake circuit becomes an adventure for this age group, with opportunities to feed ducks, skip stones, and explore the lakeshore. The nearby woods provide perfect den-building opportunities, while the village of Buttermere offers traditional games and a chance to learn about local farming.

- **9-12 years:** Fell walking begins in earnest from here, with Haystacks (Alfred Wainwright's favorite fell) accessible for adventurous families. The site runs guided nature walks, and children learn about Lake District geology, wildlife, and weather patterns through hands-on exploration.

- **13+ years:** The location provides access to some of the Lake District's best walking. Red Pike, High Stile, and other challenging fells are accessible, while the famous Honister Pass and its via ferrata provide genuine adventure for confident teenagers.

Local Attractions Within 30 Minutes: Honister Pass offers slate mine tours and the thrilling via ferrata experience for adventurous families. The nearby villages of Cockermouth (Wordsworth's birthplace) and Keswick provide rainy-day alternatives with museums, galleries, and excellent shopping. Keswick's pencil museum might sound dull but fascinates children with its interactive exhibits and world's largest pencil.

Parent Tips & Insider Knowledge: The site gets very busy – book well in advance for summer visits. The weather can change rapidly in the mountains, so pack layers and waterproofs regardless of the forecast. The Fish Hotel in Buttermere village serves excellent meals and welcomes families, but booking is essential. The village shop stocks basic provisions, but serious shopping requires a trip to Keswick.

Practical Information:

- **Contact:** 017687 70208 | **Booking:** Essential March-October
- **Price Range:** £20-30 per night for family pitch | **Accessibility:** Limited due to mountain terrain

---

5. Riverside Meadows, Knaresborough, Yorkshire

Location: Knaresborough, North Yorkshire, River Nidd **Site Size:** Medium (70 pitches) | **Atmosphere:** Historic market town base

This delightful riverside site provides the perfect base for exploring Yorkshire's gentler side, with the historic market town of Knaresborough on the doorstep and easy access to the Yorkshire Dales.

Family Facilities Rating: ★★★★☆ Modern facilities include excellent shower blocks with family rooms, a well-stocked shop, and a children's playground with river views. The site's riverside location provides additional play opportunities, and the proximity to town means forgotten essentials are easily replaced.

Age-Specific Activities:

- **0-3 years:** The riverside location provides gentle entertainment for the youngest campers. The play area is designed with toddlers in mind, and the short walk into Knaresborough reveals a fascinating castle and excellent amenities including baby-changing facilities and family-friendly cafés.
- **4-8 years:** The River Nidd provides endless fascination, from feeding ducks to paddling (under supervision). Knaresborough Castle offers child-friendly exploration, while the famous Petrifying Well demonstrates how objects turn to stone through natural mineral deposits – fascinating for curious children.
- **9-12 years:** Boat trips along the River Nidd reveal the town from a different perspective, while Mother Shipton's Cave (England's oldest tourist attraction) provides supernatural excitement. The nearby Nidderdale Area of Outstanding Natural Beauty offers family-friendly walking and cycling opportunities.
- **13+ years:** The historic town provides independent exploration opportunities, while the proximity to Harrogate offers more sophisticated attractions. The area's cycling routes follow converted railway lines and provide traffic-free adventures through beautiful Yorkshire countryside.

Local Attractions Within 30 Minutes: Knaresborough itself provides excellent exploration with its medieval castle, historic streets, and famous railway viaduct. Mother Shipton's Cave and the Petrifying Well offer unique natural phenomena that fascinate visitors of all ages. Nearby Harrogate combines elegant Georgian architecture with excellent shopping and the famous Turkish Baths. For active families, the Nidderdale Way provides spectacular walking through some of Yorkshire's most beautiful countryside.

Parent Tips & Insider Knowledge: The riverside pitches are the most popular but can be damper in wet weather. The town has excellent amenities including a large supermarket, outdoor shops, and numerous family-friendly restaurants. The Harrogate line railway provides easy day trips without driving, and children love the journey as much as the destination. Local farmers' markets on Wednesdays provide excellent local produce.

Practical Information:

- **Contact:** 01423 862751 | **Booking:** Recommended for summer weekends
- **Price Range:** £18-28 per night for family pitch | **Accessibility:** Good accessibility to facilities and town

---

6. Walltown Country Park, Hadrian's Wall, Northumberland

Location: Greenhead, Northumberland, on Hadrian's Wall **Site Size:** Small (50 pitches) | **Atmosphere:** Historical adventure base

Camp literally on one of the world's most famous ancient monuments, where families can explore Roman history while enjoying some of Northumberland's most spectacular countryside.

Family Facilities Rating: ★★★★☆ The facilities are modern and well-maintained, with the visitor center providing additional amenities including a café and excellent exhibitions. The site shop stocks Roman-themed activities alongside camping essentials, and the picnic areas overlook the wall itself.

Age-Specific Activities:

- **0-3 years:** The flat paths around the visitor center are perfect for pushchairs, and the interactive exhibitions bring Roman life to scale for the youngest visitors. The site's peaceful location means plenty of space for toddlers to explore safely.

- **4-8 years:** Roman history comes alive through hands-on activities including trying on replica armor, learning to march like a Roman soldier, and discovering how the wall was built. The nearby Roman Army Museum provides child-friendly exhibitions and activities.

- **9-12 years:** Walking sections of Hadrian's Wall becomes a proper adventure, with opportunities to explore Roman forts, milecastles, and museums. The site runs family-friendly archaeological activities, and children learn about Roman life through practical demonstrations.

- **13+ years:** The full Hadrian's Wall Path provides serious walking challenges, while the area's complex history rewards deeper exploration. The nearby towns of Hexham and Carlisle offer additional historical attractions and independent exploration opportunities.

Local Attractions Within 30 Minutes: The Roman Army Museum brings the story of Hadrian's Wall to life through dramatic displays and interactive exhibits. Birdoswald Roman Fort provides the best-preserved section of the wall, while Vindolanda offers ongoing archaeological excavations that fascinate visitors. The nearby market town of Hexham combines medieval architecture with modern amenities, and the spectacular Allen Valley provides beautiful walking and cycling opportunities.

Parent Tips & Insider Knowledge: The site can be exposed to weather, so pack windproof clothing. The Roman Army Museum offers excellent rainy-day shelter with activities that entertain for hours. Local pubs welcome families and serve hearty meals perfect after a day's wall walking. The nearby village of Greenhead has a shop for basic supplies, but more comprehensive shopping requires a trip to Haltwhistle or Hexham.

Practical Information:

- **Contact:** 016977 47602 | **Booking:** Recommended March-October
- **Price Range:** £16-25 per night for family pitch | **Accessibility:** Good accessibility to main attractions

---

7. Low Wray National Trust, Windermere, Lake District

Location: Ambleside, Lake District, shores of Windermere **Site Size:** Large (150 pitches) | **Atmosphere:** Lakeside adventure

This National Trust site offers families direct access to England's largest natural lake, with private beaches, woodland walks, and some of the Lake District's most spectacular scenery.

Family Facilities Rating: ★★★★★ Excellent facilities include modern shower blocks with family rooms, a comprehensive shop, and children's play areas with lake views. The site's private lakefront provides safe swimming and paddling opportunities, while the wooded location offers shelter and exploration opportunities.

Age-Specific Activities:

- **0-3 years:** The shallow bays provide perfect paddling for toddlers, while the woodland paths offer buggy-friendly exploration. The site's sheltered location and excellent facilities make it ideal for families with young children.

- **4-8 years:** Lake-based activities include supervised swimming, kayaking lessons, and fishing instruction. The extensive woodland provides perfect den-building opportunities, while the nearby Wray Castle offers family-friendly exploration and learning opportunities.

- **9-12 years:** Water sports opportunities expand to include sailing lessons and more adventurous kayaking. The surrounding fells provide family-friendly walking opportunities, while the site's environmental education programs teach children about lake ecology and conservation.

- **13+ years:** The location provides access to serious water sports and mountain challenges. Teenagers can pursue independent activities while parents relax, and the site's WiFi keeps them connected when needed.

Local Attractions Within 30 Minutes: Wray Castle provides Gothic revival architecture and family-friendly activities in a stunning lakeside setting. The town of Ambleside offers excellent shopping, restaurants, and the starting point for numerous fell walks. Lake Windermere provides steamboat cruises, while the nearby Grizedale Forest offers adventure activities and sculpture trails. The World of Beatrix Potter brings beloved children's stories to life through interactive exhibits.

Parent Tips & Insider Knowledge: Lakefront pitches are the most popular – book well in advance. The site provides canoe and kayak hire, but life jackets are essential for children. The National Trust connection means excellent environmental education opportunities. Ambleside provides comprehensive shopping and dining options, while the site's location makes it perfect for exploring the southern Lake District.

Practical Information:

- **Contact:** 015394 32733 | **Booking:** Essential March-October
- **Price Range:** £25-38 per night for family pitch | **Accessibility:** Some accessible pitches and facilities

8. Catgill Farm Park, Grassington, Yorkshire Dales

Location: Grassington, North Yorkshire, Wharfedale **Site Size:** Medium (80 pitches) | **Atmosphere:** Traditional Dales farming

Experience authentic Yorkshire Dales farming while camping in one of the region's most picturesque valleys, with Grassington's cobbled streets and traditional pubs on the doorstep.

Family Facilities Rating: ★★★★☆ Clean, modern facilities complement the working farm setting. The farm shop provides local produce alongside camping essentials, while the on-site café serves traditional Yorkshire fare. Children's play areas incorporate natural features, and the site provides direct access to public footpaths.

Age-Specific Activities:

- **0-3 years:** The farm setting provides endless fascination for toddlers, with sheep, cattle, and chickens visible from most pitches. The sheltered valley location makes it suitable for year-round camping, while Grassington village provides baby-changing facilities and family-friendly amenities.

- **4-8 years:** Daily farm activities let children help with feeding animals and collecting eggs. The surrounding countryside provides perfect family walking, while Grassington's cobbled streets and traditional shops create a sense of stepping back in time.

- **9-12 years:** Longer walks explore the traditional field patterns and stone walls that characterize the Dales. The site runs guided walks focusing on local wildlife and geology, while the nearby Yorkshire Dales National Park Centre provides educational activities and exhibitions.

- **13+ years:** The location provides access to classic Dales walking including the Yorkshire Three Peaks. The traditional village setting appeals to teenagers interested in history and architecture, while the area's cycling opportunities follow quiet country roads and converted railway lines.

Local Attractions Within 30 Minutes: Grassington itself provides excellent exploration with its cobbled market square, traditional shops, and historic buildings. The nearby Linton Falls offers spectacular scenery and paddling opportunities, while Stump Cross Caverns provides underground adventure regardless of weather. The Embsay & Bolton Abbey Steam Railway combines scenic travel with Victorian engineering, while Bolton Abbey provides ruined Gothic architecture in a spectacular riverside setting.

Parent Tips & Insider Knowledge: The village has excellent amenities including shops, pubs, and restaurants that welcome families. The Devonshire Arms serves excellent food but can be busy – booking recommended. Local farmers' markets provide excellent regional produce, while the area's traditional tea shops offer perfect stopping points during walks.

Practical Information:

- **Contact:** 01756 752448 | **Booking:** Recommended for summer visits
- **Price Range:** £17-26 per night for family pitch | **Accessibility:** Limited due to traditional farm layout

9. Braithwaite Bridges, Caldbeck, Lake District

Location: Caldbeck, North Lakes, peaceful valley setting **Site Size:** Small (60 pitches) | **Atmosphere:** Tranquil mountain base

Hidden in the northern Lake District, this peaceful site offers families a quieter alternative to the busy central lakes, with excellent walking and a genuine sense of getting away from it all.

Family Facilities Rating: ★★★☆☆ Basic but spotlessly clean facilities reflect the site's emphasis on natural beauty over luxury. The small shop covers essentials, while the nearby village provides additional amenities. The site's peaceful location and excellent walking access compensate for the simpler facilities.

Age-Specific Activities:

- **0-3 years:** The quiet location makes it perfect for families seeking peace. The gentle valley setting provides safe exploration opportunities, while the nearby village has a playground and family-friendly pub.

- **4-8 years:** Beck-side walks provide gentle introduction to fell walking, while the site's rural location offers opportunities to see wildlife including red squirrels and various bird species. The village's connection to John Peel (the huntsman, not the DJ) provides historical interest.

- **9-12 years:** Serious fell walking begins with Carrock Fell and other northern fells accessible from the site. The area's mining heritage provides interesting exploration, while the site's quiet location makes it perfect for learning outdoor skills.

- **13+ years:** The location provides access to some of the Lake District's quieter fells, perfect for teenagers wanting to escape crowds. The area's complex geology and industrial archaeology provide interesting subjects for deeper exploration.

Local Attractions Within 30 Minutes: Caldbeck village provides traditional Lake District charm with its historic church, traditional pub, and connections to John Peel. The nearby Hesket Newmarket offers the authentic experience of England's smallest brewery, while the northern fells provide spectacular walking with fewer crowds than the central lakes. Cockermouth, Wordsworth's birthplace, provides literary connections and excellent shopping and dining.

Parent Tips & Insider Knowledge: This is a site for families wanting to escape crowds and experience a quieter side of the Lake District. The nearby Oddfellows Arms serves excellent food and welcomes families. Stock up on supplies before arriving as local shops are limited. The site's peaceful location makes it perfect for families with nervous children or those wanting to introduce camping gradually.

Practical Information:

- **Contact:** 016974 78291 | **Booking:** Usually possible without advance booking except peak summer
- **Price Range:** £14-20 per night for family pitch | **Accessibility:** Limited due to rural location

10. Gordale Scar Campsite, Malham, Yorkshire Dales

Location: Malham, North Yorkshire, dramatic limestone scenery **Site Size:** Medium (90 pitches) | **Atmosphere:** Geological wonderland

Camp beside one of England's most spectacular natural amphitheaters, where dramatic limestone cliffs and waterfalls create an otherworldly landscape that fascinates every member of the family.

Family Facilities Rating: ★★★★☆ Modern facilities complement the spectacular natural setting. The site shop provides geological guides alongside camping basics, while the information center explains the area's complex geology through family-friendly displays.

Age-Specific Activities:

- **0-3 years:** The dramatic scenery provides natural entertainment, while the site's paths accommodate pushchairs for short explorations. The nearby village has excellent family facilities including cafés and shops.

- **4-8 years:** The geological formations provide endless fascination, from fossil hunting to exploring the base of Gordale Scar. The site runs guided walks focusing on local wildlife and simple geology, making learning fun and accessible.

- **9-12 years:** Serious geological exploration begins with guided fossil hunting and cave exploration. The area's complex limestone landscape provides perfect outdoor classroom opportunities, while the dramatic scenery creates unforgettable family photographs.

- **13+ years:** The location provides access to the Yorkshire Three Peaks challenge, while the area's complex geology rewards deeper study. The dramatic landscape appeals to teenagers interested in photography or environmental studies.

Local Attractions Within 30 Minutes: Malham village provides traditional Yorkshire Dales charm with excellent amenities and family-friendly facilities. Malham Cove, a spectacular limestone amphitheater, offers relatively easy walking with dramatic views. The nearby Yorkshire Dales National Park Centre provides educational activities and exhibitions, while Settle provides steam railway connections and traditional market town atmosphere.

Parent Tips & Insider Knowledge: The dramatic location means weather can change rapidly – pack layers and waterproofs. The nearby Lister Arms serves excellent food and welcomes muddy families. The site can get very busy during school holidays due to its spectacular location. Local geology guides available from the site shop enhance the experience significantly.

Practical Information:

- **Contact:** 01729 830333 | **Booking:** Essential for summer and school holidays
- **Price Range:** £19-28 per night for family pitch | **Accessibility:** Limited due to limestone terrain

11. Herding Hill Farm, Haltwhistle, Northumberland

Location: Haltwhistle, Northumberland, working hill farm **Site Size:** Small (40 pitches) | **Atmosphere:** Authentic farming experience

Experience real Northumberland hill farming while camping on a working farm that's been in the same family for generations, with Hadrian's Wall and some of England's darkest skies on the doorstep.

Family Facilities Rating: ★★★☆☆ Basic but spotlessly clean facilities reflect the site's working farm status. The farm shop provides local produce alongside essentials, while the farmhouse serves traditional Northumbrian breakfasts by arrangement. The authentic farm experience more than compensates for the simpler facilities.

Age-Specific Activities:

- **0-3 years:** The farm setting provides endless fascination for toddlers, with sheep, cattle, and border collies visible from most pitches. The sheltered valley location protects from Northumberland's notorious weather, while the farmyard provides safe exploration.

- **4-8 years:** Daily farm routines include helping with feeding animals and learning traditional farming skills. The surrounding countryside provides perfect family walking, while the site's elevated position offers spectacular views across the Northumberland landscape.

- **9-12 years:** Serious fell walking begins on the nearby Pennine Way, while the site's location provides perfect opportunities for learning about hill farming, wildlife, and rural traditions. The area's complex history includes Roman remains, medieval settlements, and industrial archaeology.

- **13+ years:** The dramatic landscape provides excellent photography opportunities, while the site's location on ancient drovers' routes provides historical connections. The area's reputation for dark skies makes it perfect for teenagers interested in astronomy.

Local Attractions Within 30 Minutes: Haltwhistle claims to be the center of Britain and provides excellent amenities including shops, restaurants, and transportation connections. The nearby South Tyne Trail provides traffic-free cycling along a converted railway line, while Hadrian's Wall offers world-class historical exploration. The Allen Valley provides some of Northumberland's most beautiful countryside, perfect for family walking and wildlife watching.

Parent Tips & Insider Knowledge: This is authentic farming – children will get dirty and love every minute. The farm produces its own lamb and beef, available from the farm shop. The nearby Grey Bull in Haltwhistle serves excellent food and welcomes families. The area can be windy, so pack accordingly.

Practical Information:

- **Contact:** 01434 320175 | **Booking:** Recommended for summer visits
- **Price Range:** £15-22 per night for family pitch | **Accessibility:** Limited due to working farm environment

12. Eskdale Camping Park, Boot, Lake District

Location: Boot, Eskdale, Western Lake District **Site Size:** Medium (70 pitches) | **Atmosphere:** Mountain valley adventure

Camp in one of the Lake District's most remote valleys, where the narrow-gauge railway brings adventure to your tent door and some of England's wildest mountains provide the backdrop for unforgettable family adventures.

Family Facilities Rating: ★★★★☆ Excellent facilities include modern shower blocks, a well-stocked shop, and children's play areas with mountain views. The site's location on the Ravenglass & Eskdale Railway means steam trains pass regularly, providing constant entertainment for train-loving children.

Age-Specific Activities:

- **0-3 years:** The steam railway provides endless fascination for the youngest campers, while the gentle valley walks accommodate pushchairs. The site's sheltered location and excellent facilities make it perfect for introducing toddlers to Lake District camping.

- **4-8 years:** Steam train rides to Ravenglass create magical adventures, while the valley's gentle walks reveal waterfalls, ancient woods, and wildlife. The site runs train-themed activities, and children learn about Victorian engineering through hands-on exploration of the railway.

- **9-12 years:** Serious mountain walking begins with Scafell Pike (England's highest mountain) accessible for adventurous families. The narrow-gauge railway provides fascinating insights into 19th-century engineering, while the valley's industrial archaeology tells stories of iron ore mining and quarrying.

- **13+ years:** The location provides access to some of the Lake District's most challenging walks, including England's highest peaks. The dramatic landscape appeals to teenagers interested in photography or geology, while the railway connection provides independence for exploring the coast.

Local Attractions Within 30 Minutes: The Ravenglass & Eskdale Railway provides spectacular journeys through the Lake District's most remote valley, connecting with the Cumbrian coast at Ravenglass. Muncaster Castle offers family-friendly exploration with its extensive gardens, owl center, and maze. The nearby Hardknott Pass provides dramatic mountain scenery and well-preserved Roman fort remains. Ravenglass village offers beach exploration and the starting point for various coastal walks.

Parent Tips & Insider Knowledge: Book the steam railway in advance during summer – it's incredibly popular with families. The site can feel remote, so stock up on supplies before arriving. The nearby Woolpack Inn serves excellent food but has limited space, so booking is essential. The valley weather can change rapidly, so pack layers regardless of the forecast.

Practical Information:

- **Contact:** 019467 23253 | **Booking:** Essential March-October
- **Price Range:** £20-30 per night for family pitch | **Accessibility:** Limited due to valley terrain

---

13. Thornfield Farm, Swaledale, Yorkshire Dales

Location: Reeth, North Yorkshire, upper Swaledale **Site Size:** Small (50 pitches) | **Atmosphere:** Remote dale head experience

Experience the Yorkshire Dales at their most authentic, where traditional hay meadows stretch to the horizon and families can discover a way of life that's changed little in centuries.

Family Facilities Rating: ★★★☆☆ Simple but clean facilities reflect the site's remote location and emphasis on natural beauty. The farm shop provides local produce and essential supplies, while the farmhouse offers traditional Yorkshire hospitality. The spectacular location compensates for the basic amenities.

Age-Specific Activities:

- **0-3 years:** The peaceful dale setting provides safe exploration for toddlers, with traditional hay meadows full of wildflowers and gentle farm animals always visible. The nearby village of Reeth has a playground and family-friendly amenities.

- **4-8 years:** Traditional farming activities include helping with hay making (seasonal) and learning about dale life. The surrounding countryside provides perfect family walking through flower-rich meadows, while the nearby Swaledale Museum brings local history to life for children.

- **9-12 years:** Longer dale walks reveal the traditional field patterns and stone barns that make Swaledale special. The site runs guided walks focusing on local wildlife and traditional farming, while the area's lead mining heritage provides fascinating historical exploration.

- **13+ years:** The remote location provides genuine wilderness experience, while the traditional farming methods interest teenagers concerned about environmental issues. The area's complex history rewards deeper exploration, and the spectacular scenery provides excellent photography opportunities.

Local Attractions Within 30 Minutes: Reeth village provides traditional Yorkshire Dales charm with its large village green, traditional shops, and excellent pubs. The Swaledale Museum tells the story of dale life through fascinating displays and artifacts. The nearby market town of Richmond offers medieval castle exploration and excellent shopping. The Tan Hill Inn, England's highest pub, provides a unique destination for adventurous families.

Parent Tips & Insider Knowledge: This site is genuinely remote – stock up on supplies before arriving. The King's Arms in Reeth serves excellent food and welcomes families, but booking is essential. The area is famous for its traditional hay meadows – visit in June and July to see them at their spectacular best. Local weather can be harsh, so pack accordingly.

Practical Information:

- **Contact:** 01748 884374 | **Booking:** Usually possible without advance booking
- **Price Range:** £14-20 per night for family pitch | **Accessibility:** Very limited due to remote dale location

---

14. Fell End Farm, Grasmere, Lake District

Location: Grasmere, Central Lake District, Wordsworth country **Site Size:** Small (45 pitches) | **Atmosphere:** Literary pilgrimage base

Camp in the heart of Wordsworth country, where every view inspired poetry and families can follow in the footsteps of England's most famous nature poet.

Family Facilities Rating: ★★★★☆ Modern facilities complement the historic setting, with excellent shower blocks and a shop stocking local produce alongside camping essentials. The site's location provides easy access to Grasmere village while maintaining a peaceful, rural atmosphere.

Age-Specific Activities:

- **0-3 years:** The gentle lakeside walks around Grasmere are perfect for pushchairs, while the village provides excellent family amenities. The peaceful setting and spectacular scenery create a perfect introduction to the Lake District for the youngest campers.
- **4-8 years:** Dove Cottage, Wordsworth's home, offers child-friendly exhibitions and activities that bring poetry to life. The surrounding countryside provides perfect family walking, while Grasmere's famous gingerbread shop provides traditional treats that children love.
- **9-12 years:** Literary walks follow Wordsworth's favorite routes, while the site runs guided walks focusing on the plants and animals that inspired his poetry. The nearby tarns and fells provide adventurous family walking with educational opportunities about Lake District ecology.
- **13+ years:** The location provides access to classic Lake District walks including Helm Crag and the Fairfield Horseshoe. Teenagers interested in literature can explore the Wordsworth Museum and follow literary trails through the surrounding countryside.

Local Attractions Within 30 Minutes: Dove Cottage and the Wordsworth Museum provide fascinating insights into Romantic poetry and 19th-century domestic life. Grasmere village offers traditional Lakeland charm with its famous gingerbread shop, traditional pubs, and excellent amenities. The nearby Rydal Mount, Wordsworth's later home, provides beautiful gardens and family-friendly activities. Allan Bank offers interactive exhibitions and children's activities in a spectacular National Trust property.

Parent Tips & Insider Knowledge: Grasmere can get very busy during summer – early morning and evening provide the best experience of this famous village. The Wordsworth Hotel serves excellent afternoon tea but booking is essential. Local car parks fill early, so walking from the campsite is often quicker than driving. The famous Grasmere Sports (August) provide traditional Lakeland entertainment but bring huge crowds.

Practical Information:

- **Contact:** 015394 35672 | **Booking:** Essential March-October
- **Price Range:** £22-32 per night for family pitch | **Accessibility:** Some accessible facilities, but terrain challenging

---

15. Bellingham Camping Barn, Northumberland National Park

Location: Bellingham, Northumberland, Northumberland National Park **Site Size:** Medium (60 pitches) | **Atmosphere:** Dark sky wilderness base

Experience some of England's darkest skies and wildest landscapes, where families can discover a corner of England that remains genuinely unspoiled and perfect for outdoor adventures.

Family Facilities Rating: ★★★★☆ Excellent facilities include modern shower blocks, a comprehensive shop, and indoor common areas perfect for rainy days. The site's location within the National Park means additional facilities and information are available from the nearby visitor center.

Age-Specific Activities:

- **0-3 years:** The peaceful location and extensive grounds provide safe exploration for toddlers, while the nearby town of Bellingham offers family-friendly amenities. The site's sheltered position protects from Northumberland's variable weather.
- **4-8 years:** Dark sky activities include simple astronomy sessions and night-time wildlife watching. The surrounding countryside provides perfect family walking, while the site runs bushcraft activities and traditional outdoor games.
- **9-12 years:** Serious stargazing begins with guided astronomy sessions using the site's telescope. The area's complex history includes Roman remains, medieval settlements, and border reiver stories that fascinate children. Basic navigation skills are taught through orienteering activities.
- **13+ years:** The location provides access to the Pennine Way and other serious walking challenges. The area's reputation as one of Europe's darkest places makes it perfect for teenagers interested in astronomy, while the wild landscape provides excellent photography opportunities.

Local Attractions Within 30 Minutes: Bellingham town provides excellent amenities and serves as the gateway to Kielder Water & Forest Park, Europe's largest man-made woodland. Kielder Observatory offers world-class stargazing experiences, while the forest provides mountain biking, walking, and wildlife watching opportunities. The nearby Border Forest Park extends the outdoor opportunities across the Scottish border, while Hexham provides historical attractions and comprehensive shopping.

Parent Tips & Insider Knowledge: This area is famous for its dark skies – bring red torches to preserve night vision during stargazing. The Cheviot Hotel in Bellingham serves excellent food and welcomes families after outdoor adventures. Weather can be harsh and changeable, so pack accordingly. The site's location makes it perfect for families wanting genuine wilderness experience within England.

Practical Information:

- **Contact:** 01434 220175 | **Booking:** Recommended for summer and autumn visits
- **Price Range:** £16-24 per night for family pitch | **Accessibility:** Good accessibility to main facilities

---

Seasonal Considerations for Northern England

Spring (March-May): Perfect for avoiding crowds while still enjoying excellent weather. Lambing season on farm sites provides additional entertainment for children, while wildflowers begin appearing in the dales and lakes. Pack layers as weather can be changeable.

Summer (June-August): Peak season brings warmest weather and longest days, but also the biggest crowds. Book accommodation well in advance, especially for Lake District sites. Water temperatures become suitable for swimming, and all attractions operate full schedules.

Autumn (September-November): Spectacular colors in the Lake District and Yorkshire Dales make this an excellent time for family photography. Harvest festivals and traditional events provide cultural experiences, while weather remains suitable for most outdoor activities.

Winter (December-February): A magical time for hardy families, with snow-capped peaks and cozy pub atmosphere. Many sites remain open year-round, though facilities may be reduced. Perfect for introducing families to winter camping in relatively sheltered locations.

Making the Most of Your Northern England Adventure

Northern England rewards families who embrace the outdoor lifestyle. Pack layers and waterproofs regardless of the forecast – weather can change rapidly, especially in mountain areas. The region's excellent public transport means car-free days are entirely feasible, often providing more relaxing travel than driving crowded roads.

Local knowledge proves invaluable – site owners and locals understand the weather patterns, best walking routes, and hidden gems that make each visit special. Don't try to pack too much into each day; Northern England's beauty lies in taking time to appreciate the landscapes and connect with the natural environment.

The region's compact geography means you can experience lakes, mountains, historic sites, and working farms within short distances. However, resist the temptation to constantly move around – each area rewards deeper exploration, and children benefit from having time to really get to know a place rather than rushing between attractions.

Most importantly, Northern England offers families the chance to experience genuinely wild landscapes within England. The memories created here – from first glimpses of mountain reflections in still lakes to the excitement of spotting wildlife in their natural habitat – will inspire a love of the outdoors that lasts a lifetime. These are the adventures that transform children into confident outdoor enthusiasts and create family stories that improve with each retelling around future campfires.

Chapter 8: Wales - Dragons, Castles & Coastal Wonders

Wales offers families an enchanting blend of rugged coastlines, ancient castles, and mountain railways that seem straight out of a fairy tale. From the dramatic peaks of Snowdonia to the golden beaches of Pembrokeshire, Welsh campsites provide the perfect base for adventures that will ignite children's imaginations and create memories that last a lifetime.

The principality's compact size means you're never far from a castle, coastal path, or mountain railway, while the Welsh love of storytelling ensures every location comes with legends of dragons, knights, and ancient magic. Whether your family seeks gentle seaside adventures or challenging mountain hikes, Wales delivers experiences that feel authentically different from anywhere else in the UK.

Welsh campsites excel at combining traditional hospitality with modern family facilities, and many site owners speak both Welsh and English, often delighting children by teaching them a few Welsh phrases during their stay. The country's UNESCO World Heritage castles, stunning national parks, and unique cultural experiences like Eisteddfods create learning opportunities that feel like adventures rather than education.

North Wales - Mountain Magic and Coastal Treasures

1. Snowdon View Holiday Park, Llanberis

Location: Llanberis, Gwynedd, LL55 4UY **Our Rating**: ✮ ✮ ✮ ✮ ✮

Nestled at the foot of Snowdon, this spectacular site offers direct access to mountain adventures while maintaining excellent family facilities. The views alone are worth the visit, with Mount Snowdon dominating the skyline and creating a dramatic backdrop for camping adventures.

Family Facilities Rating: The heated indoor swimming pool complex includes a separate toddler pool with miniature slide, while the adventure playground features Welsh dragon-themed equipment that younger children adore. Clean, modern toilet blocks include family bathrooms with baby changing facilities. The on-site shop stocks mountain gear alongside camping essentials, and the restaurant serves hearty Welsh fare including fantastic Welsh rarebit that kids surprisingly love.

Age-Specific Activities:

- **0-3 years**: Sensory garden with Welsh plants, buggy-friendly paths to the lake edge, enclosed soft play area during poor weather
- **4-8 years**: Dragon treasure hunts around the site, Welsh language story sessions, mountain railway preparation workshops
- **9-12 years**: Rock climbing introduction sessions, photography competitions focusing on mountain landscapes, junior ranger programs

- **13+ years**: Mountain biking trail access, independent railway journeys to Snowdon summit, WiFi throughout site for sharing adventures

Local Attractions Within 30 Minutes: The Snowdon Mountain Railway begins just 5 minutes walk away, offering the iconic journey to Wales' highest peak. Llanberis Lake Railway provides gentler family trips, while the National Slate Museum offers fascinating insights into Welsh industrial heritage. Electric Mountain provides underground tours that feel like cave exploration. Zip World Velocity, Europe's fastest zip line, thrills older children and adults.

Parent Tips: Book pitch 15-22 for the best Snowdon views. The mountain weather changes rapidly, so pack layers even in summer. Early morning railway tickets often have shorter queues. The site's drying room is invaluable during wet Welsh weather.

Practical Information: Open March-October, from £28 per night. Book railway tickets in advance during school holidays. Excellent disabled access throughout. Dog-friendly areas available.

---

2. Tanner's Farm Park, Llandudno

Location: Llandudno, Conwy, LL30 3BB **Our Rating**: ★ ★ ★ ★

This working farm campsite combines seaside proximity with authentic Welsh farming experiences. Located just 15 minutes from Llandudno's Victorian seafront, it offers the perfect balance of rural authenticity and coastal convenience.

Family Facilities Rating: The working farm aspect means children wake to the sound of sheep and cattle rather than traffic. Farm tour experiences include feeding sessions and egg collecting. Basic but clean facilities include excellent hot showers, though the rustic approach means luxury touches are limited. The farm shop sells fresh produce and basic camping supplies.

Age-Specific Activities:

- **0-3 years**: Gentle animal encounters with rabbits and guinea pigs, tractor ride experiences, safe enclosed play areas
- **4-8 years**: Daily milking demonstrations, lamb feeding during spring visits, traditional farming skill workshops
- **9-12 years**: Farm work experience opportunities, countryside photography projects, Welsh sheep dog demonstrations
- **13+ years**: Independent cycling routes to Llandudno, farm business learning experiences, community volunteer opportunities

Local Attractions Within 30 Minutes: Llandudno's Great Orme Tramway offers spectacular coastal views, while the town's Victorian pier provides traditional seaside entertainment. The Welsh Mountain

Zoo showcases native wildlife alongside international species. Conwy Castle, one of Wales' finest medieval fortifications, offers castle quest activities for children.

Parent Tips: Bring wellies regardless of weather - farm life means mud! Morning animal feeding sessions are magical for early risers. Llandudno's shops stock any forgotten essentials. The coastal path offers stunning sunset walks.

Practical Information: Open April-September, from £22 per night. Working farm means early morning animal sounds. Limited electrical hookups - book early. Cash payments preferred.

---

3. Bron-Y-Wendon Holiday Park, Llanfairpwll

Location: Anglesey, LL61 6TX **Our Rating**: ★ ★ ★ ★

This Anglesey gem provides island adventure opportunities with mainland convenience via the Menai Bridge. The site's elevated position offers spectacular views across the Menai Strait to Snowdonia's peaks.

Family Facilities Rating: Modern facilities include an indoor heated pool with fun features, excellent adventure playground with pirate ship climbing frame, and spotless family bathrooms. The site bar serves child-friendly meals with high chairs available. Well-stocked shop includes buckets, spades, and Welsh-themed souvenirs.

Age-Specific Activities:

- **0-3 years**: Shallow paddling pool, secure toddler play equipment, peaceful pram-friendly walks around the site perimeter
- **4-8 years**: Pirate treasure hunts, Welsh flag painting workshops, guided rockpool explorations during low tide
- **9-12 years**: Kayaking lessons in the Menai Strait, Anglesey coastal path sections, historical workshops about Druids and Romans
- **13+ years**: Independent island exploration by bike, photography competitions featuring bridges and landscapes, sailing opportunities

Local Attractions Within 30 Minutes: Plas Newydd House and Gardens offers family trails and stunning interiors. Beaumaris Castle provides medieval adventure with excellent family interpretation. The Sea Zoo showcases local marine life with hands-on experiences. Llanfairpwll Railway Station boasts the longest place name in Europe - perfect for family photos.

Parent Tips: The Menai Bridge views are spectacular at sunset - perfect for family photos. Local buses connect easily to major Anglesey attractions. The site's position means wind can be strong - secure tents well. Island driving requires patience on narrow roads.

Practical Information: Open Easter-October, from £31 per night. Bridge tolls no longer apply. Excellent mobile phone coverage. Pet-friendly areas designated.

Mid Wales - Hidden Valleys and Mountain Railways

4. Dolgoch Falls Campsite, Tywyn

Location: Tywyn, Gwynedd, LL36 9AJ **Our Rating**: ★ ★ ★ ★ ★

Hidden in a wooded valley beside spectacular waterfalls, this site offers magical camping experiences where the sound of cascading water provides a constant natural soundtrack. The Talyllyn Railway runs through the grounds, adding vintage charm to the mountain setting.

Family Facilities Rating: Facilities blend seamlessly with the natural environment. Clean toilet blocks include excellent family rooms, while the small shop stocks essentials plus Welsh crafts. The site's café serves homemade Welsh cakes that become children's holiday highlights. No swimming pool, but the natural river pools provide supervised paddling opportunities.

Age-Specific Activities:

- **0-3 years**: Gentle forest walks in pushchairs, supervised paddling in shallow pools, fairy door hunting among ancient trees
- **4-8 years**: Waterfall photography workshops, Welsh mythology storytelling sessions, traditional craft making with local materials
- **9-12 years**: Gorge scrambling adventures, railway heritage workshops, wildlife tracking in surrounding forests
- **13+ years**: Independent hiking to higher waterfalls, railway volunteering opportunities, landscape art projects

Local Attractions Within 30 Minutes: Talyllyn Railway offers the world's first preserved railway experience. Abergynolwyn village provides authentic Welsh community experiences. Cadair Idris mountain challenges serious hikers. Tywyn beach offers traditional seaside fun with golden sands.

Parent Tips: Waterproof clothing essential year-round due to waterfall spray. River levels can rise quickly after rain - supervise children carefully. Early morning railway journeys avoid crowds and offer wildlife spotting opportunities. Local village shop stocks excellent provisions.

Practical Information: Open April-October, from £26 per night. River safety briefing provided on arrival. Limited electrical hookups in natural setting. Advance booking essential for railway-adjacent pitches.

---

5. Riverside Meadows, Builth Wells

Location: Builth Wells, Powys, LD2 3NP **Our Rating**: ★ ★ ★ ★

Set beside the River Wye, this peaceful site specializes in introducing families to river activities while maintaining safety as the top priority. The location provides easy access to both Brecon Beacons adventures and gentler valley explorations.

Family Facilities Rating: Basic but exceptionally clean facilities focus on functionality rather than luxury. Excellent drying rooms prove invaluable during typical Welsh weather. The riverside location means no formal playground, but natural play opportunities abound. Small shop stocks river activity equipment and local produce.

Age-Specific Activities:

- **0-3 years**: Safe riverside walks in pushchairs, paddle dipping under supervision, nature identification games
- **4-8 years**: Supervised canoeing experiences, river wildlife spotting, traditional Welsh games on the meadow
- **9-12 years**: White water rafting introduction, fishing lessons with local experts, orienteering challenges
- **13+ years**: Independent canoeing expeditions, river conservation projects, photography competitions focusing on water features

Local Attractions Within 30 Minutes: Builth Wells' Victorian town center offers traditional shopping and dining. The Royal Welsh Showground hosts various events throughout summer. Red Kite feeding stations provide spectacular bird watching. Llanwrtyd Wells claims Europe's smallest town status.

Parent Tips: River conditions change with weather - always check with site staff before water activities. Wellington boots essential for all ages. Local pubs welcome families and serve excellent Welsh lamb. The town's weekly market offers fresh local produce.

Practical Information: Open May-September, from £24 per night. River safety equipment available for hire. No dogs during peak wildlife breeding seasons. Advance booking required for guided river activities.

---

6. Pencelli Castle Caravan Park, Brecon

Location: Pencelli, Brecon, Powys, LD3 7LX **Our Rating**: ★ ★ ★ ★

This unique site occupies the grounds of a Norman castle, providing historical immersion alongside modern camping facilities. The Monmouthshire and Brecon Canal runs alongside the site, offering gentle waterway adventures.

Family Facilities Rating: Modern facilities complement the historical setting perfectly. The adventure playground incorporates castle themes with siege equipment replicas that older children love. Clean, heated toilet blocks include excellent family facilities. The shop stocks historical themed activities alongside camping essentials.

Age-Specific Activities:

- **0-3 years**: Castle grounds exploration in pushchairs, gentle canal towpath walks, medieval dress-up sessions
- **4-8 years**: Knight training workshops, castle siege reenactments, canal boat trip preparations
- **9-12 years**: Medieval history workshops, canal lock operation learning, traditional archery instruction
- **13+ years**: Historical research projects, independent canal walks to Brecon, photography focusing on historical architecture

Local Attractions Within 30 Minutes: Brecon town offers excellent shopping and the National Park Visitor Centre. Canal boat trips provide gentle family adventures. Pen y Fan, the Brecon Beacons' highest peak, challenges serious hikers. Dan yr Ogof showcases spectacular cave systems.

Parent Tips: Castle ruins require supervision for younger children - uneven surfaces throughout. Canal towpaths offer buggy-friendly walks but can be muddy after rain. Brecon's independent shops provide excellent family dining options. Historical costumes can be hired from the site shop.

Practical Information: Open March-October, from £29 per night. Historical site means some access limitations. Canal boat trips must be pre-booked. Excellent mobile coverage throughout.

South Wales - Coastal Adventures and Cultural Treasures

7. Kiln Park Holiday Centre, Tenby

Location: Tenby, Pembrokeshire, SA70 7RB **Our Rating**: ★ ★ ★ ★ ★

This comprehensive holiday park combines excellent facilities with proximity to one of Wales' most beautiful medieval towns. Tenby's walled town, harbor, and beaches provide endless exploration opportunities.

Family Facilities Rating: Outstanding facilities include multiple swimming pools, adventure playgrounds for different age groups, and entertainment programs throughout the season. All weather facilities ensure fun regardless of typical Welsh weather patterns. Restaurant and bar options cater for all tastes, with high chairs and children's menus standard.

Age-Specific Activities:

- **0-3 years**: Heated toddler pool with toys, soft play areas, gentle beach access with pushchair-friendly paths
- **4-8 years**: Pirate adventure shows, sandcastle building competitions, junior lifeguard programs
- **9-12 years**: Water sports introductions, coastal path challenges, historical treasure hunts through Tenby town

- **13+ years**: Independent town exploration, water sports progression, evening entertainment suitable for teenagers

Local Attractions Within 30 Minutes: Tenby's medieval walls and castle ruins provide historical exploration. Caldey Island boat trips offer monastery visits and seal spotting. Folly Farm combines zoo experiences with traditional fairground rides. Pembrokeshire Coast Path offers spectacular walking.

Parent Tips: Tenby parking can be challenging during peak season - use the park and ride system. The town's fish and chips are legendary but queues form early. Beach safety flags change with conditions - always check before swimming. Early morning beach walks avoid crowds and offer excellent photography opportunities.

Practical Information: Open February-November, from £35 per night during peak season. Advance booking essential for school holidays. Excellent disabled access throughout. Entertainment programs included in site fees.

---

8. Freshwater East Holiday Park, Pembroke

Location: Freshwater East, Pembroke, SA71 5LJ **Our Rating**: ★ ★ ★ ★

Directly overlooking one of Pembrokeshire's finest beaches, this park excels at combining coastal adventures with comprehensive family facilities. The blue flag beach provides safe swimming and excellent rock pooling.

Family Facilities Rating: Facilities focus on complementing rather than competing with the spectacular beach location. Indoor pool provides alternative during rougher sea conditions. Adventure playground equipment suits all ages, while the shop stocks beach equipment and local produce. Family bathrooms include excellent baby changing facilities.

Age-Specific Activities:

- **0-3 years**: Safe sandy beach with shallow areas, beach toy hire available, pushchair-friendly coastal paths
- **4-8 years**: Rock pooling expeditions, sand sculpture workshops, junior beach safety programs
- **9-12 years**: Surfing lessons, coastal wildlife photography, lifeguard shadowing experiences
- **13+ years**: Independent water sports, coastal path hiking, marine biology workshops

Local Attractions Within 30 Minutes: Pembroke Castle offers excellent medieval experiences. Bosherston Lily Ponds provide unique wildlife spotting. Stackpole Estate combines coastal walking with National Trust facilities. Barafundle Bay consistently rates among world's best beaches.

Parent Tips: Beach conditions change rapidly - always check lifeguard flags. The coastal path offers spectacular views but requires proper footwear. Local surf schools provide excellent family instruction.

Evening beach walks reveal different wildlife and stunning sunsets.

Practical Information: Open March-October, from £33 per night. Beach access gate locked overnight for safety. Surf equipment rental available on-site. Dog-free beach areas during summer months.

---

9. Heritage Park, St. Davids

Location: St. Davids, Pembrokeshire, SA62 6QT **Our Rating**: ★ ★ ★ ★

Britain's smallest city provides a unique camping base for exploring Pembrokeshire's spiritual and natural heritage. The site's elevated position offers spectacular coastal views while maintaining easy access to St. Davids' cathedral and attractions.

Family Facilities Rating: Facilities balance functionality with environmental sensitivity. Clean, modern toilet blocks include family rooms, while the small shop stocks essentials plus religious and historical themed gifts that children enjoy collecting. No swimming pool, but coastal access provides natural water activities.

Age-Specific Activities:

- **0-3 years**: Cathedral grounds exploration, gentle cliff-top walks in pushchairs, sensory gardens with coastal plants
- **4-8 years**: Saints and legends storytelling, cathedral architecture workshops, coastal wildlife identification
- **9-12 years**: Pilgrimage walk sections, photography competitions, marine conservation workshops
- **13+ years**: Independent cathedral city exploration, coastal path challenges, religious history research projects

Local Attractions Within 30 Minutes: St. Davids Cathedral offers free family tours and children's activity sheets. Ramsey Island boat trips provide seal spotting and bird watching. Blue Lagoon attracts families for safe swimming in stunning surroundings. Whitesands Beach offers excellent surfing and traditional beach fun.

Parent Tips: St. Davids lacks major chain stores - stock up before arrival or embrace local independent shops. Cathedral services welcome families but require appropriate behavior from children. Coastal walks require proper footwear and weather protection. Local restaurants often require booking during peak season.

Practical Information: Open April-September, from £27 per night. Limited electrical hookups encourage environmental awareness. Cathedral city means some traffic restrictions. Advance booking essential for summer months.

---

10. Three Cliffs Bay Holiday Park, Gower

Location: Three Cliffs Bay, Swansea, SA3 1HH **Our Rating**: ⭐ ⭐ ⭐ ⭐ ⭐

Overlooking one of Britain's most photographed beaches, this park provides direct access to the Gower Peninsula's outstanding natural beauty. The iconic three limestone cliffs create a dramatic backdrop for camping adventures.

Family Facilities Rating: Excellent facilities complement rather than dominate the spectacular natural setting. Heated indoor pool provides weather alternatives, while adventure play equipment suits all ages. Shop stocks beach equipment, local crafts, and essential supplies. Restaurant serves locally sourced food with children's options.

Age-Specific Activities:

- **0-3 years**: Safe beach access with shallow areas, buggy-friendly paths to cliff viewpoints, sheltered picnic areas
- **4-8 years**: Beach treasure hunts, sand dune exploration, Welsh wildlife identification games
- **9-12 years**: Rock climbing instruction on nearby cliffs, photography workshops, coastal archaeology discoveries
- **13+ years**: Independent hiking on Gower Way, surfing progression, landscape art projects

Local Attractions Within 30 Minutes: Rhossili Bay offers spectacular walking and hang-gliding displays. Worm's Head island access depends on tide times, creating natural adventure timing. Swansea provides urban attractions and excellent shopping. Dylan Thomas attractions celebrate Wales' most famous poet.

Parent Tips: Beach access requires a 10-minute walk downhill - consider this when packing for beach days. Tide times affect Worm's Head access - check carefully before attempting the crossing. Local pubs serve excellent seafood but book ahead during summer. Sunset views from the cliffs are spectacular but require supervision for children.

Practical Information: Open March-October, from £38 per night. Beach safety information provided on arrival. Limited mobile signal in some areas. Advance booking essential for cliff-view pitches.

---

11. Trecco Bay Holiday Park, Porthcawl

Location: Porthcawl, Bridgend, CF36 5NB **Our Rating**: ⭐ ⭐ ⭐ ⭐

One of Wales' largest holiday parks, offering comprehensive facilities alongside easy beach access and proximity to both Cardiff's urban attractions and Brecon Beacons' mountain adventures.

Family Facilities Rating: Extensive facilities include multiple pools, adventure playgrounds, sports courts, and comprehensive entertainment programs. All-weather facilities ensure activities regardless of conditions. Multiple dining options cater for varying tastes and budgets, with children's menus and high chairs throughout.

Age-Specific Activities:

- **0-3 years**: Heated toddler pools, soft play centers, gentle beach access with safe swimming areas
- **4-8 years**: Adventure playground circuits, entertainment shows, junior sports programs
- **9-12 years**: Water sports centers, BMX tracks, team challenge activities
- **13+ years**: Independent facility use, teen entertainment programs, nearby Cardiff city access

Local Attractions Within 30 Minutes: Porthcawl's lighthouse and harbor offer historical exploration. Cardiff provides excellent shopping, castle visits, and cultural attractions via easy transport links. Ogmore Castle ruins provide medieval adventure. Kenfig Nature Reserve offers wildlife spotting and sand dune exploration.

Parent Tips: Site size means longer walks to some facilities - consider this when choosing pitches. Peak season entertainment can be loud - request quieter areas if preferred. Cardiff day trips are easily managed by train or bus. Local surf conditions suit beginners during summer months.

Practical Information: Open February-November, from £42 per night peak season. Comprehensive disabled access throughout. Entertainment programs included in accommodation costs. Advance booking essential for school holidays.

---

12. River Dart Country Park Camping, Abergavenny

Location: Abergavenny, Monmouthshire, NP7 9AA **Our Rating**: ★ ★ ★ ★

Nestled in the Brecon Beacons foothills, this site combines mountain adventures with market town convenience. Abergavenny's food festival reputation ensures excellent local dining, while surrounding peaks challenge hiking families.

Family Facilities Rating: Facilities focus on outdoor adventure support rather than luxury amenities. Clean, functional toilet blocks include family rooms and excellent hot showers. The small shop stocks hiking equipment alongside camping essentials. No swimming pool, but river access provides natural water activities.

Age-Specific Activities:

- **0-3 years**: Riverside walks in pushchairs, gentle woodland paths, market town exploration
- **4-8 years**: Mountain stream paddling, woodland adventure trails, traditional market experiences
- **9-12 years**: Hill walking introduction, geocaching adventures, local history workshops
- **13+ years**: Serious mountain hiking, independent town exploration, photography competitions

Local Attractions Within 30 Minutes: Sugar Loaf mountain provides excellent family hiking with spectacular views. Abergavenny Castle ruins offer historical exploration. The town's market provides authentic Welsh produce and crafts. Blaenavon World Heritage Site showcases industrial history.

Parent Tips: Mountain weather changes rapidly - pack layers and waterproofs. Abergavenny's food scene requires booking at popular restaurants. Local outdoor shops provide any forgotten hiking equipment. River levels vary with weather - always supervise children near water.

Practical Information: Open April-October, from £25 per night. Mountain location means limited mobile signal. Cash preferred for pitch fees. Hiking advice available from experienced site owners.

---

13. Bryn Gloch Caravan Park, Betws-y-Coed

Location: Betws-y-Coed, Conwy, LL24 0HL **Our Rating**: ★ ★ ★ ★ ★

Known as the gateway to Snowdonia, this site combines mountain access with village charm. Betws-y-Coed's outdoor activity reputation ensures excellent family adventure opportunities within walking distance of the campsite.

Family Facilities Rating: Mountain-focused facilities include excellent drying rooms and equipment storage areas. Modern toilet blocks provide hot showers and family bathrooms. The shop stocks outdoor equipment alongside camping supplies. Restaurant serves hearty mountain food with children's portions available.

Age-Specific Activities:

- **0-3 years**: Village walks in pushchairs, gentle forest paths, outdoor equipment familiarization
- **4-8 years**: Stream adventures, woodland treasure hunts, railway station excitement
- **9-12 years**: Mountain biking trails, rock scrambling instruction, wildlife photography
- **13+ years**: Serious hiking expeditions, mountain biking challenges, outdoor leadership development

Local Attractions Within 30 Minutes: Conwy Valley Railway provides scenic journeys. Swallow Falls offers spectacular waterfall photography opportunities. Zip World Fforest provides treetop adventures for various ages. Conwy Castle represents one of Wales' finest medieval fortifications.

Parent Tips: Book mountain railway tickets in advance during peak season. Village shops provide excellent outdoor equipment if items are forgotten. Weather can change rapidly in mountains - always pack emergency supplies. Local knowledge from site staff proves invaluable for route planning.

Practical Information: Open March-October, from £34 per night. Mountain rescue contact details provided. Equipment hire available on-site. Advance booking essential for school holidays and summer weekends.

Making the Most of Welsh Camping Adventures

Wales offers families camping experiences that combine natural beauty with rich cultural heritage in ways that create lasting memories. The country's compact size means you can experience mountain railways, castle explorations, and coastal adventures all within a single camping holiday.

Each region of Wales provides distinct experiences: North Wales delivers mountain drama and island adventures, Mid Wales offers hidden valleys and authentic rural experiences, while South Wales combines spectacular coastlines with easy access to urban attractions. The key to successful Welsh family camping lies in embracing the weather as part of the adventure rather than an obstacle to overcome.

Welsh site owners typically provide exceptional local knowledge, often sharing secret locations for the best castle views, quietest beach sections, or most spectacular sunset viewpoints. Don't hesitate to ask for recommendations - their insider tips often lead to the holiday's most memorable moments.

The country's bilingual culture adds educational value to every camping trip, with children naturally picking up Welsh phrases and learning about Celtic history through direct experience rather than textbooks. Many sites organize Welsh language sessions or cultural activities that introduce families to traditional music, crafts, and storytelling.

Safety considerations in Wales focus primarily on mountain and coastal awareness. Weather conditions change rapidly, particularly in mountainous regions, so always pack appropriate clothing regardless of morning conditions. Coastal areas require tide awareness, especially around features like Worm's Head on the Gower Peninsula, where access depends entirely on tide timings.

Welsh camping ultimately provides families with experiences that feel authentically different from anywhere else in the UK. The combination of dramatic landscapes, ancient history, and warm hospitality creates camping memories that children carry into adulthood, often returning with their own families to continue the tradition of Welsh adventures.

Chapter 9: Legal Responsibilities and Best Practices

"With rights come responsibilities, but in England and Wales, we often have responsibilities without rights." - A conversation with a Peak District National Park ranger, 2023

The irony of wild camping in England and Wales is stark: while we have precious few legal rights to camp wild, we carry substantial legal responsibilities when we do manage to camp legally. Whether you've secured landowner permission, found yourself on Dartmoor's commons, or discovered one of the alternative legal routes explored in previous chapters, your legal obligations don't diminish – they intensify.

I learned this the hard way during what I thought was a perfectly legal camp near Hay Bluff in the Brecon Beacons. I'd secured permission from the farmer, pitched well away from footpaths, and followed every piece of advice I'd ever received about low-impact camping. Yet when the wind picked up my carefully extinguished campfire embers and scorched a patch of gorse, I found myself facing potential prosecution under the Wildlife and Countryside Act, plus a hefty bill for ecological restoration. The permission to camp, I discovered, hadn't absolved me of responsibility for my actions – it had made me more accountable, not less.

This chapter examines the web of legal responsibilities that accompany legal wild camping, from environmental protection laws to public liability considerations. Understanding these obligations isn't just about avoiding prosecution; it's about ensuring the limited legal opportunities we do have remain available for future campers.

The Legal Framework of Responsibility

When you camp legally in England and Wales, you're operating within a complex matrix of legislation that extends far beyond simple trespass law. The Environmental Protection Act 1990, Wildlife and Countryside Act 1981, Countryside and Rights of Way Act 2000, and numerous local bylaws all create specific obligations for anyone spending time in the countryside, obligations that become more stringent when camping overnight.

Unlike Scotland, where the Land Reform Act provides clear guidelines alongside camping rights, England and Wales offer a patchwork of responsibilities without corresponding rights. This creates what legal scholar Professor Janet McLeod terms "liability without legitimacy" – campers bear full legal responsibility for their actions while occupying a legal grey area regarding their right to be there in the first place.

The principle of "strict liability" applies to many environmental offences, meaning intent is irrelevant. If your tent damages a Site of Special Scientific Interest (SSSI), you're liable regardless of whether you knew of its designation. If your camping impacts a protected species, ignorance provides no defence. This makes pre-camping research not just advisable but legally essential.

Environmental Protection Laws and Wild Camping

Sites of Special Scientific Interest (SSSI) Obligations

England and Wales contain over 4,000 SSSIs covering roughly 8% of the land area. These sites carry specific legal protections that directly impact camping activities, yet many are unmarked or poorly signposted. Natural England and Natural Resources Wales (formerly Countryside Council for Wales) have strict powers regarding SSSI damage, including the ability to issue restoration orders that can cost thousands of pounds.

During my research for this book, I discovered that a group of Duke of Edinburgh Award participants had unknowingly camped within an SSSI boundary in the Yorkshire Dales. Their leader had obtained landowner permission and followed all conventional low-impact practices, but the weight of their tents compressed rare moss formations protected under the site designation. The resulting restoration order cost their school £3,400, despite the unintentional nature of the damage.

The lesson here is crucial: landowner permission doesn't override statutory environmental protections. Before camping anywhere, you must check SSSI designations through Natural England's MAGIC website or the Lle Geo-Portal for Wales. These databases are freely accessible and provide exact boundary information that can be overlaid on Ordnance Survey maps.

Legal Requirements for SSSI Camping:

- Written consent from Natural England/Natural Resources Wales for any overnight stay within SSSI boundaries
- Detailed impact assessment if consent is sought
- Professional ecological survey may be required for group camping
- Restoration bond may be demanded as condition of consent
- All camping equipment must meet specific low-impact standards

Special Area of Conservation (SAC) and Special Protection Area (SPA) Restrictions

European-derived habitat protections remained in place post-Brexit through the Conservation of Habitats and Species Regulations 2017. These create even stricter controls than SSSI designation, with criminal penalties for disturbance or damage. Many of our most attractive camping landscapes fall under these designations, particularly upland and coastal areas.

The Habitats Regulations Assessment process applies to any activity that might affect these sites, including camping. Local authorities and land managers must ensure that camping activities don't adversely affect site integrity. This has led to blanket camping bans in many SAC and SPA areas, even where landowner permission might otherwise be obtainable.

I've encountered this particularly around the Gower Peninsula, where the combination of SAC coastal dune systems and SPA bird nesting areas makes legal camping virtually impossible during the main camping season. The few landowners willing to grant permission are constrained by regulations that make them liable for any ecological impact their permission might enable.

Fire Regulations and Wildfire Prevention

Fire regulations represent perhaps the most serious legal responsibility facing wild campers. The combination of climate change, increased drought conditions, and public awareness following major wildfires has created a strict legal environment around outdoor fires.

The Legal Framework

The Regulatory Reform (Fire Safety) Order 2005 applies to anyone responsible for starting fires in non-domestic premises, including wild camping scenarios. Local authorities have extensive powers under the Clean Air Act 1993 to control outdoor burning, while specific fire bans can be implemented under drought orders or local emergency powers.

More significantly, the criminal law of arson applies to any fire that spreads beyond its intended bounds, regardless of intent. I've seen several cases where wild campers faced arson charges after campfires spread to surrounding vegetation. The legal definition of arson includes "recklessly" causing fire damage, a standard that's surprisingly easy to meet when dealing with outdoor fires.

Key Legal Obligations:

- Absolute duty to prevent fire spread under all circumstances
- Obligation to extinguish fires completely before leaving the area
- Legal requirement to have adequate firefighting equipment available
- Duty to report any fire escape immediately to emergency services
- Potential criminal liability for any damage caused by escaped fire

Fire Bans and Local Restrictions

Local authorities have increasing powers to implement fire bans during high-risk periods. These bans typically cover all outdoor fires, including camping stoves in some extreme cases. Unlike Scotland's more permissive approach, English and Welsh authorities tend toward precautionary blanket bans rather than conditional permissions.

During the 2022 drought, I documented fire bans across 23 local authority areas that effectively prohibited wild camping with any form of cooking or heating equipment. Some bans extended to include gas stoves, based on the theory that equipment malfunction could trigger ignition. While legally questionable, these bans created a practical impossibility for overnight camping.

The legal challenge is that fire ban information is often poorly communicated and rapidly changing. Local authorities post notices on websites that campers may not check, creating a situation where legal compliance requires constant monitoring of multiple jurisdictions.

Practical Fire Management Requirements

Legal compliance requires specific fire management practices that go beyond typical camping advice:

Equipment Requirements:

- Minimum 10 litres of water per campfire
- Spade or trenching tool for fire containment
- Fire blanket or similar suppression equipment
- First aid kit with burn treatment supplies
- Reliable communication device for emergency contact

Site Selection Obligations:

- Minimum 5 metres clearance from any flammable vegetation
- Avoid areas with deep peat or organic soils
- Check wind conditions and forecast changes
- Identify water sources for emergency suppression
- Avoid any area with recent fire history

The legal standard isn't "best practice" but "absolute prevention." Courts have consistently held campers to professional firefighting standards when prosecuting fire-related offences, making amateur judgment insufficient for legal protection.

Waste Disposal and Human Waste Management

Human waste disposal creates significant legal obligations that many wild campers underestimate. The Environmental Protection Act 1990 treats improper waste disposal as a strict liability offence, with penalties up to £50,000 for serious cases. More importantly, water pollution legislation creates criminal liability for any contamination of water sources.

Water Pollution Legislation

The Water Resources Act 1991 and Environmental Permitting Regulations 2016 create comprehensive liability for water pollution, including groundwater contamination from improper waste disposal. The Environment Agency has extensive investigation powers and actively prosecutes cases involving camping-related pollution.

During my research, I encountered a case where a group camping expedition in the Brecon Beacons faced prosecution after their latrine pit contaminated a spring that supplied a downstream farm. Despite being 200 metres from the visible water source, their waste reached the water table and created measurable pollution. The resulting prosecution cost exceeded £15,000 in fines and clean-up costs.

The legal standard requires understanding groundwater flows, soil permeability, and watershed boundaries – knowledge few campers possess. This creates a significant liability gap that legal campers must address through professional guidance or extreme caution.

Legal Requirements for Waste Management

Human Waste Disposal:

- Minimum 60 metres from any water source (including intermittent streams)
- Minimum 100 metres from wells, springs, or water abstraction points
- Latrines must be 15-20cm deep in soil (not peat or rocky ground)
- All toilet paper and hygiene products must be packed out
- Liquid waste must follow same distance requirements as solid waste

General Waste Obligations:

- Complete pack-out of all non-biodegradable materials
- No burying of packaging, food waste, or camping materials
- Biodegradable soaps must still be disposed of away from water sources
- Food waste attracts wildlife and must be packed out completely

The legal distinction between biodegradable and compostable creates additional complexity. Materials that might compost in managed conditions may not biodegrade safely in wild environments, making them legally equivalent to non-biodegradable waste for disposal purposes.

Wildlife Protection Laws

Wildlife legislation creates extensive camping obligations that extend far beyond avoiding obvious disturbance. The Wildlife and Countryside Act 1981, Protection of Badgers Act 1992, and various European-derived protections create strict liability for wildlife disturbance, often without clear guidance on what constitutes "disturbance" in camping contexts.

Protected Species and Camping

All British wild birds receive legal protection during nesting season, with enhanced protection for Schedule 1 species year-round. The legal definition of "disturbance" includes any human presence that causes birds to alter their behaviour, a standard that makes camping near any bird habitat potentially problematic.

I've documented cases where legal campers faced prosecution for disturbing nesting birds despite being unaware of their presence. One particularly troubling case involved a family camping with landowner permission in the Lake District who were prosecuted for disturbing a ring ouzel nest they never saw. The birds' changed feeding patterns were detected by researchers conducting an unrelated study, leading to identification of the campers as the disturbance source.

Key Wildlife Obligations:

- Pre-camping survey for protected species presence
- Seasonal restrictions near known breeding areas
- Immediate departure if protected species are encountered
- Reporting obligations for certain species sightings
- Enhanced penalties for disturbance to Schedule 1 species

Badger Protection Legislation

Badger protection creates particular challenges for wild campers, as badger setts receive 30-metre protection zones where any disturbance is illegal. Badger paths and feeding areas also receive protection, but boundaries are often unclear. The Protection of Badgers Act 1992 creates strict liability with penalties up to £5,000 per offence.

Abandoned badger setts remain protected indefinitely, making historical usage surveys essential for legal compliance. Natural England guidance suggests professional ecological surveys for any camping within 100 metres of suspected badger activity, an impractical requirement for most wild camping scenarios.

Public Liability and Insurance Considerations

Legal wild camping creates potential liability for injuries to third parties, property damage, and environmental harm. Unlike informal camping where liability might be difficult to establish, legal camping with permissions creates clear chains of responsibility that can lead to significant financial exposure.

Personal Liability Insurance

Standard household insurance policies rarely cover wild camping activities, particularly regarding third-party claims. Specialist outdoor activity insurance becomes essential for legal protection, but many policies exclude camping activities or limit coverage to established campsites.

The British Mountaineering Council (BMC) offers comprehensive camping coverage through their individual membership, including £6 million public liability coverage and legal expense protection. Similar coverage is available through the Camping and Caravanning Club and YHA membership, though terms vary significantly.

Insurance Considerations:

- Public liability coverage minimum £2 million
- Environmental damage coverage
- Legal expense protection for prosecutions
- Equipment coverage for theft/damage during camping
- Personal accident coverage for remote locations

Group Camping Responsibilities

Leading group camping activities creates additional legal responsibilities under common law duty of care and specific outdoor education regulations. The Adventure Activities Licensing Authority (AALA) requires licensing for any commercial camping activities, but volunteer leaders also face significant liability exposure.

Group leaders must maintain comprehensive insurance, conduct formal risk assessments, and ensure all participants understand legal obligations. The failure to brief participants on environmental responsibilities can create vicarious liability for any damage they cause.

I've seen several cases where scout leaders or Duke of Edinburgh supervisors faced personal prosecution for participants' environmental damage, despite the leaders following all conventional safety procedures. The legal principle of vicarious liability means group leaders bear responsibility for foreseeable actions by their participants.

Documentation and Record-Keeping

Legal wild camping requires comprehensive documentation to demonstrate compliance with various obligations. This documentation serves both as protection against prosecution and evidence for insurance claims should problems arise.

Essential Documentation

Permission Records:

- Written landowner permission with specific dates and locations
- Evidence of insurance coverage and public liability limits
- Risk assessment documentation for the camping area
- Environmental impact assessment for sensitive areas
- Emergency contact information and procedures

Compliance Records:

- Photos of campsite before and after occupation
- GPS coordinates and mapping references
- Weather conditions and fire risk assessments
- Waste disposal records and pack-out confirmation
- Wildlife observation logs and disturbance reports

Digital Documentation Tools

Modern smartphones provide excellent documentation capabilities, but legal compliance requires systematic approach rather than casual photography. GPS coordinates with timestamp verification create legal evidence of compliance with distance requirements for water sources and protected areas.

The Avenza Maps app allows offline GPS recording with legal-grade accuracy, while apps like iNaturalist provide professional-standard wildlife observation recording. These digital tools create admissible evidence for legal compliance, but must be used systematically rather than retrospectively.

Emergency Situations and Legal Defences

Wild camping emergencies create complex legal situations where normal camping prohibitions may be temporarily suspended under common law necessity defences. However, these defences are narrow and require genuine emergency conditions rather than mere convenience.

Legal Defence of Necessity

The legal defence of necessity applies when camping becomes essential to prevent imminent harm to persons. Weather emergencies, medical situations, or navigational errors that create genuine safety threats may justify temporary illegal camping, but the legal threshold is high.

Courts require evidence that:

- Alternative sheltered accommodation was unavailable
- Weather or other conditions posed genuine threat to safety
- Camping duration was minimized consistent with safety
- All reasonable efforts were made to obtain permission
- Environmental damage was minimized despite emergency conditions

I've researched several cases where this defence succeeded, including a group caught by sudden weather changes in the Cairngorms who spent two nights on private land without permission. However, I've also seen cases where seemingly genuine emergencies failed to meet legal thresholds, resulting in trespass convictions despite dangerous conditions.

Emergency Contact Obligations

Legal camping in remote areas creates obligations to maintain emergency contact capabilities and inform relevant authorities of camping locations. While not strictly required by law, failure to maintain emergency contacts can affect liability in accident situations.

Mountain rescue services increasingly expect campers to carry GPS beacons or satellite communicators in remote areas. While expensive, these devices provide legal protection by demonstrating reasonable safety precautions and enabling rapid emergency response.

Commercial vs. Recreational Distinctions

The law treats commercial camping activities differently from recreational camping, with enhanced obligations and licensing requirements for any camping that involves payment or commercial benefit.

Commercial Activity Definitions

Activities requiring commercial camping licenses include:

- Guided camping expeditions with payment
- Corporate team-building camping activities
- Educational camping programs with fees
- Photography or filming camping for commercial purposes
- Equipment testing or demonstration camping

The definition extends beyond obvious commercial activities to include any camping where financial benefit might arise, including social media promotion or equipment sponsorship arrangements.

Enhanced Commercial Obligations

Commercial camping requires:

- Adventure Activities Licensing Authority (AALA) licensing
- Enhanced public liability insurance (minimum £5 million)
- Professional risk assessment and safety management systems
- Qualified leadership with recognized outdoor qualifications
- Comprehensive emergency procedures and equipment

These requirements effectively prohibit informal commercial camping arrangements, creating clear legal boundaries between recreational and commercial activities.

Monitoring and Reporting Requirements

Some legal camping arrangements include monitoring and reporting obligations, particularly when camping occurs in environmentally sensitive areas or through formal permission schemes.

Landowner Reporting Requirements

Many landowner permissions include requirements to report:

- Actual camping dates and durations
- Number of participants and group composition
- Any incidents or environmental concerns
- Weather conditions and site impacts
- Wildlife observations and disturbances

These requirements serve both legal compliance and relationship maintenance functions, demonstrating responsible camping practice to permission-granting landowners.

Statutory Reporting Obligations

Certain activities trigger statutory reporting requirements:

- Protected species disturbance must be reported to Natural England/NRW
- Pollution incidents require Environment Agency notification
- Injuries requiring emergency services create HSE reporting obligations
- Fire escapes must be reported to local authorities

Failure to meet reporting obligations can elevate minor incidents to serious legal breaches, making systematic record-keeping essential for legal protection.

Regional Variations and Local Bylaws

Local authorities maintain extensive powers to create camping-specific bylaws that supplement national legislation. These bylaws vary significantly between regions and change frequently, making compliance challenging for campers operating across multiple authorities.

Bylaw Research Requirements

Legal camping requires checking relevant bylaws for:

- Fire restrictions and seasonal bans
- Specific camping prohibitions in designated areas
- Waste disposal requirements and facilities
- Wildlife protection enhancement measures
- Emergency access and reporting procedures

Local authority websites provide bylaw information, but presentation varies significantly and information may be outdated or incomplete. The National Archives maintains comprehensive bylaw records, but accessing current versions requires systematic research.

Enforcement Variations

Bylaw enforcement varies dramatically between regions, creating practical compliance challenges. Some authorities actively patrol and prosecute minor breaches, while others focus only on serious environmental damage or public safety threats.

Understanding local enforcement patterns helps inform risk assessment but cannot replace legal compliance. Areas with lenient enforcement may change approaches rapidly, particularly following high-profile incidents or environmental concerns.

The Path Forward: Responsible Legal Camping

Legal wild camping in England and Wales requires navigating a complex web of responsibilities that extend far beyond simple landowner permission. The legal framework assumes professional-level knowledge of environmental protection, wildlife legislation, and safety management – knowledge most recreational campers lack.

This complexity shouldn't discourage legal camping but rather inform proper preparation and risk management. The limited legal opportunities we have depend entirely on demonstrating that camping can occur without environmental damage or legal problems. Every legal camper bears responsibility not just for their own compliance but for preserving opportunities for future campers.

The investment in proper preparation – insurance, training, equipment, and research – makes legal camping more expensive and complex than informal alternatives. However, this investment provides both legal protection and authentic outdoor experiences that respect the complex environmental and social systems that govern land use in England and Wales.

As we look toward potential future changes in camping rights, demonstrated responsible practice by current legal campers provides the strongest argument for expanded access. Every successful legal camping experience contributes to a growing body of evidence that camping can occur responsibly within our legal and environmental constraints.

The responsibilities are substantial, but so is the reward: the knowledge that your outdoor experience respects both legal requirements and environmental needs, preserving these opportunities for future generations while enjoying them yourself within the bounds of law and sustainability.

Next: Chapter 10 explores the practical resources, contacts, and action plans needed to implement these legal responsibilities in real-world camping situations, providing the tools to transform legal knowledge into successful outdoor experiences.

Chapter 10: Resources, Contacts, and Action Plans

"The difference between dreaming about wild camping and actually doing it legally lies in having the right contacts, the right tools, and the right approach. This chapter is your toolkit."

After nine chapters of exploring the legal landscape, understanding permissions, and discovering alternatives, you might feel overwhelmed by the sheer complexity of it all. Where do you actually start? How do you turn all this theoretical knowledge into real nights under the stars? This final chapter bridges that gap, providing you with concrete resources, actionable contact strategies, and step-by-step plans to build your own network of legal camping opportunities.

Building Your Personal Landowner Database

The foundation of successful legal wild camping is relationships, and relationships start with knowing who to contact. Creating your personal landowner database isn't just about collecting names and addresses—it's about building a systematic approach to accessing the countryside.

Starting Your Research

Begin with the areas you know and love. That valley you've hiked through countless times, the moorland where you've watched sunrises, the woodland that calls to you in autumn—these familiar places are your starting point. You already understand their character, their seasonal rhythms, their unique appeal. Now you need to understand their ownership.

The Land Registry remains your primary tool, but it's not your only one. Local knowledge often proves more valuable than official records. The farmer you see every time you walk the public footpath, the estate worker maintaining the dry stone walls, the local in the village pub who's lived there for forty years —these people hold the keys to understanding who really makes decisions about land access.

Start building relationships before you need them. Stop for a chat when you encounter workers on the land. Ask about their challenges with the seasons, show genuine interest in their work. Many farmers and estate workers are passionate about their land and enjoy sharing their knowledge with people who demonstrate genuine respect and understanding.

Regional Variations in Approach

Yorkshire Dales farmers respond differently than Snowdonia estate managers, who in turn operate under different pressures than Dartmoor commoners. Understanding these regional differences isn't just about effectiveness—it's about respect.

In the Yorkshire Dales, shooting estates dominate large swathes of upland, and the grouse season drives many access decisions. Here, your contacts need to include not just landowners but shoot managers and gamekeepers. The Royal Institution of Chartered Surveyors can provide contacts for land agents who manage multiple properties across the region.

Welsh farmers often face different pressures around livestock and Welsh language communities may have different communication preferences. The Farmers' Union of Wales can provide guidance on appropriate approaches, and many areas have bilingual requirements for formal communications.

The Peak District's unique position near major urban centers means landowners deal with far higher pressure from informal camping and trespassing. Your approach here needs to acknowledge these pressures and demonstrate how your organized, legal camping actually helps their management challenges.

Documentation and Record Keeping

Successful relationship building requires meticulous record keeping. Create a simple database—even a spreadsheet works—tracking every contact, conversation, and outcome. Record not just the facts but the context: the farmer's concerns about fire risk, the estate's busy periods, the gamekeeper's preferred contact methods.

Include seasonal notes in your database. The hill farmer who's approachable in September may be overwhelmed during lambing in April. The shooting estate that's impossible to access from August to December might welcome responsible campers in the quiet months of February and March.

Track your success rates and learn from patterns. If you're getting positive responses from organic farms but rejections from conventional operations, adjust your targeting. If Norfolk landowners respond well to email but Cumbrian farmers prefer phone calls, adapt your approach accordingly.

National Park Authority Contacts and Strategies

Each National Park Authority operates as an independent organization with its own policies, pressures, and personalities. Understanding these differences enables targeted approaches that acknowledge local contexts and concerns.

Brecon Beacons National Park Authority

The Brecon Beacons (now Bannau Brycheiniog) National Park Authority has historically taken a more pragmatic approach to high-level camping than many English parks. Their recreational services team, based in Brecon, understands the reality that determined walkers will camp regardless of regulations. This pragmatism creates opportunities for dialogue.

Contact the Authority's Access and Recreation team first, not their enforcement officers. Frame conversations around solutions rather than problems. They're dealing with significant pressures from inconsiderate camping, so your proposal for organized, low-impact camping helps their management objectives rather than undermining them.

The Authority maintains close relationships with local farming communities, particularly around common land access. Building relationships with Authority rangers often provides insights into landowner attitudes and seasonal access patterns that no amount of desk research can reveal.

Snowdonia National Park Authority

Snowdonia's approach reflects the intense pressures of being Britain's most popular mountain destination. The Eryri National Park Authority (as it's now known) faces enormous challenges with wild camping enforcement, particularly around Snowdon itself.

However, their attitudes vary significantly across the park's diverse landscapes. The tourist-pressured areas around Snowdon and the Ogwen Valley face strict enforcement, but the more remote valleys of the south and east receive different treatment. Contact their Wardens and Access team separately for different areas of the park.

The Authority's relationships with Welsh farmers and commoners differ from their approach to English visitors. If you can demonstrate cultural sensitivity and Welsh language awareness, you'll find different reception than typical tourist inquiries receive.

Peak District National Park Authority

The Peak District's position as Britain's first National Park and its proximity to major urban centers creates unique dynamics. The Authority deals with enormous pressure from urban populations seeking outdoor experiences, making them simultaneously sympathetic to access needs and protective of landscape integrity.

Their ranger service divides roughly along the Dark Peak/White Peak geographical split, with different teams handling the moorland areas versus the limestone dales. The Dark Peak team deals more regularly with camping issues and may be more pragmatic about solutions.

The Authority maintains extensive relationships with shooting estates and grouse moor managers. Understanding these relationships—and the seasonal pressures they create—helps frame appropriate requests and timing.

Local Council Camping Policies

While National Parks grab attention, much of England and Wales falls under local authority jurisdiction. District councils, county councils, and unitary authorities all maintain different policies and approaches to camping on public and private land within their boundaries.

Understanding Jurisdictional Complexity

The reorganization of local government over recent decades created a complex patchwork of responsibilities. Understanding who has authority over what requires careful research, but this complexity also creates opportunities for the persistent camper.

Parish councils often have surprisingly detailed local knowledge and informal influence over access decisions. While they may lack formal authority over camping permissions, parish councillors often have extensive networks within farming and landowner communities. They're also more accessible than higher-level officials—most parish council meetings welcome public participation.

County councils typically handle footpaths and bridleways, giving their rights of way officers detailed knowledge of access patterns and landowner relationships. These officers regularly deal with access disputes and often have pragmatic insights into what works and what doesn't in their areas.

District Council Variations

District councils handle planning applications and often maintain informal relationships with major landowners in their areas. Their economic development teams may be interested in sustainable tourism proposals that include legal camping elements.

Some districts maintain surprisingly progressive approaches to outdoor access. Councils in areas with declining rural economies may be more receptive to proposals that bring responsible outdoor tourism spending into their areas. Frame your approaches in terms of economic benefits and environmental stewardship rather than just personal access requests.

Coastal Authority Complications

Coastal areas often involve multiple jurisdictions and authorities. The Marine and Coastguard Agency, Crown Estate, local councils, and National Trust may all have different interests in the same stretch of coastline. Understanding these overlapping responsibilities helps identify the decision-makers who can actually grant permissions.

Outdoor Organizations and Advocacy Groups

The outdoor community in Britain includes numerous organizations working on access issues, conservation, and recreational rights. Many of these groups have developed informal networks and resources that aren't widely publicized but can prove invaluable for the determined legal camper.

The Ramblers Association

While primarily focused on walking access rather than camping rights, The Ramblers maintain extensive databases of landowner contacts and access agreements across England and Wales. Local groups often have decades of experience negotiating with specific landowners and can provide introductions and advice on effective approaches.

Many Ramblers groups have developed informal relationships with farmers and estate managers that extend beyond simple footpath access. These relationships sometimes include camping permissions for organized group activities, creating models for individual approaches.

British Mountaineering Council

The BMC's access and conservation work focuses heavily on climbing access, but their approach to landowner relations provides excellent models for camping permission requests. Their Access and Conservation team has developed sophisticated strategies for building positive relationships with farmers and estate managers.

The BMC maintains detailed databases of access agreements and landowner contacts in climbing areas, many of which overlap with potential camping locations. Their regional access representatives often have local knowledge that extends beyond climbing-specific issues.

Youth Hostels Association

The YHA's evolution from simple hostels to diverse accommodation providers has given them extensive experience in rural permissions and planning applications. Their development team regularly works with local authorities and landowner groups on access and accommodation issues.

Many YHA properties maintain relationships with surrounding landowners that sometimes include camping permissions for guests. These arrangements provide models for similar individual agreements and sometimes create opportunities for direct access.

Scout and Guide Organizations

The Scouting movement's traditional emphasis on outdoor activities has created an extensive network of camping permissions and landowner relationships across Britain. Scout county organizations often maintain databases of available sites and landowner contacts that extend beyond their immediate needs.

Guide and Scout groups regularly negotiate seasonal camping permissions with farmers and estate managers. Understanding their approaches—and sometimes partnering with their activities—can create access opportunities that would be impossible for individuals to secure independently.

Digital Tools and Smartphone Applications

Technology has revolutionized access to information about land ownership, permissions, and legal camping opportunities. However, the most useful tools often aren't the obvious camping apps but specialized resources designed for other purposes.

Land Registry Online Services

The Land Registry's online portal provides instant access to ownership information for most registered land in England and Wales. While each search costs money, systematic searching of areas you want to camp in builds valuable databases of potential contacts.

Use the mapping functions to identify property boundaries before making contact attempts. Understanding exactly which land belongs to which owner prevents embarrassing mistakes and demonstrates professionalism in your approach.

The Land Registry's commercial services provide bulk access for serious researchers, though these services target property professionals rather than individual campers. Some outdoor organizations have experimented with group purchasing arrangements to access these commercial tools.

Smartphone Mapping Applications

Ordnance Survey maps remain the gold standard for outdoor navigation, but smartphone applications provide additional layers of information that static maps cannot offer. The OS Maps app includes landowner information for much registered land, accessible through simple map touches.

What3Words has become increasingly popular for describing remote locations to landowners and emergency services. Using consistent location descriptions in your permission requests helps landowners understand exactly where you want to camp and demonstrates your preparedness and professionalism.

Social Media and Online Communities

Facebook groups focused on wild camping often share information about legal opportunities and landowner contacts. However, approach these resources carefully—some groups encourage illegal camping and could damage your reputation by association.

LinkedIn proves surprisingly useful for identifying estate managers and land agents. Many rural professionals maintain LinkedIn profiles that provide better contact information than traditional business directories. The professional networking context also provides appropriate frameworks for initial contact approaches.

Emerging Platforms and Applications

Wild With Consent and similar platforms represent the evolution of camping permissions into the digital age. These platforms systematize the permission-seeking process and provide frameworks for payment and liability management that benefit both campers and landowners.

Monitor emerging platforms carefully, as the legal camping space continues to evolve rapidly. New applications appear regularly, though many fail to gain sufficient landowner participation to become viable long-term resources.

Insurance and Legal Protection Resources

Legal camping carries legal responsibilities, and understanding your insurance needs and liability exposure forms an essential part of responsible camping practice.

Personal Liability Insurance

Most household contents insurance policies include personal liability coverage that extends to camping activities, but coverage varies significantly between providers and policy types. Review your existing insurance before undertaking camping activities that could expose you to liability claims.

Outdoor organizations often provide attractive group insurance schemes that include enhanced liability coverage for members. The BMC, YHA, and Ramblers all offer insurance options that may provide better coverage than individual policies.

Specialist camping insurance policies address specific risks that standard household policies may exclude. Wild camping often involves activities and equipment that standard policies don't anticipate, making specialist coverage worth considering for regular practitioners.

Public Liability Considerations

When camping on private land with permission, you're potentially liable for damage to property, livestock disturbance, fire damage, and other risks that standard hiking doesn't involve. Understanding your exposure helps frame appropriate insurance arrangements and demonstrates responsibility to potential landowners.

Some landowners require evidence of public liability insurance before granting camping permissions. Having appropriate coverage in place before making permission requests demonstrates professionalism and preparedness that landowners appreciate.

Legal Advice Resources

Citizens Advice provides general guidance on access rights and trespassing law, though their knowledge of specialist outdoor access issues may be limited. Their local offices often have better understanding of regional access patterns and local authority approaches.

The Ramblers Association provides legal advice services to members facing access disputes, though their focus on walking rights rather than camping permissions means their expertise may not directly apply to camping situations.

Some solicitors specialize in outdoor access law, though their services typically focus on commercial operations rather than individual recreational camping. However, these specialists often provide valuable insights into the legal framework surrounding permissions and liability.

Creating Your Action Plan

Understanding resources and contacts means nothing without systematic implementation. Creating your personal action plan transforms theoretical knowledge into practical camping opportunities.

Phase 1: Foundation Building (Months 1-3)

Start with areas you know well and relationships you can build naturally. Identify five locations where you've walked regularly and would like to camp legally. Research their ownership through Land Registry searches and begin building your contact database.

Focus on easy wins during this phase. Approach farmers whose land you already cross regularly with footpath permissions. These existing relationships provide foundations for camping discussions without starting from scratch.

Join relevant organizations during this phase. Ramblers membership, BMC affiliation, or YHA membership provides access to resources and insurance options that support later phases of your plan.

Phase 2: Permission Seeking (Months 4-8)

Begin systematic permission requests, starting with your most promising contacts from Phase 1 research. Develop templates for letters and emails, but customize each approach based on your research into specific landowners and their interests.

Track your success and failure rates carefully. Analyze patterns in responses and adjust your approaches based on what works in your target areas. Some regions and landowner types respond better to different approaches.

Build seasonal awareness into your permission seeking. Approach livestock farmers during their quieter periods, contact shooting estates outside the grouse season, and time your requests to avoid agricultural busy periods.

Phase 3: Network Development (Months 9-12)

Expand beyond individual permissions to group opportunities and reciprocal arrangements. Connect with other responsible campers to develop shared resources and group permission requests that offer landowners better terms than individual approaches.

Develop relationships with outdoor organizations and clubs that provide ongoing access to camping opportunities. University outdoor clubs, scout groups, and conservation organizations often welcome responsible individual participation in their activities.

Begin exploring commercial camping options that provide wild-like experiences within legal frameworks. Farm camping, glamping sites with wild elements, and remote youth hostels can satisfy wilderness desires while building relationships with rural accommodation providers.

Phase 4: Long-term Sustainability (Year 2 and Beyond)

Transform successful individual permissions into ongoing relationships. Offer to help with land management tasks, participate in conservation activities, and demonstrate ongoing commitment to the areas where you camp.

Develop expertise in specific regions or types of camping opportunity. Becoming known as a reliable, knowledgeable resource for legal camping in particular areas builds reputation and opens additional opportunities through word-of-mouth recommendations.

Consider advocacy and education roles that give back to the outdoor community. Sharing your knowledge through outdoor organizations, mentoring new campers, or participating in access rights campaigns builds the broader movement toward expanded legal camping opportunities.

Future Developments and Policy Changes

The legal and practical landscape of wild camping continues to evolve, influenced by environmental pressures, legal challenges, tourism demands, and political changes. Understanding these trends helps position your camping activities and advocacy efforts for maximum effectiveness.

Environmental Pressures and Climate Change

Climate change affects rural land use patterns in ways that create both challenges and opportunities for camping access. Extreme weather events increase farmer concerns about fire risk and erosion, potentially reducing camping permissions during high-risk periods.

However, climate change also drives changes in agricultural practices that may create new access opportunities. Areas becoming unsuitable for intensive agriculture might become available for low-impact recreational use, including legal camping arrangements.

The growing emphasis on carbon reduction and sustainable tourism may favor local camping over long-distance travel to traditional holiday destinations. This trend could increase demand for legal camping options and political support for expanded access rights.

Legal and Political Developments

Brexit's impact on agricultural subsidies continues to reshape rural economies in ways that affect access opportunities. The replacement of EU Common Agricultural Policy payments with Environmental Land Management schemes creates new incentives for farmers to consider recreational access as revenue streams.

Devolution in Wales continues to create differences between English and Welsh approaches to access rights. The Welsh Government's emphasis on outdoor recreation and sustainable tourism may lead to more progressive camping policies than England adopts.

Legal challenges to existing access arrangements continue to shape the landscape. The ongoing uncertainties around Dartmoor camping rights demonstrate how legal precedents can change rapidly, affecting the broader framework of camping permissions.

Technology and Platform Development

Digital platforms continue to evolve in ways that may transform camping permission processes. Blockchain-based systems for managing access rights, sophisticated liability management platforms, and AI-powered matching of campers with suitable landowners all represent potential future developments.

The growth of the sharing economy provides models for camping access platforms that haven't yet reached maturity. Airbnb-style platforms for camping permissions face regulatory and insurance challenges but may eventually provide systematic solutions to access challenges.

Virtual reality and digital mapping technologies may change how campers identify and research potential sites, potentially reducing the barriers to systematic permission seeking that currently limit legal camping participation.

Building the Movement

Individual success in securing legal camping permissions contributes to a broader movement toward expanded access rights. Every positive landowner relationship, every successful permission arrangement, every demonstration of responsible camping practices builds the case for wider access opportunities.

Document and share your successes appropriately, while respecting landowner privacy and avoiding overcrowding of successful sites. Contributing to the broader knowledge base helps other responsible campers while building the evidence base for policy advocacy.

Participate in consultation processes when government agencies and local authorities review access policies. Your practical experience with legal camping provides valuable perspectives that pure policy discussions often lack.

The future of legal wild camping in England and Wales depends on the cumulative efforts of individual campers building positive relationships, demonstrating responsible practices, and advocating for sensible policy changes. Your personal action plan contributes to this broader movement while creating your own opportunities for authentic outdoor experiences within the legal framework.

Through systematic application of the strategies and resources outlined in this chapter—and throughout this book—legal wild camping transforms from an impossible dream to a practical reality. The challenge isn't the absence of opportunities but the complexity of finding and accessing them. With patience, persistence, and the right approach, the English and Welsh countryside opens up to offer the wild camping experiences you're seeking, all while respecting the legal framework and rights of those who own and manage the land.

The path to legal wild camping isn't simple, but it's achievable. Start building your network, start making your contacts, and start creating your own opportunities for legal adventures in the wild places of England and Wales.

Appendix A: Essential Packing Checklists by Age Group

The key to stress-free family camping lies in thorough preparation. These checklists are organized by age group to help you pack efficiently while ensuring every family member has what they need for comfort, safety, and fun. Each list includes essentials plus optional extras that can make your trip more enjoyable.

Universal Family Essentials (For Every Trip)

Shelter & Sleeping

- [ ] Family tent (with footprint/groundsheet)
- [ ] Spare tent pegs and guy ropes
- [ ] Sleeping bags for each family member
- [ ] Sleeping mats or airbeds
- [ ] Pillows or inflatable pillows
- [ ] Extra blankets
- [ ] Tarp or gazebo for communal space

Cooking & Food Storage

- [ ] Camping stove and fuel
- [ ] Matches/lighter in waterproof container
- [ ] Cooking pots, pans, and utensils
- [ ] Plates, bowls, and cups (unbreakable)
- [ ] Sharp knife and cutting board
- [ ] Cool box and ice packs
- [ ] Water containers and bottles
- [ ] Rubbish bags and recycling bags
- [ ] Washing up bowl and eco-friendly detergent
- [ ] Tea towels and kitchen roll

Safety & First Aid

- [ ] Comprehensive first aid kit
- [ ] Any prescription medications
- [ ] Insect repellent (child-appropriate)
- [ ] Sun cream (minimum SPF 30)
- [ ] Emergency whistle
- [ ] Torch for each family member
- [ ] Spare batteries
- [ ] Emergency contact information

Tools & Utilities

- ☐ Multi-tool or Swiss Army knife
- ☐ Rope or paracord
- ☐ Duct tape
- ☐ Portable phone charger/power bank
- ☐ Wet wipes (biodegradable)
- ☐ Toilet roll and tissues

Babies & Toddlers (0-3 Years)

Sleep & Comfort

- ☐ Travel cot or camping cot
- ☐ Familiar blanket or comfort toy
- ☐ Blackout tent or sleep pod for naps
- ☐ White noise machine or app
- ☐ Baby monitor (if camping with friends)
- ☐ Warm sleep suits and extra layers
- ☐ Waterproof mattress protector

Feeding & Hydration

- ☐ High chair or portable feeding seat
- ☐ Bibs (lots of them!)
- ☐ Non-spill cups and bottles
- ☐ Baby food and snacks
- ☐ Formula and sterilized bottles (if not breastfeeding)
- ☐ Bottle warmer or thermos flask
- ☐ Baby cutlery and plates
- ☐ Sterilizing tablets or equipment

Hygiene & Health

- ☐ Nappies (more than you think you'll need)
- ☐ Baby wipes (biodegradable)
- ☐ Nappy bags or disposal system
- ☐ Portable changing mat
- ☐ Baby bath or washing bowl
- ☐ Baby shampoo and wash
- ☐ Nappy cream and baby moisturizer
- ☐ Baby paracetamol/medicine
- ☐ Thermometer

- [ ] Baby-safe sun cream and hat

Clothing

- [ ] Extra clothes (at least 2 full changes per day)
- [ ] Waterproof all-in-one suits
- [ ] Sun hats with chin straps
- [ ] Warm layers for evening
- [ ] Wellies or waterproof shoes
- [ ] Non-slip socks
- [ ] Swimming nappies and UV suits

Entertainment & Development

- [ ] Favorite books (board books ideal)
- [ ] Soft toys and teething toys
- [ ] Stacking cups or rings
- [ ] Bubbles (always a winner!)
- [ ] Portable playmat
- [ ] Musical toys or rattle
- [ ] Ball (soft and large)

Safety & Mobility

- [ ] Portable travel gates or barriers
- [ ] Pushchair suitable for rough terrain
- [ ] Baby carrier or sling
- [ ] Reins or wrist straps for toddlers
- [ ] Socket covers and safety locks
- [ ] Corner guards for sharp table edges

Optional Extras

- [ ] Portable baby swing or bouncer
- [ ] Travel potty
- [ ] UV tent or sun shelter
- [ ] Paddling pool (small, inflatable)
- [ ] Sand toys for beach camping

Young Children (4-8 Years)

Sleep & Comfort

- [ ] Child-sized sleeping bag

- [ ] Favorite teddy or comfort item
- [ ] Small pillow or pillowcase from home
- [ ] Pajamas and dressing gown
- [ ] Slippers or camp shoes
- [ ] Eye mask if sensitive to early morning light

Clothing

- [ ] Clothes for each day plus 2 spare sets
- [ ] Waterproof jacket and trousers
- [ ] Warm fleece or hoodie
- [ ] Sun hat and sunglasses
- [ ] Sturdy walking shoes/boots
- [ ] Wellies
- [ ] Swimming costume and towel
- [ ] Underwear and socks (extras essential)

Personal Care

- [ ] Child toothbrush and toothpaste
- [ ] Hair brush and hair ties
- [ ] Child-friendly shampoo
- [ ] Any special skincare products
- [ ] Tissues and handkerchiefs

Entertainment & Learning

- [ ] Activity books and coloring books
- [ ] Crayons, pencils, and felt tips
- [ ] Playing cards or simple card games
- [ ] Small board games or travel games
- [ ] Nature identification books
- [ ] Magnifying glass
- [ ] Collection bags for treasures
- [ ] Kite (if appropriate for location)
- [ ] Ball games equipment
- [ ] Skipping rope
- [ ] Bubbles and bubble wands

Technology (If Allowed)

- [ ] Tablet with downloaded content
- [ ] Headphones (child-safe volume)
- [ ] Portable chargers

Safety Equipment

- [ ] High-vis vest or bright clothing
- [ ] Whistle on lanyard
- [ ] ID bracelet with parent contact details
- [ ] Child-specific first aid items

Optional Adventure Gear

- [ ] Child-sized backpack for day trips
- [ ] Water bottle with name label
- [ ] Disposable camera
- [ ] Binoculars (child-friendly)
- [ ] Head torch with red light option
- [ ] Nature journal and pencil

Older Children (9-12 Years)

Personal Responsibility Items

- [ ] Their own packing list (teach them to pack!)
- [ ] Personal toiletry bag with essentials
- [ ] Own water bottle and snacks
- [ ] Pocket money for treats
- [ ] Small backpack for independence

Clothing & Gear

- [ ] Weather-appropriate clothing layers
- [ ] Good quality waterproofs
- [ ] Proper hiking boots (broken in)
- [ ] Hat and gloves for cool weather
- [ ] Multiple pairs of socks and underwear
- [ ] Quick-dry towels
- [ ] Swimming gear

Adventure Equipment

- [ ] Child-appropriate multi-tool or knife (with supervision rules)
- [ ] Compass and basic map
- [ ] Whistle and emergency procedures card
- [ ] Head torch with spare batteries
- [ ] Small first aid kit (teach basic use)
- [ ] Binoculars

☐ Camera (disposable or old digital)

Entertainment & Education

☐ Books appropriate to reading level
☐ Journal or diary for trip memories
☐ Art supplies for nature sketching
☐ Nature identification guides
☐ Star chart for night sky viewing
☐ Geocaching app and treasure hunt ideas
☐ Craft supplies for rainy days

Technology

☐ Tablet/e-reader with offline content
☐ Portable speaker (consider campsite rules)
☐ Power bank and charging cables
☐ Games or apps for educational fun

Independence Building

☐ Own tent space organization system
☐ Responsibility for specific family camping tasks
☐ Emergency contact information memorized
☐ Basic camping skills checklist

Teenagers (13+ Years)

Personal Essentials

☐ Let them pack their own bags (with guidance)
☐ Personal hygiene products
☐ Any required medications
☐ Contact lens supplies if needed
☐ Feminine hygiene products

Technology & Communication

☐ Smartphone with camping apps
☐ Portable charger and cables
☐ Bluetooth speaker (respectful use)
☐ Camera for social media memories
☐ Offline entertainment (downloaded music, books)

Clothing for Independence

- [ ] Weather-appropriate gear they've chosen
- [ ] Comfortable hiking/walking shoes
- [ ] Layering system they understand
- [ ] Swimming gear and UV protection
- [ ] Evening wear for campsite social areas

Adventure & Responsibility

- [ ] Their own small rucksack
- [ ] Water bottle and healthy snacks
- [ ] Map and compass skills
- [ ] Basic first aid knowledge
- [ ] Emergency whistle and procedures
- [ ] Pocket knife (with safety training)
- [ ] Head torch and spare batteries

Entertainment & Social

- [ ] Books, magazines, or e-readers
- [ ] Art supplies or hobby materials
- [ ] Musical instrument (if portable)
- [ ] Games to play with family or friends
- [ ] Journal for reflection and memories

Life Skills Development

- [ ] Responsibility for cooking one meal
- [ ] Tent setup and maintenance tasks
- [ ] Navigation and planning involvement
- [ ] Weather monitoring responsibilities
- [ ] Environmental awareness checklist

Seasonal Considerations

Spring Camping (March-May)

- [ ] Extra layers for temperature changes
- [ ] Waterproof everything
- [ ] Warm hats and gloves
- [ ] Antihistamine for hay fever
- [ ] Wellington boots for muddy conditions

Summer Camping (June-August)

- [ ] High SPF sun cream and after-sun
- [ ] Lots of water containers
- [ ] Sun hats and UV clothing
- [ ] Insect repellent and bite relief
- [ ] Light, breathable clothing
- [ ] Portable shade or umbrellas

Autumn Camping (September-November)

- [ ] Warm sleeping gear
- [ ] Waterproof outer layers
- [ ] Hand warmers and toe warmers
- [ ] Extra batteries (cold drains them faster)
- [ ] Thermos flasks for warm drinks

Winter Camping (December-February)

- [ ] 4-season sleeping bags
- [ ] Insulated sleeping mats
- [ ] Thermal underwear layers
- [ ] Ice scraper and snow brush
- [ ] Emergency heating options
- [ ] High-calorie foods

Memory-Making Extras

Documentation & Memories

- [ ] Camera for family photos
- [ ] Notebook for trip journaling
- [ ] Materials for leaf/flower pressing
- [ ] Scrapbook supplies for later

Comfort Items

- [ ] Camping chairs for relaxation
- [ ] String lights for ambiance (battery-powered)
- [ ] Outdoor games for family time
- [ ] Musical instruments for campfire songs

Special Considerations

- ☐ Extra supplies for wet weather
- ☐ Backup entertainment for confined spaces
- ☐ Comfort foods for homesick moments
- ☐ Special treats for celebration

Remember: This list looks extensive, but not everything is needed for every trip. Start with the essentials and add items based on your family's specific needs, the season, and the type of camping you're doing. The goal is preparation without overpacking!

Pro Tip: Create a family camping box that stays packed year-round with non-perishable essentials. This makes trip preparation much quicker and ensures you never forget the basics.

Appendix B: Campfire Cooking Recipes for Families

Safety First: Essential Campfire Cooking Guidelines

Before diving into delicious recipes, remember these crucial safety points when cooking with children around campfires:

- Always supervise children near open flames
- Keep a bucket of water or sand nearby for emergencies
- Use long-handled utensils and heat-resistant gloves
- Create a designated "safe zone" at least 3 feet from the fire for children
- Never leave a fire unattended, even for a moment
- Check campsite fire regulations and restrictions before lighting

Equipment Essentials for Family Campfire Cooking

Must-Have Items:

- Cast iron or heavy-bottomed camping pots
- Long-handled spoons and spatulas
- Heat-resistant gloves
- Aluminum foil (lots of it!)
- Camping grill grate
- Sharp knife and cutting board
- Can opener and bottle opener
- Plates, bowls, and utensils for everyone

Nice-to-Have Extras:

- Pie iron for toasted sandwiches
- Dutch oven with legs
- Camping tripod for hanging pots
- Mesh bag for washing up in streams

Breakfast Adventures

1. Sunrise Breakfast Burritos

Prep: 15 minutes | Cook: 10 minutes | Serves: 4-6

Ingredients:

- 8 large flour tortillas
- 12 eggs, scrambled
- 2 cups grated cheese
- 1 tin black beans, drained
- 1 jar salsa
- 1 avocado, diced
- Aluminum foil

Method:

1. Scramble eggs in a large camping pan over medium coals
2. Warm tortillas by the fire (kids love this job!)
3. Let each family member build their own burrito with preferred fillings
4. Wrap tightly in foil and warm by the fire for 2-3 minutes
5. Unwrap carefully - contents will be hot!

Kid-Friendly Tips: Let little ones help crack eggs (expect some shell!) and older children can manage their own tortilla assembly.

2. Campfire French Toast

Prep: 10 minutes | Cook: 15 minutes | Serves: 4-6

Ingredients:

- 8 thick slices bread
- 4 eggs
- 1/2 cup milk
- 2 tbsp sugar
- 1 tsp vanilla extract
- Pinch of cinnamon
- Butter for frying
- Maple syrup and fresh berries

Method:

1. Whisk eggs, milk, sugar, vanilla, and cinnamon in a shallow bowl
2. Heat butter in a large camping pan
3. Dip bread slices in egg mixture, ensuring both sides are coated

4. Cook 2-3 minutes each side until golden brown

5. Serve immediately with syrup and berries

Parent Hack: Pre-mix the egg mixture at home and transport in a sealed container to save morning prep time.

Lunch Favourites

3. Hobo Packets (Personalised Meals)

Prep: 20 minutes | Cook: 25 minutes | Serves: 4-6

Basic Ingredients (per packet):

- 150g diced potatoes
- 100g protein (chicken, sausage, or halloumi)
- Handful of vegetables (carrots, onions, peppers)
- Knob of butter
- Salt, pepper, and herbs
- Heavy-duty aluminum foil

Method:

1. Give each family member their own large sheet of foil
2. Let them choose their preferred ingredients
3. Place ingredients in center of foil, add seasonings and butter
4. Fold foil into secure packets (adults should double-check seals)
5. Place on hot coals for 20-25 minutes, turning once
6. Open carefully with tongs - steam will be very hot!

Age Adaptations:

- **2-5 years:** Pre-cut all ingredients, let them choose combinations
- **6-12 years:** Can help with chopping soft vegetables with supervision
- **13+ years:** Can prepare entire packets independently

4. Campfire Grilled Cheese & Tomato Soup

Prep: 10 minutes | Cook: 20 minutes | Serves: 4-6

For Grilled Cheese:

- 8 slices bread
- Butter
- Cheese slices
- Cast iron pan or pie iron

For Tomato Soup:

- 2 tins chopped tomatoes
- 2 cups vegetable stock
- 1 onion, diced
- 2 cloves garlic
- 1 tbsp olive oil
- Salt, pepper, and basil

Method:

1. Heat olive oil in Dutch oven, sauté onion and garlic
2. Add tomatoes and stock, simmer 15 minutes
3. Meanwhile, butter bread and assemble sandwiches
4. Cook sandwiches in hot pan, 2-3 minutes each side
5. Blend soup with camp blender or leave chunky
6. Serve together for the ultimate comfort meal

Dinner Delights

5. Campfire Chili with Cornbread

Prep: 15 minutes | Cook: 45 minutes | Serves: 6-8

For Chili:

- 500g mince beef or turkey
- 2 tins kidney beans
- 2 tins chopped tomatoes
- 1 onion, diced
- 2 peppers, diced
- 2 tbsp chili powder (adjust for family taste)
- 1 tbsp cumin
- Salt and pepper

For Easy Cornbread:

- 2 boxes cornbread mix
- Ingredients as specified on box
- Dutch oven with lid

Method:

1. Brown mince in Dutch oven over hot coals
2. Add vegetables, cook 5 minutes
3. Add tomatoes, beans, and spices
4. Simmer 30 minutes, stirring occasionally
5. Meanwhile, prepare cornbread batter according to package
6. Pour into greased Dutch oven, cover with lid
7. Place on coals with more coals on lid for 25 minutes

Serving Suggestion: Top with grated cheese, sour cream, and chopped spring onions. Perfect for feeding hungry families!

6. Foil-Packet Fish with Vegetables

Prep: 15 minutes | Cook: 20 minutes | Serves: 4

Ingredients:

- 4 fish fillets (cod, salmon, or trout)
- 2 courgettes, sliced
- 1 red onion, sliced
- 2 lemons, sliced
- 4 tbsp olive oil
- Fresh herbs (dill, parsley, or thyme)
- Salt and pepper

Method:

1. Create 4 large foil sheets, brush with olive oil
2. Place fish fillet in center of each sheet
3. Top with vegetables and lemon slices
4. Drizzle with olive oil, season well
5. Seal packets tightly

6. Cook on medium coals for 15-20 minutes

Kid Appeal: Let children help arrange vegetables and herbs - they're more likely to eat what they've helped prepare!

Sweet Treats & Desserts

7. Classic S'mores (with Variations)

Prep: 5 minutes | Cook: 5 minutes | Serves: As many as you like!

Traditional S'mores:

- Graham crackers (or digestive biscuits)
- Marshmallows
- Milk chocolate bars

Gourmet Variations:

- **Peanut Butter Cup:** Use peanut butter cups instead of plain chocolate
- **Strawberry:** Add fresh strawberry slices
- **Cookie Dough:** Use cookies instead of crackers
- **Adult Version:** Dark chocolate with a sprinkle of sea salt

Method:

1. Roast marshmallows over glowing coals (not flames!)
2. Sandwich between crackers with chocolate
3. Press gently and wait for chocolate to melt
4. Enjoy the delicious mess!

Toasting Tips for Kids:

- Use long roasting forks or clean sticks
- Golden brown is perfect - burnt tastes bitter
- Have wet wipes ready!

8. Campfire Baked Apples

Prep: 10 minutes | Cook: 30 minutes | Serves: 4-6

Ingredients:

- 6 large cooking apples

- 6 tbsp brown sugar
- 3 tbsp butter
- 1 tsp cinnamon
- 1/2 cup chopped nuts or dried fruit
- Aluminum foil

Method:

1. Core apples, leaving bottom intact
2. Mix sugar, butter, cinnamon, and nuts
3. Stuff mixture into apple centers
4. Wrap each apple in foil
5. Nestle in hot coals for 25-30 minutes
6. Serve with vanilla ice cream if available

Tip: These can cook while you're eating dinner - perfect timing for dessert!

9. Campfire Banana Boats

Prep: 10 minutes | Cook: 10 minutes | Serves: 4-6

Ingredients:

- 6 bananas (slightly green work best)
- Mini marshmallows
- Chocolate chips
- Crushed biscuits
- Aluminum foil

Method:

1. Make a deep slit along length of banana (keep peel on)
2. Stuff with marshmallows and chocolate chips
3. Wrap in foil
4. Place on warm coals for 8-10 minutes
5. Open carefully and eat with a spoon

Kid-Friendly: Perfect for little hands to prepare, and eating is half the fun!

Drinks & Beverages

10. Campfire Hot Chocolate

Prep: 5 minutes | Cook: 10 minutes | Serves: 4-6

Ingredients:

- 4 cups whole milk
- 100g dark chocolate, chopped
- 2 tbsp sugar (optional)
- Marshmallows for topping
- Pinch of cinnamon

Method:

1. Heat milk in heavy pot over medium coals
2. Add chocolate and whisk until melted
3. Add sugar if desired
4. Serve in camping mugs topped with marshmallows

Adult Addition: Add a splash of rum or Bailey's to grown-up mugs after kids are served!

11. Fresh Fruit Camping Sangria (Non-Alcoholic)

Prep: 15 minutes | Chill: 2 hours | Serves: 6-8

Ingredients:

- 4 cups apple juice
- 2 cups sparkling water
- 1 apple, diced
- 1 orange, sliced
- 1 cup grapes, halved
- 1 cup strawberries, sliced
- Fresh mint leaves
- Ice

Method:

1. Combine all ingredients in large camping pitcher
2. Chill in cool box for at least 2 hours
3. Serve over ice in camping cups

4. Perfect for hot summer days!

One-Pot Wonders for Easy Cleanup

12. Campfire Pasta Bake

Prep: 15 minutes | Cook: 25 minutes | Serves: 6-8

Ingredients:

- 500g pasta shapes
- 2 jars pasta sauce
- 2 cups grated mozzarella
- 1 cup grated parmesan
- 500g cooked sausage or chicken, diced
- 2 cups water
- Dutch oven

Method:

1. Combine uncooked pasta, sauce, meat, and water in Dutch oven
2. Cover and cook on coals for 20 minutes, stirring occasionally
3. Top with cheeses, cover again
4. Cook 5 more minutes until cheese melts
5. Let stand 5 minutes before serving

Time-Saver: Pre-cook meat at home and store in cool box.

13. Hearty Camping Stew

Prep: 20 minutes | Cook: 1 hour | Serves: 8-10

Ingredients:

- 1kg stewing beef, cubed
- 4 potatoes, chunked
- 4 carrots, sliced
- 2 onions, diced
- 2 tbsp tomato purée
- 4 cups beef stock
- 2 bay leaves

- Salt, pepper, and thyme

Method:

1. Brown beef in Dutch oven
2. Add onions, cook until soft
3. Add remaining ingredients
4. Cover and simmer 45 minutes to 1 hour
5. Check occasionally, add water if needed

Perfect For: Rainy days when everyone needs warming up!

Cooking Tips for Different Ages

Ages 2-5 Years

- **Safe Jobs:** Washing vegetables, stirring (with help), arranging toppings
- **Equipment:** Child-safe plastic knives for soft foods
- **Special Considerations:** Keep meals simple, familiar flavors work best

Ages 6-12 Years

- **Safe Jobs:** Chopping soft vegetables, measuring ingredients, tending (not lighting) fire
- **Equipment:** Real knives with close supervision, long-handled utensils
- **Learning Opportunities:** Basic fire safety, food hygiene, following recipes

Ages 13+ Years

- **Responsibilities:** Planning meals, full food preparation, fire management
- **Skills Development:** Advanced cooking techniques, camp kitchen organization
- **Independence:** Can handle their own cooking projects

Emergency Meal Solutions

When the Fire Won't Light

- **Cold Options:** Wraps, sandwiches, pasta salads prepared at home
- **Camping Stove Backup:** Quick pasta, tinned soup, jacket potatoes
- **No-Cook Treats:** Trail mix, fresh fruit, cheese and crackers

When It's Pouring Rain

- **Tarp Cooking:** Set up cooking area under large tarp
- **Quick Options:** Anything that cooks in 15 minutes or less
- **Comfort Food:** Hot soup, grilled cheese, hot chocolate

Dietary Requirements

- **Vegetarian:** Replace meat with halloumi, extra vegetables, or plant proteins
- **Gluten-Free:** Use GF bread, pasta, and check all packaged ingredients
- **Allergies:** Always pack safe alternatives and check campsite shop options

---

Campfire Cooking Games & Activities

While Food Cooks

- **Story Chain:** Each person adds one sentence to a group story
- **20 Questions:** Classic camping game that never gets old
- **Shadow Puppets:** Use firelight to create entertainment
- **Gratitude Circle:** Share best parts of the day

Teaching Moments

- **Fire Science:** Explain how different woods burn differently
- **Nutrition Talk:** Discuss why we need different food groups
- **Local History:** Research what people ate in the area historically
- **Environmental Awareness:** Discuss Leave No Trace principles

---

Shopping & Preparation Lists

Pre-Trip Shopping

Pantry Staples:

- Salt, pepper, basic herbs and spices
- Olive oil in small container
- Aluminum foil (heavy-duty)
- Matches in waterproof container

Fresh Items (Buy Just Before Trip):

- Meat and fish

- Fresh vegetables and fruits

- Dairy products

- Bread

Don't Forget:

- Cool box ice packs

- Food storage containers

- Washing up liquid and sponges

- Tea towels and kitchen roll

Home Preparation Ideas

- Pre-chop vegetables and store in containers

- Make spice mixes in small containers

- Freeze meat in meal-sized portions

- Prepare marinades in advance

Remember, campfire cooking is about more than just food - it's about creating memories, teaching life skills, and bringing families together around the ancient ritual of sharing meals by the fire. Don't worry if things don't go perfectly; the best camping stories often come from the meals that went slightly wrong!

Final Safety Reminder: Always ensure your fire is completely extinguished before leaving it unattended or going to sleep. Pour water over the ashes, stir, and pour more water. The ashes should be cold to the touch.

Appendix D: Emergency Contacts and Safety Information

Essential Emergency Numbers

National Emergency Services

- **999** - Police, Fire, Ambulance, Coastguard (free from any phone)
- **112** - European emergency number (works on mobile phones even without signal to your network)
- **101** - Non-emergency police (for reporting crimes that don't require immediate response)
- **111** - NHS non-emergency medical advice (24/7 health helpline)

Specialized Emergency Services

- **Coastguard (Maritime emergencies)**: 999 or VHF Channel 16
- **Mountain Rescue**: 999 (ask for Police, then Mountain Rescue)
- **Cave Rescue**: 999 (ask for Police, then Cave Rescue)
- **RNLI Lifeboat Service**: 999 (ask for Coastguard)

Regional Emergency Contacts

England

NHS Direct: 111 **Environment Agency Floodline**: 0345 988 1188 **Public Health England**: 0344 225 4524

Wales

NHS Direct Wales: 0845 4647 **Natural Resources Wales**: 0300 065 3000 **Welsh Ambulance Service**: 999

Scotland

NHS 24: 111 **Scottish Environment Protection Agency**: 0800 80 70 60 **Police Scotland non-emergency**: 101

Northern Ireland

Health and Social Care: 028 9536 3220 **Northern Ireland Environment Agency**: 0800 80 70 60

Poison Control and Medical Emergencies

National Poisons Information Service

- **Telephone**: 0344 892 0111 (for healthcare professionals)
- **Public advice**: Contact 111 or 999 for poisoning emergencies

Common Camping-Related Poisoning Risks

- **Plant poisoning** (berries, mushrooms, leaves)
- **Carbon monoxide** (faulty camping stoves, heaters)
- **Cleaning products** and camping chemicals
- **Insect bites and stings**

Immediate Actions for Poisoning:

1. Call 999 if the person is unconscious, having difficulty breathing, or having seizures
2. Call 111 for advice if conscious but showing symptoms
3. Keep the substance container or take a photo of the plant
4. Do NOT induce vomiting unless specifically told to do so

Weather Emergency Services

Met Office Weather Warnings

- **Website**: metoffice.gov.uk
- **Weather warnings app**: Download for real-time alerts
- **Severe weather helpline**: 0370 900 0100

Flood Warnings

- **Environment Agency Floodline**: 0345 988 1188
- **Flood warnings direct**: Sign up at gov.uk/sign-up-for-flood-warnings
- **Scottish Flood Warning**: floodlinescotland.org.uk (0345 988 1188)
- **Welsh Flood Warning**: 0345 988 1188

Lost Child Protocol

Immediate Actions (First 10 Minutes)

1. **Alert other family members** - assign search areas
2. **Check obvious places first**:
   - Toilets and shower blocks
   - Play areas and adventure zones
   - Water features (priority check)
   - Other families' pitches nearby
3. **Inform campsite staff immediately**
4. **Ask other campers** to join the search

5. **Take photos** of the search area with your phone

If Child Not Found After 10 Minutes

1. **Call 999 immediately**

2. **Contact campsite management** to lock down exits

3. **Provide clear description**:
   - Age, height, hair color, clothing
   - Any medical conditions or medications
   - Recent photo on your phone

4. **Designate one person** to stay at your pitch in case child returns

5. **Expand search** to surrounding areas with police guidance

Prevention Strategies

- Use **matching bright t-shirts** for family outings
- **Wristbands with contact details** for children under 8
- **Establish meeting points** at each new location
- **Practice "stranger danger"** but also teach children to find "safe adults" (families with children, shop workers in uniform)
- **Take daily photos** of children in their outfits

Medical Emergency Action Plan

Severe Allergic Reactions (Anaphylaxis)

Call 999 immediately if:

- Difficulty breathing or wheezing
- Swelling of face, lips, or throat
- Rapid pulse and dizziness
- Widespread rash or hives
- Severe nausea or vomiting

Immediate actions:

1. Call 999
2. Use EpiPen if prescribed (inject into outer thigh)
3. Help person lie flat with legs raised (unless breathing difficulties)
4. Loosen tight clothing
5. Be prepared to perform CPR

Burns and Scalds

For serious burns (large area, deep, or on face/hands):

1. Call 999
2. Cool burn with cold running water for 20 minutes
3. Remove rings/tight items before swelling
4. Cover with cling film or clean cloth
5. Do NOT use ice, butter, or adhesive bandages

Cuts and Bleeding

For severe bleeding:

1. Call 999 if bleeding won't stop or is spurting
2. Apply direct pressure with clean cloth
3. Raise injured area above heart level if possible
4. Do NOT remove objects embedded in wounds
5. Treat for shock if person becomes pale and cold

Head Injuries

Call 999 if person has:

- Lost consciousness (even briefly)
- Severe headache or dizziness
- Nausea or vomiting
- Confusion or memory loss
- Clear fluid from ears or nose
- Different sized pupils

Natural Hazards and Wildlife

Coastal Hazards

Coastguard: 999

- **Rip currents**: Swim parallel to shore, then toward beach
- **Cut off by tide**: Stay calm, call for help, climb to highest point
- **Cliff falls**: Never go to cliff edges to help; call 999

River and Lake Safety

- **Cold water shock**: Get out immediately, warm gradually
- **Swift water rescue**: Throw rope or flotation device; don't enter water
- **Hypothermia**: Remove from cold, warm slowly, seek medical help

Wildlife Encounters

Most UK wildlife is harmless, but be aware of:

- **Adders** (only venomous UK snake): Keep calm, back away slowly, seek medical attention for bites
- **Wasps/bees**: Remove stinger, apply cold compress, watch for allergic reactions
- **Ticks**: Remove with tweezers, clean area, watch for spreading rash over following days
- **Wild animals**: Never feed or approach; secure food storage

Technology and Communication

Mobile Phone Considerations

- **Download offline maps** before traveling to remote areas
- **Carry portable chargers** and keep phones above 20% battery
- **Emergency SOS features**: Most smartphones have emergency features that work even with poor signal
- **What3Words app**: Helps emergency services find your exact location using three-word combinations

Communication When Mobile Signal Is Poor

- **Move to higher ground** for better signal
- **Try different networks** (emergency calls can use any available network)
- **Landline phones**: Ask at campsite reception or local businesses
- **Satellite communicators**: Consider for very remote camping

Campsite-Specific Emergency Information

Upon Arrival at Any Campsite

Always locate and note:

- Nearest hospital with A&E department
- Local GP surgery or walk-in centre
- Campsite manager contact details
- Water shut-off valves and electrical panels

- Fire assembly points
- Nearest pharmacy
- Local police station

Fire Safety on Campsites

In case of fire:

1. **Ensure everyone is out** of tent/caravan
2. **Alert neighboring campers**
3. **Call 999**
4. **Report to campsite reception**
5. **Move to assembly point**
6. **Never re-enter** burning accommodation

Fire prevention:

- Check all gas connections regularly
- Keep fire extinguisher/fire blanket accessible
- Clear escape routes
- No candles in tents
- Proper disposal of cigarettes and barbecue ashes

Mental Health and Emotional Support

Crisis Support Services

- **Samaritans**: 116 123 (free, 24/7, confidential)
- **Crisis Text Line**: Text HOME to 85258
- **CALM (Campaign Against Living Miserably)**: 0800 58 58 58
- **Childline**: 0800 1111 (for children and young people)

Managing Camping Stress and Anxiety

For children experiencing camping anxiety:

- Maintain familiar routines where possible
- Pack comfort items (favorite toy, blanket)
- Have backup accommodation plans
- Stay calm and reassuring yourself

For adults feeling overwhelmed:

- Don't try to be the "perfect" camping family
- Ask for help from other campers
- Have an exit strategy if needed
- Remember that some trips don't go as planned, and that's okay

Insurance and Legal Considerations

Travel Insurance for UK Camping

- **Check existing policies**: Home, car, and health insurance may provide some coverage
- **Camping-specific coverage**: Equipment theft, cancellation due to weather
- **Activity coverage**: Ensure adventurous activities are covered
- **Emergency evacuation**: Particularly important for remote locations

Legal Responsibilities

- **Supervision of children**: Parents remain legally responsible for children's actions
- **Damage to property**: You may be liable for damage caused by your family
- **Environmental protection**: Follow Leave No Trace principles
- **Privacy and photography**: Be mindful when taking photos that include other families

Creating Your Personal Emergency Plan

Before You Travel

1. **Medical information sheet** for each family member:
   - Allergies and medications
   - Medical conditions
   - Emergency contacts
   - Doctor's contact details
   - Insurance information

2. **Share your plans** with someone at home:
   - Where you're staying (exact address/GPS coordinates)
   - Duration of stay
   - Expected return date
   - Contact schedule

3. **Prepare emergency cash**:
   - Keep some cash separate from cards
   - Know locations of nearest ATMs

- Have coins for phone boxes (rare but useful backup)

Emergency Kit for Every Camping Trip

Basic first aid supplies:

- Plasters, bandages, antiseptic wipes
- Thermometer, pain relief medication
- Any prescription medications (plus spares)
- Emergency contact cards
- Whistle for each family member
- Torch with extra batteries
- Emergency blanket (space blanket)

Communication tools:

- Fully charged mobile phones
- Portable charger/power bank
- Important phone numbers written down
- Map of local area (paper backup)

Remember: Stay Calm, Act Quickly, Ask for Help

The most important advice in any emergency is to stay as calm as possible, act quickly when needed, and never hesitate to ask for help. Fellow campers, campsite staff, and emergency services are there to help, and most camping emergencies can be resolved quickly with the right response.

Camping should be fun and adventurous, but being prepared for emergencies ensures that your family can handle whatever comes your way and get back to making those precious memories together.

Keep this information easily accessible during your camping trips. Consider taking photos of relevant sections with your phone for quick reference.

Appendix C: Rainy Day Activities and Games

When the British weather shows its true colours, these activities will keep your family entertained and create some of your most treasured camping memories.

The Camping Parent's Rainy Day Mindset

Before diving into activities, remember that rainy days often become the stories your children tell for years to come. The key is preparation and attitude. Pack these activities before you leave home, and when the rain starts, approach it as an adventure rather than a setback.

Golden Rules for Rainy Day Success:

- Stay dry but don't hide away completely
- Rotate activities every 30-45 minutes to maintain interest
- Involve all ages with adaptable games
- Use the rain as part of the fun when safe to do so
- Have backup plans for your backup plans

Indoor Tent & Caravan Activities

Storytelling Adventures (All Ages)

Campfire Stories Without the Fire Create atmospheric storytelling sessions using a torch as your "campfire." Each family member contributes one sentence to build collaborative stories.

Age Adaptations:

- **0-3 years:** Simple sound effect stories with animal noises
- **4-8 years:** Adventure tales with familiar characters
- **9-12 years:** Mystery stories with plot twists
- **13+ years:** Comedy improv or dramatic storytelling

Story Starter Prompts:

- "The tent that could fly discovered its power when..."
- "Deep in the British countryside, three children found a map that..."
- "When the rain started talking, it said..."

Card and Board Games by Age

Ages 0-3: Simple Recognition Games

- **Colour Hunt:** Using picture cards, spot colours around your tent

- **Animal Sounds Bingo:** Match picture cards to sounds you make
- **Stack and Tumble:** Build soft block towers (pack foam blocks)

Ages 4-8: Engaging Strategy Games

- **Travel Scrabble or Boggle:** Word building in compact form
- **Uno or Skip-Bo:** Fast-paced card games
- **Magnetic Travel Chess/Checkers:** Won't slide around in the tent
- **I Spy Journals:** Create illustrated lists of everything spotted

Ages 9-12: Complex Thinking Games

- **Settlers of Catan (Travel Edition):** Strategy and negotiation
- **Ticket to Ride: First Journey:** Geography meets strategy
- **Phase 10:** Rummy-style card game with progressive challenges
- **Travel Trivia:** Create UK-specific questions about your journey

Ages 13+: Social and Strategic Games

- **Exploding Kittens:** Quick, humorous card game
- **Codenames Duet:** Two-player word association
- **Pandemic:** Cooperative world-saving strategy
- **Cards Against Humanity Family Edition:** Age-appropriate humor

Creative Activities

Art Projects Using Natural Materials

- **Leaf Pressing:** Collect leaves before rain, press between heavy books
- **Rain Painting:** Let raindrops create art on paper (briefly outside tent)
- **Nature Journals:** Draw and document wildlife spotted from tent entrance
- **Camping Memory Books:** Collage daily adventures with tickets, photos, drawings

DIY Craft Supplies to Pack:

- Washable markers and crayons
- Small sketch pads or notebooks
- Glue sticks and child-safe scissors
- Washi tape for decorating
- Sticker collections
- Modelling clay in sealed containers

Covered Outdoor Activities

Under Gazebos or Shelter

Water Play Games (Using Rain Creatively)

- **Rain Catch Challenge:** Use different sized containers to catch raindrops
- **Puddle Science:** Measure rainfall, test floating objects
- **Rain Music:** Set up pots and pans to create rain orchestras
- **Weather Prediction Games:** Track weather patterns and make forecasts

Active Games in Covered Spaces

- **Camping Charades:** Act out camping activities, British wildlife, local landmarks
- **Twenty Questions:** Focus on camping gear, local attractions, British animals
- **Human Knots:** Physical puzzle game for older children
- **Dance Party:** Bring a portable speaker for tent discos

Educational Weather Activities

Weather Science Experiments

- **Rain Gauge Creation:** Measure daily rainfall using marked containers
- **Cloud Identification Charts:** Spot different cloud types and predict weather
- **Wind Direction Games:** Create simple wind vanes using sticks and paper
- **Temperature Tracking:** Monitor changes throughout the day

Geography Games

- **Map Adventures:** Plan future trips using OS maps
- **County Challenge:** Name counties, capitals, famous landmarks
- **Distance Guessing:** Estimate distances between campsites visited
- **Compass Skills:** Learn basic navigation (even indoors)

Age-Specific Rainy Day Schedules

Toddlers (0-3 Years) - 2 Hour Rainy Session

9:00-9:30: Quiet story time with picture books **9:30-10:00:** Sensory play with textured toys and soft blocks **10:00-10:15:** Snack break and brief outside observation of rain **10:15-10:45:** Simple singing games and nursery rhymes **10:45-11:00:** Naptime preparation or quiet cuddle time

Young Children (4-8 Years) - 3 Hour Schedule

9:00-9:45: Creative drawing project - camping adventure comic strips **9:45-10:30:** Card games or travel board games **10:30-10:45:** Active break - tent dancing or stretching **10:45-11:30:** Nature scavenger hunt (items visible from tent) **11:30-12:00:** Cooking preparation help or snack creation

Pre-teens (9-12 Years) - 4 Hour Schedule

9:00-10:00: Journal writing and trip documentation **10:00-11:00:** Strategy board games or complex card games **11:00-11:15:** Physical activity break **11:15-12:15:** Science experiments or weather tracking **12:15-1:00:** Lunch preparation and cooking activities

Teenagers (13+ Years) - Flexible Schedule

Morning: Photography project documenting rainy day camping **Mid-morning:** Reading time or podcast listening **Late morning:** Planning next day's activities using guidebooks and maps **Afternoon:** Creative writing, blogging, or social media content creation **Evening:** Movie night on tablet/laptop with downloaded content

Rainy Day Cooking Adventures

No-Cook Options Perfect for Wet Weather

Build-Your-Own Sandwich Bar Set up ingredients for creative sandwich making:

- Various breads and wraps
- Multiple protein options
- Fresh vegetables and spreads
- Let each family member create themed sandwiches

Trail Mix Creation Station Combine various ingredients for custom trail mixes:

- Nuts, dried fruits, chocolate chips
- Cereal pieces, pretzels, seeds
- Create family blend recipes to remember trips

Cold Pasta Salad Assembly Pre-cook pasta before the rain arrives:

- Add vegetables, cheese, dressing
- Each person customizes their portion
- Perfect for varying tastes and dietary needs

Simple Hot Options Using Camping Stoves

One-Pot Wonders

- **Camping Risotto:** Rice, stock, vegetables, cheese
- **Hearty Soup:** Canned base with added fresh ingredients
- **Pasta Bakes:** Pre-cook pasta, add sauce and cheese, heat through

Hot Drink Specialties

- **Camping Hot Chocolate:** Various toppings bar with marshmallows, cream, sprinkles
- **Herbal Tea Tasting:** Bring selection of caffeine-free options for children
- **Warm Fruit Drinks:** Heat fruit juices with spices

Technology-Enhanced Rainy Day Fun

Educational Apps and Games (When WiFi Available)

Geography and Nature Apps:

- **iNaturalist:** Identify plants and animals spotted around campsite
- **Star Walk:** Plan evening stargazing for when clouds clear
- **Weather Apps:** Track storm patterns and clearing predictions
- **Geocaching:** Plan treasure hunts for when weather improves

Creative Apps:

- **Stop Motion Studio:** Create camping adventure animations
- **Drawing Apps:** Digital art projects documenting trip
- **Music Creation Apps:** Compose camping theme songs
- **Photo Editing:** Enhance daily photos into travel albums

Offline Entertainment Options

Pre-Downloaded Content:

- **Audiobooks:** British authors, adventure stories, educational content
- **Podcasts:** Family-friendly shows, nature programs, comedy
- **Educational Videos:** Local history, wildlife documentaries
- **Movies:** Camping-themed films, British comedies, family favorites

Digital Games for Rainy Days:

- **Trivia Apps:** UK-specific questions about areas you're visiting
- **Word Games:** Crosswords, word searches, anagram challenges
- **Strategy Games:** Chess, checkers, puzzle games
- **Creative Apps:** Drawing, music, storytelling applications

Rainy Day Emergency Kit Essentials

Entertainment Supplies Checklist

Creative Materials:

- ☐ Sketchbooks and colored pencils
- ☐ Sticker books and activity books
- ☐ Playing cards and travel games
- ☐ Craft supplies in waterproof container
- ☐ Puzzles appropriate for tent space

Comfort Items:

- ☐ Extra blankets for cozy fort building
- ☐ Pillows for comfortable seating
- ☐ Favorite stuffed animals or comfort objects
- ☐ Special treats reserved for rainy days
- ☐ Hot water bottles for warmth

Practical Supplies:

- ☐ Battery-powered lanterns for adequate lighting
- ☐ Waterproof storage bags for keeping things dry
- ☐ Backup power banks for devices
- ☐ First aid supplies easily accessible
- ☐ Emergency contact information

Making Rainy Days Memorable

Photography Projects

Rainy Day Photo Challenges:

- Document tent life during storms
- Capture artistic shots of rain on tent fabric
- Take portraits of family members enjoying indoor activities
- Create time-lapse videos of weather patterns
- Photograph creative solutions to rainy day challenges

Memory Making Activities:

- Write family camping journals together
- Create collaborative photo albums

- Start camping tradition collections (pressed flowers, ticket stubs)
- Record video messages to future selves
- Document funny moments and quotes

Connection Building Exercises

Family Bonding Games:

- Share favorite memories from the trip so far
- Play "Would You Rather" with camping scenarios
- Create family camping rules and traditions
- Plan next year's camping adventures together
- Share stories from parents' childhood camping experiences

Learning Opportunities:

- Research local history and legends
- Practice new skills (card tricks, origami, basic knots)
- Learn about weather patterns and forecasting
- Study maps of areas you plan to visit
- Practice foreign language phrases for future travels

Regional Rainy Day Specialties

Lake District Rainy Day Activities

- **Fell Walking Planning:** Study routes and difficulty levels
- **Local Legend Research:** Investigate area folklore and stories
- **Wildlife Spotting:** Learn about native birds and animals
- **Photography Planning:** Scout locations for clear weather shots

Cornwall Coastal Activities

- **Tide Pool Research:** Plan low-tide explorations
- **Maritime History:** Study local shipwrecks and maritime heritage
- **Geological Learning:** Understand coastal formation and rock types
- **Surf Condition Monitoring:** Track weather for future surf lessons

Scottish Highland Preparations

- **Clan History Research:** Investigate family names and Scottish heritage
- **Highland Games Planning:** Learn about traditional Scottish sports

- **Gaelic Language Basics:** Learn simple phrases and pronunciation
- **Monster Mythology:** Research local legends and sighting locations

When the Sun Returns

Transition Activities

- **Gear Drying Station Setup:** Organize wet equipment efficiently
- **Outdoor Activity Planning:** Prioritize activities missed during rain
- **Energy Release Games:** Help children transition from indoor to outdoor play
- **Weather Appreciation:** Discuss how rain makes outdoor time more precious

Rainy Day Memory Preservation

- **Photo Organization:** Sort and caption rainy day photos
- **Story Recording:** Write down funny moments and quotes
- **Souvenir Creation:** Make something to remember the rainy day adventure
- **Thank You Notes:** Write appreciation notes for campsite staff who helped

Emergency Weather Protocols

Safety Considerations During Severe Weather

When to Stay Put:

- Heavy rain with lightning
- Strong winds that could affect tent stability
- Flooding warnings in the area
- Severe weather warnings issued by authorities

When to Seek Additional Shelter:

- Tent leaking significantly
- Family members feeling unwell due to dampness
- Equipment failure compromising safety
- Local emergency services recommendations

Emergency Contact Information:

- Campsite emergency numbers
- Local emergency services
- Weather warning hotlines

- Family emergency contacts

Health and Comfort During Extended Rainy Periods

Preventing Dampness Issues:

- Maintain good ventilation in tents and caravans
- Change into dry clothes regularly
- Use moisture-absorbing products if available
- Keep sleeping areas as dry as possible

Mood Management:

- Maintain regular meal and sleep schedules
- Ensure everyone gets some physical activity
- Practice gratitude exercises focusing on positive aspects
- Plan special treats or activities for mood lifting

Remember, rainy days often become the most talked-about parts of camping trips. Embrace the adventure, stay flexible, and focus on the unique bonding opportunities that only come when families are "stuck" together in a small space. These moments often create the strongest memories and the best family stories.

The key to successful rainy day camping is preparation, attitude, and remembering that every camping trip - regardless of weather - is an adventure worth celebrating.

Appendix E: UK Camping Associations and Resources

National Camping Organizations

The Camping and Caravanning Club

Website: campingandcaravanningclub.co.uk
Phone: 024 7647 5448
What they offer: Britain's oldest camping organization with over 100 sites nationwide, comprehensive insurance options, expert advice, and discounted stays. Their Red Pennant site awards guarantee quality standards. Membership includes monthly magazine, route planning service, and access to overseas sites.

Family benefits: Special children's entertainment programs, family rallies, and beginner camping courses. Their sites are specifically chosen for family-friendly facilities and safe environments.

The Caravan and Motorhome Club

Website: caravanclub.co.uk
Phone: 01342 326944
What they offer: Premium camping sites with excellent facilities, travel services, insurance, and breakdown cover. Their David Bellamy Conservation Awards recognize environmentally responsible sites.

Family benefits: Playground standards certification, family activity programs, and dedicated family areas on many sites.

Independent Holiday Parks Association (IHPA)

Website: ihpa.co.uk
What they offer: Represents over 300 independent family-run holiday parks across the UK. These smaller operators often provide more personalized service and unique local experiences.

Family benefits: Many IHPA members specialize in family holidays with creative children's activities and local area expertise.

Regional Tourism Boards and Resources

Visit England

Website: visitengland.com
Family camping section: Comprehensive database of quality-assessed campsites with detailed facility information and honest reviews.

Visit Wales

Website: visit.wales
Camping resources: Specialist outdoor adventure guidance and Welsh language cultural programs for

families.

Visit Scotland

Website: visitscotland.com
Family focus: Highland adventure planning, island camping guides, and Scottish heritage experiences.

Specialist Family Camping Resources

Cool Camping

Website: coolcamping.com
Specialty: Boutique and unique camping experiences, glamping options, and hidden gems perfect for adventurous families.

Pitchup.com

Website: pitchup.com
Features: Real-time availability, verified reviews from families, and instant booking. Excellent filtering options for family-specific needs.

UK Campsite Reviews

Website: ukcampsite.co.uk
Strength: Honest, detailed reviews from real camping families. Their forum is invaluable for getting answers to specific questions.

Safety and Training Organizations

Royal Society for the Prevention of Accidents (RoSPA)

Website: rospa.com
Camping safety resources: Free guides on campsite safety, water safety for families, and fire safety around camps.

Mountain Training

Website: mountain-training.org
Family courses: Family-oriented outdoor skills courses, navigation training, and age-appropriate adventure skills.

British Canoeing

Website: britishcanoeing.org.uk
Family programs: "Go Canoeing" family introduction courses and safe water activity guidance.

Environmental and Educational Resources

The National Trust

Website: nationaltrust.org.uk
Camping connections: Many NT properties have nearby family-friendly campsites. Their family membership includes activity guides and special events.

English Heritage

Website: english-heritage.org.uk
Family camping tie-ins: Castle-based camping experiences and educational programs that complement historical site visits.

Wildlife Trusts

Website: wildlifetrusts.org
Nature camping: Local wildlife watching guides, family nature activities, and conservation camping experiences.

Forest Holidays

Website: forestholidays.co.uk
Forest camping: Specialist woodland camping with ranger-led activities and forest adventure courses for children.

Weather and Planning Resources

Met Office

Website: metoffice.gov.uk
Camping weather: Detailed regional forecasts essential for camping trip planning. Their app provides hour-by-hour updates perfect for outdoor activities.

Environment Agency

Website: gov.uk/environment-agency
Flood warnings: Essential for riverside camping. Real-time flood warnings and river level information.

Ordnance Survey

Website: ordnancesurvey.co.uk
Family mapping: Their OS Maps app is invaluable for family walking and local area exploration. Includes family-friendly route suggestions.

Specialist Equipment and Advice

Go Outdoors

Website: gooutdoors.co.uk

Family expertise: Nationwide stores with family camping specialists. Regular family camping workshops and equipment advice.

Blacks

Website: blacks.co.uk

Family focus: Comprehensive family camping equipment range with knowledgeable staff and seasonal family camping events.

Millets

Website: millets.co.uk

Budget-friendly: Good value family camping equipment with practical advice for families starting their camping journey.

Online Communities and Forums

UK Camping and Caravanning Forums

Platform: Multiple active Facebook groups and dedicated forums

Value: Real-time advice from experienced family campers, site recommendations, and equipment reviews from parents.

Mumsnet Travel Forum

Website: mumsnet.com

Family focus: Practical advice from parents, honest campsite reviews, and solutions to common family camping challenges.

Family Camping Facebook Groups

- UK Family Camping
- Wild Camping with Kids UK
- Budget Family Camping UK

Emergency and Medical Resources

NHS 111

Phone: 111

Service: 24/7 medical advice. Essential contact for camping families, especially when camping in remote areas.

HM Coastguard

Phone: 999 (emergency) or VHF Channel 16

Coverage: Essential for coastal camping. Their RNLI partnership provides water safety education for families.

Mountain Rescue

Phone: 999 (ask for Mountain Rescue)
Coverage: Available across UK mountain and hill regions. Their prevention advice is valuable for families planning upland camping.

Accessibility Resources

Tourism for All

Website: tourismforall.org.uk
Focus: Detailed accessibility information for campsites and local attractions. Specialist advice for families with diverse access needs.

Disabled Ramblers Association

Website: disabledramblers.co.uk
Resources: Accessible walking routes and outdoor activity advice for families with disabled members.

Booking and Discount Resources

Camping Club Discounts

Many supermarket loyalty programs (Tesco Clubcard, Nectar) offer camping vouchers and discounts.

Youth Hostel Association (YHA)

Website: yha.org.uk
Family rooms: Budget-friendly accommodation alternative with many locations near excellent camping sites.

National Trust and English Heritage Family Memberships

Both offer significant discounts at associated campsites and include free entry to hundreds of family attractions.

Local Authority Resources

Local Council Tourism Departments

Most UK councils maintain comprehensive local camping information, including smaller municipal sites often overlooked by commercial directories.

Tourist Information Centres

Still invaluable for local knowledge, weather updates, and last-minute availability. Many offer free local activity guides specifically designed for families.

Seasonal and Weather-Specific Resources

UK Snow Sports

Website: snowsport.org
Winter camping: Specialist advice for families interested in winter camping and snow-based activities.

Beach Safety Information

RNLI Website: rnli.org
Essential for coastal camping: Tide times, beach safety flags, and family water safety education.

Remember to check websites and contact details before traveling, as these can change. Many organizations offer mobile apps that provide real-time updates and offline access to essential information - perfect for camping locations with limited connectivity.

Most of these resources offer free advice and information, though some membership organizations provide additional benefits for a small annual fee that often pays for itself through discounts and exclusive access.

Appendix F: Seasonal Activity Calendar

Your month-by-month guide to the best family camping activities across the UK

How to Use This Calendar

This calendar highlights the optimal activities and experiences available during each month of the year across different regions of the UK. Weather patterns, wildlife behaviour, local events, and seasonal attractions all influence when certain activities are at their peak. Use this guide to plan your camping trips around what matters most to your family.

Key Symbols:

- ☀ Peak season activity
- ★ Good time for activity
- 🌧 Weather-dependent
- ⬤ Suitable for toddlers (0-3 years)
- ⬤ Great for children (4-8 years)
- ⬤ Perfect for tweens (9-12 years)
- ⬤ Teen-friendly (13+ years)

JANUARY ❄

Cozy camping and winter wonders

Southwest England

- **Beach walking and storm watching** ☀ 🌧 (Cornwall & Devon coasts)
  - Ages: All ages with proper gear ⬤ ⬤ ⬤ ⬤
  - Best locations: Woolacombe, St. Ives, Weymouth
  - Pack: Waterproofs, warm layers, flask with hot chocolate
- **Winter wildlife spotting** ★ (Exmoor, Dartmoor)
  - Ages: 4+ years ⬤ ⬤ ⬤
  - Highlights: Red deer, winter birds, frost-covered landscapes
  - Equipment needed: Binoculars, field guides

Southeast England

- **Winter gardens exploration** ☀ (Kent, Sussex)

- Ages: All ages ● ● ● ●
- Featured: RHS Wisley winter borders, Leeds Castle grounds
- Activities: Snowdrop hunting, winter tree identification

Heart of England

- **Indoor attractions focus** ☀·
  - Ages: All ages ● ● ● ●
  - Highlights: Warwick Castle winter events, Cadbury World
  - Camping tip: Book sites with good indoor facilities

Northern England

- **Winter stargazing** ☀· (Lake District, Yorkshire Dales)
  - Ages: 8+ years ● ●
  - Best conditions: Clear, cold nights
  - Equipment: Star charts, red torch, warm blankets

Wales

- **Mountain railway adventures** ⭐ 🚂
  - Ages: All ages ● ● ● ●
  - Featured: Snowdon Mountain Railway, Ffestiniog Railway
  - Bonus: Spectacular winter mountain views

Scotland

- **Highland winter landscapes** ⭐ 🚂
  - Ages: 6+ years ● ● ●
  - Activities: Short winter walks, Highland visitor centres
  - Safety note: Experienced winter hikers only for mountain areas

---

FEBRUARY ❀

Early signs of spring

Southwest England

- **Lambing season begins** ☀· (Devon & Somerset farms)
  - Ages: Perfect for toddlers and young children ● ● ●
  - Farm visits: Pennywell Farm, Totnes Rare Breeds Farm

- Activities: Bottle feeding, meeting newborn animals
- **Surfing lessons** ⭐ 🐾 (Cornwall beaches)
  - Ages: 8+ years with wetsuit ● ●
  - Best beaches: Polzeath, Croyde, Woolacombe
  - Equipment: Full wetsuit essential

Southeast England

- **Snowdrop trails** ☀ (Sussex, Hampshire)
  - Ages: All ages ● ● ● ●
  - Prime locations: Wakehurst Place, Sheffield Park
  - Photography opportunity: Capture carpets of white flowers

Heart of England

- **Half-term indoor adventures** ☀
  - Ages: All ages ● ● ● ●
  - Featured: Think Tank Birmingham, National Space Centre
  - Camping strategy: Book early for half-term week

Wales

- **Castle exploration** ⭐ (All regions)
  - Ages: 4+ years ● ● ●
  - Highlights: Caerphilly Castle, Conwy Castle
  - Activity: Medieval themed treasure hunts

MARCH ●

Spring awakening

Southwest England

- **Puffin return** ☀ (Cornwall islands and cliffs)
  - Ages: 6+ years ● ● ●
  - Best viewing: RSPB Bempton Cliffs, Skomer Island
  - Equipment: Binoculars, camera with zoom
- **Daffodil season** ⭐ (Cornwall, Devon)
  - Ages: All ages ● ● ● ●
  - Activities: Flower photography, nature crafts

Southeast England

- **Spring garden visits** ☀· (All counties)
  - Ages: All ages ● ● ● ●
  - Featured: Kew Gardens, RHS Wisley
  - Activities: Nature scavenger hunts, garden sketching

Eastern England

- **Seal pupping** ★ (Norfolk coast)
  - Ages: 6+ years ● ● ●
  - Best spots: Blakeney Point, Horsey Beach
  - Important: Observe from distance, no dogs allowed

Wales

- **St. David's Day celebrations** ☀· (All Wales)
  - Ages: All ages ● ● ● ●
  - Activities: Welsh culture workshops, traditional music
  - Try: Welsh cakes around the campfire

APRIL ☀

Easter holidays and spring blooms

Southwest England

- **Easter egg hunts** ☀· (Devon & Cornwall attractions)
  - Ages: 0-12 years ● ● ●
  - Featured: National Trust properties, theme parks
  - Book ahead: Popular Easter weekend activities
- **Beach combing season begins** ★
  - Ages: All ages ● ● ● ●
  - Best beaches: Chesil Beach, Lyme Regis
  - Equipment: Collecting bags, identification guides

Southeast England

- **Bluebell woods** ☀· (All counties)
  - Ages: All ages ● ● ● ●

- Prime locations: Kew Gardens, Ashridge Estate
- Photography tip: Early morning for best light

Heart of England

- **Theme park season opens** ☀️
  - Ages: Height restrictions apply ⬛ ⬛ ⬛
  - Featured: Alton Towers, Thorpe Park
  - Strategy: Mid-week visits for smaller crowds

Northern England

- **Lake District walking season** ⭐ 🌧️
  - Ages: 4+ years ⬛ ⬛ ⬛
  - Easy walks: Tarn Hows, Buttermere
  - Essential: Waterproof gear, proper footwear

Wales

- **Coastal path walking** ⭐ (Pembrokeshire, Gower)
  - Ages: 6+ years ⬛ ⬛ ⬛
  - Highlights: Barafundle Bay, Rhossili Bay
  - Wildlife: Early puffin sightings

Scotland

- **Highland spring** ⭐ 🌧️
  - Ages: 8+ years ⬛ ⬛
  - Activities: Loch-side walks, Highland visitor centres
  - Bonus: Longer daylight hours begin

MAY 🦋

Perfect family camping weather

Southwest England

- **Beach season launches** ☀️ (All coastal areas)
  - Ages: All ages ⬛ ⬛ ⬛ ⬛
  - Activities: Sandcastle building, rock pooling
  - Water temperature: Still cold, wetsuits recommended

- **Eden Project outdoor activities** ☀ (Cornwall)
  - Ages: All ages 🧑 🧑 🧑 🧑
  - Special: Spring plant displays, outdoor concerts
  - Family tip: All-day tickets allow re-entry

Southeast England

- **Historic house gardens** ☀ (All counties)
  - Ages: All ages 🧑 🧑 🧑 🧑
  - Featured: Sissinghurst, Great Dixter
  - Activities: Garden trails, outdoor picnics

Heart of England

- **Outdoor adventure season** ☀ (Peak District, Cotswolds)
  - Ages: 4+ years 🧑 🧑 🧑
  - Activities: Hill walking, cycling, geocaching
  - Equipment: Comfortable walking boots, day packs

Eastern England

- **Norfolk Broads boating** ☀ (Norfolk, Suffolk)
  - Ages: All ages with life jackets 🧑 🧑 🧑 🧑
  - Options: Day boat hire, guided tours
  - Wildlife: Marsh harriers, kingfishers

Wales

- **Mountain walking season** ★ (Snowdonia, Brecon Beacons)
  - Ages: 8+ years for lower peaks 🧑 🧑
  - Easy options: Pen y Fan, Snowdon railway
  - Essential: Mountain weather awareness

Scotland

- **Edinburgh Festival season begins** ★
  - Ages: All ages depending on shows 🧑 🧑 🧑 🧑
  - Activities: Street performances, family shows
  - Accommodation: Book early for festival periods

JUNE ✹

Long days and perfect weather

Southwest England

- **Surfing peak season** ✹ (All Cornwall beaches)
  - Ages: 6+ years with lessons ⬤ ⬤ ⬤
  - Best beaches: Fistral, Watergate Bay
  - Family packages: Many surf schools offer family deals
- **Fossil hunting** ✹ (Jurassic Coast)
  - Ages: 4+ years ⬤ ⬤ ⬤
  - Best locations: Charmouth, Lyme Regis
  - Equipment: Collecting bags, safety helmets

Southeast England

- **Castle events season** ✹ (All counties)
  - Ages: All ages ⬤ ⬤ ⬤ ⬤
  - Featured: Warwick Castle, Leeds Castle
  - Activities: Medieval tournaments, falconry displays

Heart of England

- **Peak outdoor season** ✹ (All regions)
  - Ages: All ages ⬤ ⬤ ⬤ ⬤
  - Activities: Long hikes, mountain biking, outdoor festivals
  - Daylight: Up to 17 hours in northern areas

Eastern England

- **Seaside resort season** ✹ (Norfolk, Suffolk coasts)
  - Ages: All ages ⬤ ⬤ ⬤ ⬤
  - Featured: Great Yarmouth, Southwold
  - Activities: Beach games, pier entertainment

Northern England

- **Lake activities peak** ✹ (Lake District, Yorkshire Dales)
  - Ages: All ages ⬤ ⬤ ⬤ ⬤
  - Water sports: Kayaking, sailing, swimming

- Safety: Always wear life jackets

Wales

- **Festival season** ☀ (All regions)
  - Ages: Check individual events ● ● ● ●
  - Featured: Hay Festival, Royal Welsh Show
  - Camping: Festival campsites often available

Scotland

- **Highland Games season** ☀ (Highlands)
  - Ages: All ages ● ● ● ●
  - Activities: Caber tossing, Highland dancing
  - Cultural experience: Try traditional Scottish food

JULY 🏖

Peak summer holidays

Southwest England

- **Beach holiday peak** ☀ (All coastal areas)
  - Ages: All ages ● ● ● ●
  - Activities: Swimming, beach sports, coastal walks
  - Booking tip: Reserve early for school holiday period
- **Outdoor theatre** ★ (Devon, Cornwall)
  - Ages: 6+ years ● ● ●
  - Featured: Minack Theatre, outdoor Shakespeare
  - Pack: Cushions, blankets, warm layers for evening

Southeast England

- **Summer festivals** ☀ (All counties)
  - Ages: Family events suitable for all ● ● ● ●
  - Activities: Music festivals, food festivals
  - Facilities: Many offer family camping areas

Heart of England

- **Theme park peak** ☀ (All major parks)

- Ages: Varied by attraction ● ● ●
- Strategy: Arrive early, use fast-track passes
- Heat safety: Plenty of water, regular shade breaks

Eastern England

- **Norfolk coast prime time** ☀.
  - Ages: All ages ● ● ● ●
  - Activities: Crab fishing, seal watching tours
  - Equipment: Crabbing nets, buckets, bait

Northern England

- **Fell walking season** ☀. (Lake District, Yorkshire Dales)
  - Ages: 8+ years for higher fells ● ●
  - Popular routes: Helvellyn, Pen-y-ghent
  - Essential: OS maps, compass, emergency kit

Wales

- **Coastal activities peak** ☀. (All coasts)
  - Ages: All ages ● ● ● ●
  - Activities: Coasteering, sea kayaking, rock pooling
  - Best beaches: Barafundle, Llangennith

Scotland

- **Edinburgh Festival** ☀. (Edinburgh)
  - Ages: Shows for all ages ● ● ● ●
  - Book ahead: Popular shows sell out quickly
  - Free entertainment: Street performers throughout city

AUGUST ☀

Peak holiday season continues

Southwest England

- **Warm sea swimming** ☀. (All beaches)
  - Ages: All ages with supervision ● ● ● ●
  - Best beaches: Sennen, Woolacombe, Weymouth

- Safety: Always check lifeguard flags
- **Outdoor adventure parks** ☀
  - Ages: 4+ years 🎒 🎒 🎒
  - Featured: Go Ape, high ropes courses
  - Advance booking: Essential during summer holidays

Southeast England

- **Hop picking heritage** ★ (Kent)
  - Ages: 6+ years 🎒 🎒 🎒
  - Activities: Farm tours, traditional hop picking
  - Cultural learning: Agricultural heritage

Heart of England

- **Summer shows and events** ☀
  - Ages: All ages 🎒 🎒 🎒 🎒
  - Featured: Agricultural shows, craft fairs
  - Activities: Traditional games, local food sampling

Eastern England

- **Lavender season** ☀ (Norfolk, Suffolk)
  - Ages: All ages 🎒 🎒 🎒 🎒
  - Best fields: Heacham, Hitchin Lavender
  - Activities: Photography, lavender crafts

Northern England

- **Wild swimming season** ★ (Lake District tarns)
  - Ages: Strong swimmers 10+ years 🎒 🎒
  - Popular spots: Rydal Water, Grasmere
  - Safety: Cold water, never swim alone

Wales

- **Eisteddfod season** ☀ (Various locations)
  - Ages: All ages 🎒 🎒 🎒 🎒
  - Cultural immersion: Welsh language, music, poetry
  - Activities: Workshops, performances

Scotland

- **Highland summer** ☀ (All Scotland)
  - Ages: All ages ● ● ● ●
  - Activities: Loch cruises, castle visits, clan gatherings
  - Midges warning: Pack insect repellent

SEPTEMBER 🍂

Back to school, fewer crowds

Southwest England

- **Harvest festivals** ★ (Devon, Somerset)
  - Ages: All ages ● ● ● ●
  - Activities: Apple picking, cider making demos
  - Local food: Farm shops, farmers' markets

- **Indian summer beaches** ☀ (All coasts)
  - Ages: All ages ● ● ● ●
  - Benefits: Warm sea, fewer crowds, lower prices
  - Weather: Often the sunniest month

Southeast England

- **Autumn gardens** ★ (All counties)
  - Ages: All ages ● ● ● ●
  - Featured: RHS Wisley, Sissinghurst
  - Activities: Seed collecting, autumn colour photography

Heart of England

- **Harvest time** ☀ (Cotswolds, rural areas)
  - Ages: All ages ● ● ● ●
  - Activities: Farm visits, harvest festivals
  - Learning: Agricultural cycles, seasonal foods

Eastern England

- **Migration season** ☀ (Norfolk coast)
  - Ages: 6+ years ● ● ●
  - Wildlife: Migrating birds, seals

- Equipment: Binoculars, bird identification books

Northern England

- **Autumn walking** ⭐ (Lake District, Yorkshire Dales)
  - Ages: 4+ years 🎃 🎃 🎃
  - Highlights: Autumn colours, clearer views
  - Photography: Golden hour lighting

Wales

- **Apple harvest** ⭐ (Monmouthshire, Pembrokeshire)
  - Ages: All ages 🎃 🎃 🎃 🎃
  - Activities: Orchard visits, cider tastings (adults)
  - Family fun: Apple bobbing, harvest crafts

Scotland

- **Autumn colours** 🌼 (Highland glens)
  - Ages: All ages 🎃 🎃 🎃 🎃
  - Best locations: Glen Coe, Trossachs
  - Activities: Gentle walks, photography

OCTOBER 🎃

Autumn adventures and Halloween

Southwest England

- **Storm watching** ⭐ 🌧 (Atlantic coasts)
  - Ages: 8+ years from safe distance 🎃 🎃
  - Best viewpoints: Land's End, Hartland Point
  - Safety: Observe from cliff paths, never beach level
- **Halloween trails** 🌼 (Devon, Cornwall attractions)
  - Ages: 4+ years 🎃 🎃 🎃
  - Featured: National Trust properties, theme parks
  - Activities: Pumpkin picking, spooky storytelling

Southeast England

- **Autumn leaf walks** 🌼 (All counties)

- Ages: All ages ⚫ ⚫ ⚫ ⚫
- Best locations: Ashridge, Sheffield Park
- Activities: Leaf collecting, nature crafts

Heart of England

- **Halloween events** ☀ (Theme parks, attractions)
  - Ages: Check scare levels ⚫ ⚫ ⚫
  - Featured: Alton Towers Scarefest, Warwick Castle
  - Family-friendly: Daytime events less scary

Eastern England

- **Apple and pumpkin picking** ☀ (Norfolk, Suffolk farms)
  - Ages: All ages ⚫ ⚫ ⚫ ⚫
  - Activities: Farm tours, maze challenges
  - Seasonal crafts: Pumpkin carving, apple crafts

Northern England

- **Autumn fells** ⭐ (Lake District, Yorkshire Dales)
  - Ages: 6+ years ⚫ ⚫ ⚫
  - Weather considerations: Shorter days, changeable weather
  - Essential: Head torches, warm layers

Wales

- **Half-term adventures** ⭐ (All regions)
  - Ages: All ages ⚫ ⚫ ⚫ ⚫
  - Activities: Castle ghost tours, Halloween trails
  - Cultural: Welsh ghost stories and legends

Scotland

- **Highland autumn** ⭐ 🌧
  - Ages: 8+ years ⚫ ⚫
  - Activities: Whisky distillery tours (adults), Highland games
  - Weather: Rapidly changing, pack for all conditions

NOVEMBER 🦌

Quieter camping and cozy adventures

Southwest England

- **Storm season drama** ⭐ 🌧 (All coasts)
  - Ages: 8+ years from safe viewing points ⬛ ⬛
  - Activities: Coastal centre visits, marine life discovery
  - Indoor backup: Museums, aquariums

Southeast England

- **Bonfire celebrations** ☀ (Sussex especially)
  - Ages: All ages with ear protection ⬛ ⬛ ⬛ ⬛
  - Featured: Lewes Bonfire, Rye celebrations
  - Safety: Stay in designated areas, protect young ears

Heart of England

- **Christmas market season begins** ⭐ (Birmingham, Bath)
  - Ages: All ages ⬛ ⬛ ⬛ ⬛
  - Activities: Craft shopping, seasonal foods
  - Atmosphere: Magical evening lighting

Eastern England

- **Grey seal pupping** ☀ (Norfolk, Lincolnshire coasts)
  - Ages: 6+ years ⬛ ⬛ ⬛
  - Best viewing: Donna Nook, Blakeney Point
  - Important: Observe from designated areas only

Northern England

- **Cozy pub walks** ⭐ (Lake District, Yorkshire Dales)
  - Ages: All ages ⬛ ⬛ ⬛ ⬛
  - Activities: Short walks, warm pub lunches
  - Weather gear: Full waterproofs essential

Wales

- **St. Fagans winter** ⭐ (Near Cardiff)
  - Ages: All ages ⬛ ⬛ ⬛ ⬛

- Activities: Traditional crafts, historical reenactment
- Learning: Welsh history and culture

Scotland

- **Winter preparation** ⭐ 🌧
  - Ages: 10+ years ⬤ ⬤
  - Activities: Whisky tours (adults), Highland museums
  - Daylight: Very short days in northern Scotland

DECEMBER ❄

Festive camping and winter magic

Southwest England

- **Christmas markets** ⭐ (Bath, Exeter, Truro)
  - Ages: All ages ⬤ ⬤ ⬤ ⬤
  - Activities: Festive shopping, carol singing
  - Atmosphere: Magical Christmas lighting
- **Winter beaches** ⭐ (All coasts)
  - Ages: All ages with warm clothing ⬤ ⬤ ⬤ ⬤
  - Activities: Winter walks, storm watching
  - Benefits: Peaceful, dramatic scenery

Southeast England

- **Pantomime season** ☀ (All major towns)
  - Ages: 3+ years ⬤ ⬤ ⬤
  - Traditional entertainment: Interactive family shows
  - Book ahead: Popular Christmas entertainment

Heart of England

- **Christmas attractions** ☀ (Theme parks, stately homes)
  - Ages: All ages ⬤ ⬤ ⬤ ⬤
  - Featured: Winter Wonderlands, festive trails
  - Special events: Santa experiences, carol services

Eastern England

- **Winter wildlife** ⭐ (Norfolk Broads, Suffolk coast)
  - Ages: 6+ years 🖤 🖤 🖤
  - Highlights: Winter birds, seal watching
  - Equipment: Warm clothing, binoculars

Northern England

- **Christmas markets** ❄ (Manchester, York, Chester)
  - Ages: All ages 🖤 🖤 🖤 🖤
  - German-style markets: Traditional crafts, seasonal food
  - Atmosphere: Festive music and lighting

Wales

- **Mari Lwyd traditions** ⭐ (South Wales)
  - Ages: 6+ years (can be scary for younger) 🖤 🖤 🖤
  - Cultural experience: Traditional Welsh Christmas customs
  - Activities: Carol singing, traditional games

Scotland

- **Hogmanay preparations** ⭐ (All Scotland)
  - Ages: All ages 🖤 🖤 🖤 🖤
  - Activities: Traditional Scottish celebrations
  - Cultural learning: Scottish New Year traditions

Year-Round Activity Tips

Weather-Proof Planning

- **Always pack for changeable weather** - British weather can shift quickly
- **Have indoor alternatives** - Research nearby museums, leisure centres, or covered markets
- **Check local weather forecasts** - Especially important for mountain and coastal areas
- **Seasonal gear lists** - Different months require different essential equipment

Booking Strategies

- **Peak season (July-August)**: Book 3-6 months ahead
- **Shoulder seasons (April-June, September)**: Book 1-3 months ahead

- **Off-season (October-March)**: Often book 2-4 weeks ahead, some last-minute deals available
- **School holidays**: Always book early, especially for half-terms

Budget Planning by Season

- **Most expensive**: July-August, Easter holidays
- **Good value**: May-June, September
- **Cheapest**: January-March, November (excluding Christmas)
- **Special offers**: Many sites offer midweek discounts

Regional Weather Patterns

- **Southwest**: Mildest winters, wettest region overall
- **Southeast**: Driest region, warmest summers
- **Eastern**: Cold winters, can be very windy
- **Northern**: Coolest summers, heaviest rainfall in mountains
- **Wales**: Very changeable, mountain weather unpredictable
- **Scotland**: Shortest winter days, midge season June-August

---

Remember: This calendar provides general guidance, but always check local conditions and current weather forecasts before traveling. Seasonal patterns can vary from year to year, and climate change is affecting traditional seasonal timings.

Appendix G: Budget Planning Worksheets

Introduction to Family Camping Budget Planning

Planning your family camping budget doesn't have to be overwhelming. These worksheets will help you track expenses, find savings opportunities, and ensure your camping adventures are both memorable and affordable. Remember, camping is one of the most cost-effective ways to holiday with children, and with proper planning, you can create amazing memories without breaking the bank.

Worksheet 1: Annual Family Camping Budget Planner

Family Details:

- Number of adults: _____
- Number of children (ages): _____ (), _____ (), _____ (), _____ ()
- Preferred camping season: _____
- Number of trips planned this year: _____

Annual Budget Overview

Category	Planned Budget	Actual Spent	Difference
Equipment & Gear	£_____	£_____	£_____
Campsite Fees	£_____	£_____	£_____
Transport Costs	£_____	£_____	£_____
Food & Groceries	£_____	£_____	£_____
Activities & Attractions	£_____	£_____	£_____
Emergency Fund (10%)	£_____	£_____	£_____
TOTAL	£_____	£_____	£_____

Monthly Savings Plan

Total Annual Budget: £_____ **Monthly Savings Required:** £_____ (÷ 12 months) **Weekly Savings Required:** £_____ (÷ 52 weeks)

Worksheet 2: Individual Trip Budget Planner

Trip Details:

- Destination: _____
- Dates: _____

- Number of nights: _____
- Number of people: _____

Pre-Trip Expenses

Item	Estimated Cost	Actual Cost	Notes
Campsite booking	£_____	£_____	_____
Equipment purchases	£_____	£_____	_____
Equipment rental	£_____	£_____	_____
Food shopping	£_____	£_____	_____
Travel insurance	£_____	£_____	_____
Other: _____	£_____	£_____	_____
Pre-trip subtotal	£_____	£_____	

Travel Expenses

Item	Estimated Cost	Actual Cost	Notes
Fuel/petrol	£_____	£_____	_____
Train/bus tickets	£_____	£_____	_____
Parking fees	£_____	£_____	_____
Tolls/congestion charge	£_____	£_____	_____
Travel snacks/drinks	£_____	£_____	_____
Travel subtotal	£_____	£_____	

On-Site Expenses

Item	Estimated Cost	Actual Cost	Notes
Additional site fees	£_____	£_____	_____
Local groceries	£_____	£_____	_____
Restaurant meals	£_____	£_____	_____
Ice cream/treats	£_____	£_____	_____
Laundry	£_____	£_____	_____
Gas/electric top-ups	£_____	£_____	_____
On-site subtotal	£_____	£_____	

Activities & Attractions

Activity	Estimated Cost	Actual Cost	Age Group	Worth It?
_____	£_____	£_____	_____	☐ Yes ☐ No

Activity	Estimated Cost	Actual Cost	Age Group	Worth It?
_____	£_____	£_____	_____	☐ Yes ☐ No
_____	£_____	£_____	_____	☐ Yes ☐ No
_____	£_____	£_____	_____	☐ Yes ☐ No
_____	£_____	£_____	_____	☐ Yes ☐ No
Activities subtotal	£_____	£_____		

Trip Total

Category	Amount
Pre-trip expenses	£_____
Travel expenses	£_____
On-site expenses	£_____
Activities & attractions	£_____
TRIP TOTAL	£_____

Cost per person: £_____ (÷ number of people) **Cost per night:** £_____ (÷ number of nights)

Worksheet 3: Equipment Investment Tracker

Initial Equipment Purchase Planner

Essential Items	Priority	Estimated Cost	Actual Cost	Where to Buy	Status
Tent (family size)	High	£_____	£_____	_____	☐ Owned ☐ Need
Sleeping bags (x____)	High	£_____	£_____	_____	☐ Owned ☐ Need
Sleeping mats (x____)	High	£_____	£_____	_____	☐ Owned ☐ Need
Camping chairs (x____)	Medium	£_____	£_____	_____	☐ Owned ☐ Need
Camping table	Medium	£_____	£_____	_____	☐ Owned ☐ Need
Cooking stove	High	£_____	£_____	_____	☐ Owned ☐ Need
Cooking utensils	High	£_____	£_____	_____	☐ Owned ☐ Need
Cool box	High	£_____	£_____	_____	☐ Owned ☐ Need
First aid kit	High	£_____	£_____	_____	☐ Owned ☐ Need
Torch/lanterns	High	£_____	£_____	_____	☐ Owned ☐ Need
Waterproof clothing	High	£_____	£_____	_____	☐ Owned ☐ Need
Games/entertainment	Low	£_____	£_____	_____	☐ Owned ☐ Need
TOTAL EQUIPMENT		£_____	£_____		

Equipment Upgrade Schedule

Item	Current Status	Upgrade Needed	Target Date	Estimated Cost
_____	_____	_____	_____	£_____
_____	_____	_____	_____	£_____
_____	_____	_____	_____	£_____
_____	_____	_____	_____	£_____

Worksheet 4: Money-Saving Strategies Tracker

Before You Go

Equipment Savings:

- ☐ Buy second-hand equipment from Facebook Marketplace/eBay
- ☐ Borrow equipment from friends/family for first trip
- ☐ Look for end-of-season sales (September-October)
- ☐ Join camping equipment swap groups
- ☐ Consider rental for expensive items (roof boxes, etc.)

Booking Savings:

- ☐ Book early for popular sites (save up to 20%)
- ☐ Choose off-peak dates (weekdays, shoulder season)
- ☐ Look for family deals and multi-night discounts
- ☐ Compare prices across booking platforms
- ☐ Sign up for campsite newsletters for special offers

During Your Trip

Food Savings:

- ☐ Plan meals and create shopping lists
- ☐ Shop at local supermarkets rather than site shops
- ☐ Cook at campsite rather than eating out for every meal
- ☐ Pack plenty of snacks to avoid expensive impulse buys
- ☐ Use cashback apps when shopping

Activity Savings:

- ☐ Research free activities (beaches, walking trails, parks)
- ☐ Look for family tickets and group discounts

- ☐ Check for off-peak pricing at attractions
- ☐ Use Groupon and discount voucher sites
- ☐ Pack entertainment (books, games) for rainy days

Money Saved This Trip

Savings Strategy	Amount Saved	Notes
_____	£_____	_____
_____	£_____	_____
_____	£_____	_____
_____	£_____	_____
TOTAL SAVED	£_____	

Worksheet 5: Regional Cost Comparison

Use this worksheet to compare costs across different UK regions to help plan your budget.

Region	Average Campsite Cost/Night	Fuel Cost Estimate	Average Attraction Cost	Food Cost Estimate	Total Estimated Daily Cost
Southwest England	£_____	£_____	£_____	£_____	£_____
Southeast England	£_____	£_____	£_____	£_____	£_____
Heart of England	£_____	£_____	£_____	£_____	£_____
Eastern England	£_____	£_____	£_____	£_____	£_____
Northern England	£_____	£_____	£_____	£_____	£_____
Wales	£_____	£_____	£_____	£_____	£_____
Scotland	£_____	£_____	£_____	£_____	£_____

Cost-Effective Regional Recommendations:

1. **Best Value Region:** _____

2. **Most Expensive Region:** _____

3. **Best Off-Peak Value:** _____

Worksheet 6: Family Camping Emergency Fund Calculator

Recommended Emergency Fund: 10-15% of trip budget

Trip Budget: £_____ Emergency Fund (10%): £_____ Emergency Fund (15%): £_____

Potential Emergency Expenses:

- ☐ Equipment failure/replacement: £50-200
- ☐ Medical expenses: £20-100
- ☐ Additional accommodation (if weather forces early departure): £80-150/night
- ☐ Vehicle breakdown: £100-500
- ☐ Extra food/supplies due to delays: £30-80
- ☐ Alternative activities due to weather: £40-120

Emergency Fund Usage Tracker:

Date	Emergency	Amount Used	Remaining Fund
_____	_____	£_____	£_____
_____	_____	£_____	£_____
_____	_____	£_____	£_____

Budget Planning Tips for Different Family Situations

For First-Time Campers:

- Start with a budget of £150-300 per family for a weekend trip
- Factor in £500-1,200 for initial equipment purchases
- Choose local sites to minimize travel costs
- Book all-inclusive sites with facilities to reduce unknowns

For Large Families (4+ children):

- Look for family camping pods or large pitches
- Factor in higher food costs: add 20-30% to standard estimates
- Seek group discounts at attractions
- Consider self-catering accommodations for longer stays

For Single Parents:

- Look for single-parent camping groups for shared costs

- Choose sites with good security and support
- Factor in help costs (equipment transport, etc.)
- Budget for additional entertainment during rest periods

For Families with Teenagers:

- Budget extra for WiFi costs or mobile data
- Factor in higher food costs and dietary preferences
- Include budget for independent activities
- Consider accommodation with more space/privacy

Year-End Budget Review

Annual Camping Spend Analysis

Total Planned: £_____ **Total Spent:** £_____ **Difference:** £_____ (Over/Under budget)

Cost Per Experience Analysis

- **Total nights camped:** _____
- **Cost per night:** £_____
- **Cost per family member per trip:** £_____
- **Number of different sites visited:** _____

Money-Saving Wins This Year:

1. _____
2. _____
3. _____

Areas for Improvement Next Year:

1. _____
2. _____
3. _____

Next Year's Budget Planning:

Proposed budget increase/decrease: % ***New equipment needed:*** £__ **Target number of trips:** _____
Target savings per month: £_____

Quick Reference: Typical UK Family Camping Costs (2024)

Campsite Costs:

- **Basic sites:** £15-25 per night
- **Facilities-rich sites:** £25-40 per night
- **Premium/holiday park sites:** £40-80 per night
- **Peak season premium:** +20-50%

Food Costs (family of 4):

- **Self-catering:** £40-60 per day
- **Mix of self-catering/eating out:** £60-100 per day
- **Mostly eating out:** £100-150 per day

Activity Costs (per child):

- **Free activities:** £0 (beaches, walks, playgrounds)
- **Low-cost activities:** £5-15 (mini golf, swimming)
- **Theme parks/major attractions:** £25-50
- **Outdoor activity centers:** £20-40

Transport Costs:

- **Petrol:** Budget £0.15-0.20 per mile
- **Parking:** £2-15 per day at attractions
- **Tolls:** Severn Bridge (free), Dartford Crossing £2.50

Remember, these worksheets are tools to help you plan and track your camping expenses. The goal isn't to restrict your fun, but to help you make informed decisions and get the most value from your family camping adventures. Happy camping!

Printed in Dunstable, United Kingdom